CW01239465

THE ROSE STILL GROWS BEYOND THE WALL

Near a shady wall a rose once grew,
Budded and blossomed in God's free light,
Watered and fed by morning dew,
Shedding its sweetness day and night.

As it grew and blossomed fair and tall,
Slowly rising to loftier height,
It came to a crevice in the wall,
Through which there shone a beam of light.

Onward it crept with added strength,
With never a thought of fear or pride.
It followed the light through the crevice's length
And unfolded itself on the other side.

The light, the dew, the broadening view
Were found the same as they were before;
And it lost itself in beauties new,
Breathing its fragrance more and more.

Shall claims of death cause us to grieve,
And make our courage faint or fail?
Nay! Let us faith and hope receive:
The rose still grows beyond the wall.

Scattering fragrance far and wide,
Just as it did in days of yore,
Just as it did on the other side,
Just as it will forevermore.

A.L. Frank

To Elvis
who opened hearts, emotions and minds
through his music.

To his fans for T.C.B.

ELVIS
1956
Reflections

Morrie E. Kricun
Virginia M. Kricun

Morgin Press, Inc. Wayne, PA

Photographs copyright 1991 Morgin Press, Inc.
Text copyright 1992 Morgin Press, Inc.

All rights reserved. No part of this book may be reproduced or transmitted in any form or by any means, electronic or mechanical, including photocopying, recording or by any information storage or retrieval system, without permission in writing from the Publisher.

MORGIN PRESS, INC.
303 West Lancaster Ave. Ste 283
Wayne, PA 19087 U.S.A.

Kricun, Morrie E., 1938-
  Elvis 1956 Reflections/ Morrie E. Kricun and Virginia M. Kricun
    p. cm.
  ISBN 0-9630976-0-1

Library of Congress Cataloging-in-Publication Data   CIP 91-091218

MORGIN PRESS books are available at special discounts for bulk purchases for sales promotions, premiums, fund-raising, or educational use. For details contact:
    Special Sales Director
    Morgin Press, Inc.
    303 W. Lancaster Ave. Ste 283
    Wayne, PA 19087 U.S.A.

Cover Design: Izhar Zik & Barbara Solot Graphics V, Philadelphia
Book Design: Charles Field
Editing and Production Services: Caslon, Inc.
Photographic Interpretations Prints and Design: Morrie E. Kricun
Photography Consultant: Mark Garvin
Original Photographic Negatives: Ed Braslaff 1912-1988
Phototypeset by: Digitype, Inc.
Printed and bound by: Arcata Graphics

First Edition

10 9 8 7 6 5 4 3 2

Acknowledgments

We feel fortunate to have had the support and assistance of the many caring and talented people necessary to create this book. We thank Lee Cotten and Bill Burk for their encouragement. To Betty Cagle, Robert Rickerson, Sharon Herfurth, Esther Klein and Dale Sickles for help in retrieving information, we are grateful. We are appreciative of the following wonderful libraries throughout the country that were so helpful in our research:

> Atlanta and Fulton Public Library
> Bradley Memorial Library
> Dallas Public Library (Fine Arts Division)
> The Free Library of Philadelphia
> Houston Public Library
> Jacksonville Public Library
> The Lee County Library
> The Library of Congress
> Central Library of the Los Angeles Public Library
> Louisville Free Public Library (Louisiana Division)
> Memphis Shelby County Public Library
> New Orleans Public Library
> Oakland Public Library
> Public Library of Charlotte and Mecklenburg County (Robinson-Spranger Carolina Room)
> Richmond Public Library
> St. Louis Public Library
> San Diego Public Library
> San Francisco Public Library
> Shreveport Public Library
> Van Pelt Library of the University of Pennsylvania

We wish to thank Bernadette Moore at the Archives of RCA for her patient assistance in enabling us to obtain Elvis discography information. We are deeply indebted to Melissa Zajdel for the manuscript preparation. Her hard work and dedication are very much appreciated. We also wish to thank Terrie Wigfall for her contribution. The people at Arcata Graphics have been most understanding and professional. Becky Wilson was instrumental in guiding us to correct decisions regarding printing of the book; Betty Ryan for supervising the printing of the book; and Wayne Rankin for his fine reproduction of the prints. We thank Mark Garvin for his photographic expertise, consultation, cover photo and several magnifications. We thank John Kahler for his technical advice. The book was wonderfully designed by Charles Field of Caslon, Inc., edited by Joan Powers, and the beautiful cover and the promotional material were designed by Izhar Zik and Barbara Solot of Graphics V, in Philadelphia, PA. We appreciate Morgin Press for allowing the book to reach fruition. And lastly, we thank our families and friends, whose caring support kept us going.

Preface

Creating this book has been a beautiful adventure for us, for it has brought us in contact with many wonderful people and loyal Elvis fans. In the process of researching this book, we were pleasantly surprised to discover among friends and colleagues a broad range of Elvis devotees.

Elvis 1956 Reflections is a tribute to Elvis Presley focusing on the most important year of his career. The book presents the events and happenings of that year that shaped Elvis' life and the lives of his fans. We also share with you over 100 photographs of Elvis, most of which have never been published. The photos from this photographic session that had been published appeared in *Elvis Answers Back*, a now rare collectible.

The original negatives were produced by an award winning professional photographer, Ed Braslaff on August 18, 1956, at the Hollywood Knickerbocker Hotel. The photo session took place just a few days before Elvis began filming *Love Me Tender*. We determined the date of the session by the headlines of the newspapers in the magazine rack of the gift shop in the Knickerbocker Hotel, which are seen in one of the photographs. We believe that it was an afternoon session, based on the time shown on Elvis' watch.

We acquired the negatives from the Braslaff estate and have taken great care in interpreting the negatives and printing quality photographs. We have purposely included photographs that are similar in pose yet that show different facial expressions. This allows you to see Elvis in a range of feelings and moods. We have also created close-ups that show his handsome face in greater detail. Take time in looking at each change of expression. Try to imagine his thoughts and feelings. When he is listening to the Tab Hunter record from the cover of *Hear*, was he contemplating the production of *Elvis Answers Back*? As he memorizes his script, is he feeling excited about his first film? Becoming a movie star was important to him. As he looks out over Hollywood from the roof of his hotel, does he reflect back to Mississippi? Look into his eyes and try to feel what he was experiencing at this very important time in his life.

The book is divided into parts: first is an overview of 1956 and the photographic section; the second part includes a chronology, an outline of concerts and performances, discography, filmography, and highlights from newspaper and periodical coverage that occurred in 1956. The information in the second section was gathered from extensive review of newspapers and periodicals from that year as well as books. All of these sources are listed in the bibliography.

The Chronology section lists the year's events and happenings in the order that they occurred. A letter code enables you to scan quickly for a category of personal interest.

C = Concerts and Performances
D = Discography
F = Filmography
N = Newspapers and Periodicals
T = Television Appearances

The Chronology provides an overview. More detailed information can be found in the individual sections.

In the Concerts and Performances section, Elvis' main concerts and performances for 1956 are listed. The information about the songs Elvis sang on his TV appearances was researched at the Archives of RCA.

We have presented a Discography of all of Elvis' records that were recorded or released during 1956. Some records were recorded earlier and released in 1956; others were recorded in 1956 and released later. The information in the Discography is derived almost entirely from the files of the Archives of RCA, to whom we are grateful. In a few instances, we have referred to other reference works. In cases of conflicting information, we relied on the RCA data. For example, some authors have listed shipping dates as the release date. We chose to list the RCA release date. The ratings from "The Top 100" are quoted from the charts of *The Billboard*. Occasionally, we were unable to find some bit of information; thus, a few blank spaces remain.

Elvis made his first film *Love Me Tender* in 1956. The members of the cast and others involved in the production of the film as well as the songs Elvis sang are listed in the Filmography section.

In the Newspapers and Periodicals section, we have presented excerpts, summaries, and quotations directly from the sources — articles that we reviewed. The articles are arranged chronologically to provide a perspective of Elvis happenings throughout the year. You can appreciate the increasing fame that Elvis enjoyed as the year unfolded. We have cited the date, source, page (when available), title of the article, and a summary and/or quotations. For newspapers, we chose a variety from throughout the country. For periodicals, we selected both widely circulated magazines and some with a limited circulation to show the extent of media coverage. Entertainment print media were included as well. Occasionally, we included the same subject matter from different cities to demonstrate the national coverage. We have at times presented quotations that enable you to appreciate and evaluate events for yourself. Of course, space does not allow the printing of all of the articles we discovered.

We enjoyed writing this book and creating the reflections of Elvis, and we hope that you enjoy reading it.

Contents

Reflections I
    Elvis Aron Presley

Reflections II
    Chronology
    Concerts and Performances
    Discography
    Filmography
    Newspapers and Periodicals
    Bibliography

*When you love someone
all your saved-up wishes start coming out.*

Elizabeth Bowen

Reflections I

1956 must be the most important year in the professional life of Elvis Aron Presley. It was that year he skyrocketed to international fame.

Elvis Presley entered 1956 with hope and anticipation. RCA Victor had purchased his recording contract from Sun Record Company just 6 weeks before, and his public performances were getting more and more attention. Yet, to most of America, Elvis Presley remained unknown. Elvis made recordings for Sun Record Company in 1954 and 1955, but in 1956, his songs became national hits.

Who could have foreseen as Elvis began the year that he was destined to become an international celebrity, make a recording that sold over 1 million copies (he was to have several), earn $1 million, sell over 10 million records, perform on all the major TV shows, be covered in all the major periodicals and fan magazines as well as newspapers around the world, and make his first film—all in one year! That all this and more happened to Elvis Presley in 1956 is one of the amazing testimonials to the realization of the American dream.

Elvis was hard working, performing concerts throughout the South and appearing on the Country & Western radio show "Louisiana Hayride," out of Shreveport, LA. RCA Victor had Elvis record several songs on January 10 and 11, 2 days after his 21st birthday. One of the songs, "Heartbreak Hotel" would enter *The Billboard's* "The Top 100" at position NO. 68 on February 22 and hit NO. 1 on April 25. It was Elvis' first NO. 1 song. It was only the beginning. By the end of the year, Elvis had a song in the NO. 1 position for 18 out of the last 43 weeks of 1956; a NO. 1 to NO. 3 song in 31 of the last 44 weeks of the year. This was quite an amazing accomplishment.

Elvis' performance schedule kept him moving at a dizzying pace. He frequently performed three shows a day, sometimes as many as five, and then traveled from city to city, usually by car or train, at night. It was not an easy life, but Elvis did not want the momentum to end. At this early stage of his career, he was afraid his fame might disappear as quickly as it appeared.

No entertainer worked harder than Elvis did at concerts. He was always exhausted after a concert; yet he always had time, as tired as he was, to sign autographs for any fan who managed to sneak backstage after the show. He frequently said that his fans made his fame, and he was always grateful to them. He believed they deserved his best performance. Elvis was a polite man who was appreciative of his good fortune. He always greeted people in a courteous manner and was kind even when he was stressed. He was generous to a fault and was very loyal to his friends and family. There were occasions when he performed for free, the proceeds going to a charity or another good cause.

Often the audience became overly responsive; with thousands of screaming and shrieking teenagers, the sound became so deafening that you couldn't hear Elvis sing. However, that didn't stop them. Their feelings and love for Elvis were so strong that they were happy just to be there and see him in person. Personal safety became an issue for Elvis, and after almost every show, he had to be escorted off the stage and whisked away to protect him from well meaning fans.

At the beginning of 1956, the recording industry was generally not doing well. Elvis' popularity was matched by a jump in record sales, which brought not only Elvis and RCA considerable monetary reward but it actually boosted the entire record industry financially. As merchandising took hold, Elvis-related products were to be seen everywhere. Products from lipstick to bracelets to clothing and almost anything else you could imagine were sold to the tune of over $20 million a year. In Canada, not only did Elvis' recordings break records but guitar sales soared as well. Many people benefited from the Presley Machine.

In the mid-1950s, there was no musical trend, as regional music styles dominated. In the South and Southwest, Country & Western, which grew out of "hillbilly music," was favored. The popular music to which most of America listened prior to 1956 was soft ballads and instrumentals. The rich tradition of black music, then called "race" music, first in the form of Gospel, then Jazz in the 1920s, and Rhythm & Blues in the 1950s had yet to broadly cross over to general audiences. What Elvis did in merging Country & Western with Rhythm & Blues and Rock 'n' Roll, was to create a trend that changed the direction of popular music to this day. He crossed over musical boundaries in a way that left critics buzzing and fans cheering.

Elvis worked hard in the recording sessions. Although he could not read music, he had an uncanny ear for music. He could hear a song once and would then be able to sing it in almost exactly the same style. In fact, when going over sample discs to select which songs might be right for Elvis, the demo singers would actually be imitating Elvis. Many times everyone at the recording session would feel that the last take was the one that should be the master, but Elvis would not be satisfied. He could hear something in the rendition that made him feel he could do better, and he would do a few more takes. When he was satisfied with the result, he could somehow remember the best of the takes and make a good choice for the master. For someone who never took a music lesson, he was truly remarkable in his ability to "hear" music so well.

Although Elvis was taking the teenagers and preteens by storm, he faced strong criticism from the media and adults for his style of performance and singing. His notable gyrations were unacceptable to the "grown-up" population that was part of the 1950s "generation gap." Keeping in mind the 1950 conservative moral standards, matched by relatively prudish and naive mores, one can put things in a different perspective, especially in comparison to the social behavior of the 1960s that followed. Elvis' performance style was intimidating to adults, particularly to parents of young girls and to the religious community. Parents looked at Rock 'n' Roll in general and Elvis in particular as a threat to their moral standards. Press and parents alike never made the connection to the enthusiastic singing movements typical of the Pentecostal meetings Elvis attended as a child. Yet if you listen to the songs Elvis sang, there was never anything of violence, promiscuity, anti-establishment, or anti-parent, as we so often find in today's music. Looking at the pictures of Elvis' fans at the concerts, you quickly notice what clean-cut, well dressed, nice kids they were.

Elvis' first TV appearance was on the Dorsey Brothers' "Stage Show" in the beginning of the year. He made a total of six appearances on the show. His presence on the show did not change the show's national ratings against the competition, "The Perry Como Show." In fact, it was probably due to the show's low ratings that its producers were willing to take a chance with Elvis.

In April, Elvis appeared on the "The Milton Berle Show." It was this appearance that drew so much adverse publicity because of his performance style. However, this controversy provided him with media exposure to millions of potential fans. With all this attention, no one was going to miss his performance on the "The Steve Allen Show," which had never beat its ratings competitor, "The Ed Sullivan Show." With Elvis on his show, Steve Allen decidedly beat Ed Sullivan in the ratings. Sullivan, who vowed that he would never have Presley on his "family show," relented and signed Elvis to do three shows at a handsome price. With Elvis on "The Ed Sullivan Show," ratings soared, reaching 83 percent! Elvis Presley, with radio exposure for his records, and now TV bringing him into the homes of millions, was taking the nation by storm!

Hal B. Wallis of Paramount Pictures needed to see Elvis only once to decide to give him a screen test. By his own admission, Elvis always wanted to be a movie star. He admired James Dean and at one point in 1956 related that he wanted by play Dean in a proposed biography. As Elvis' recordings were bringing him fame, Hollywood decided to take advantage of a box office "sure thing." Always wanting to give his best performance, Elvis was not satisfied with his first screen test and asked for a second. Elvis' enormous popularity, linked with a good screen test (the camera loved him), impressed the people at the studio. Five days later on April 6, Paramount signed Elvis to a 7 year, 3 picture contract for $450,000.

Although Elvis' contract was with Paramount, they did not have a suitable role for Elvis at the time, so he was "lent" to 20th Century Fox where he made his first film. The film was called *The Reno Brothers*, but the title was changed to *Love Me Tender* when the studio realized the popularity of the song of the same title that Elvis sang in the film. Filming *Love Me Tender* began on August 23, 1956 and was completed on October 8. While filming *Love Me Tender*, Elvis and his parents stayed at the Hollywood Knickerbocker Hotel, the location for the shooting of the photographs in this book.

There was a debate prior to the filming of *Love Me Tender* as to whether Elvis should be given acting lessons. Both the director and producer of the film were against Elvis receiving lessons — they wanted the natural Elvis. Elvis took his acting responsibilities seriously and studied his lines conscientiously. He was reported to have memorized not just his part, but the entire script. To his credit, in yet another performance arena where he had received no training, Elvis received praise for his acting ability in the film — even from some of his detractors.

Of course fans loved Elvis in the film. They could see and hear him close up, many for the first time, and they could see him over and over again. Fans were so into the film that they would cheer even when he cleared his throat. The press compared him to James Dean or referred to him as a singing Marlon Brando. *Love Me Tender* entered *The Billboard's* "Top Grossing Films" chart at the NO. 2 position on November 28 just 13 days after its premier in New York City! Elvis went on to make 29 feature films in 12 years.

Few times in history do all elements come together so perfectly to create such an overwhelming success. Elvis Aron Presley was like a new shining star that appeared in a flash of talent, timing, hard work, and a unique style — to brighten the musical skies forever. In one short year he had become "The King" of Rock 'n' Roll and the ruler of the hearts of his fans.

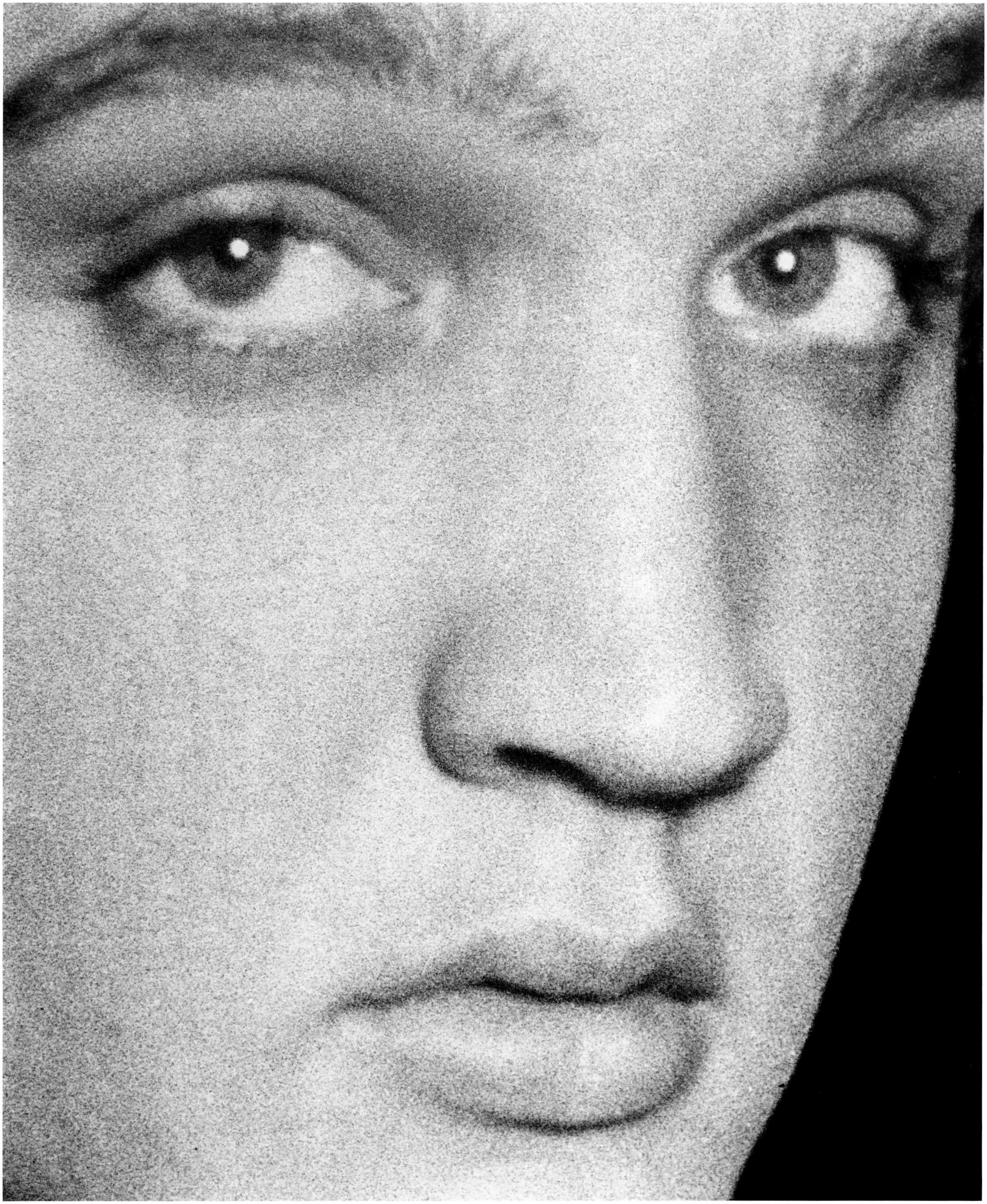

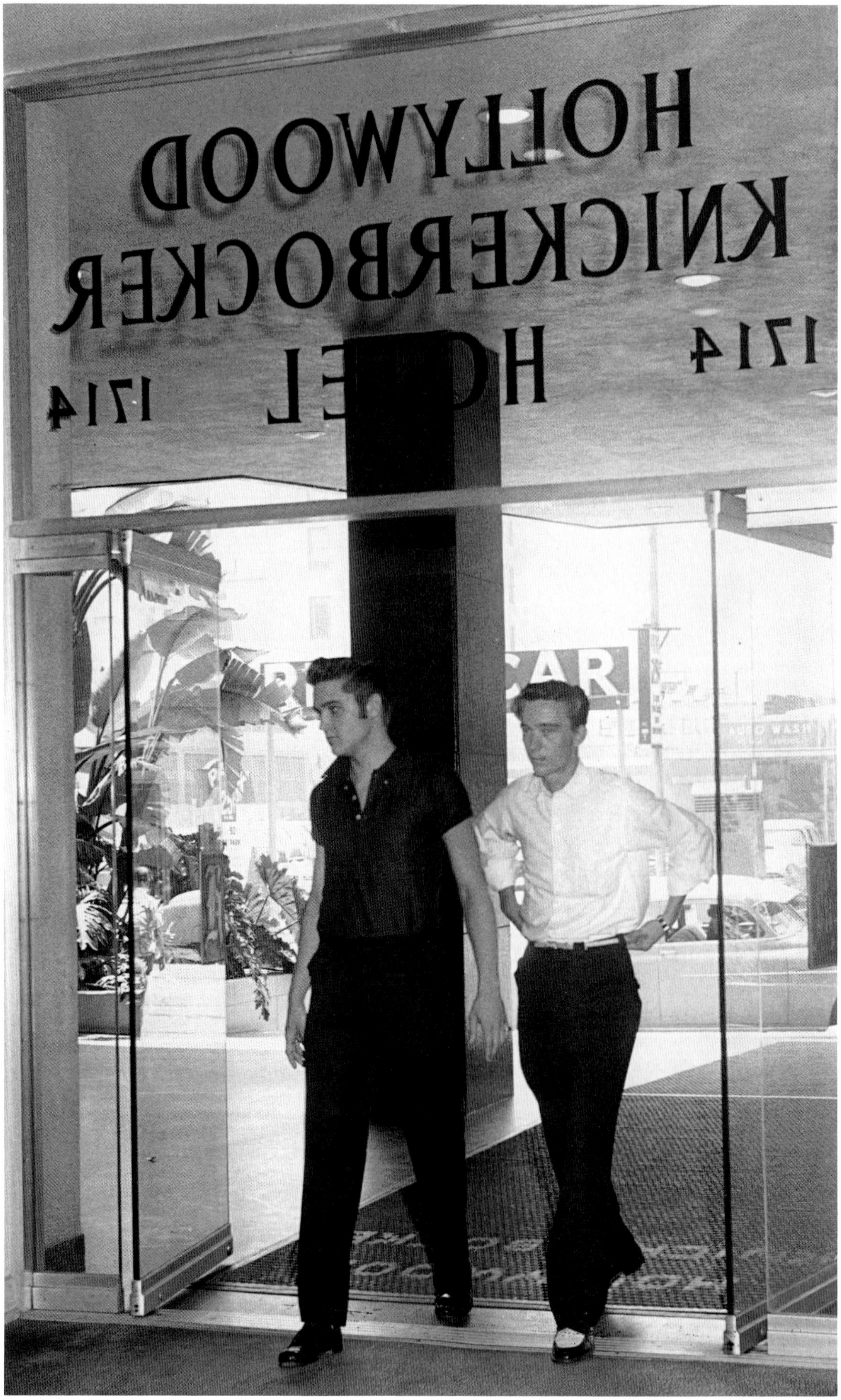
HOLLYWOOD
KNICKERBOCKER
HOTEL
1714
1714
CAR

SPORTS ILLUSTRATED
ARGOSY
TRUE
THE MAN'S MAGAZINE
stag
Har
The Atlantic
RAMS-REDSKINS GAME
KEFAUVER
CHINATOWN BRAWL
Nixon Faces Knight in
F. Caucus 'Showdown'
Thousands Cheer Dick At Airport
HERALD EXPRESS
NIGHT FINAL
MOTION
TOMORROW!
LIFE

ARGOSY
MAN'S World
MAN'S
TRUE
Newsweek
Screen stars
COSMOPO
MENNEN
FOAM SHAVE
Vaseline HAIR TONIC
MENNEN HAIR CREME FOR MEN
VICKS
SUCRETS

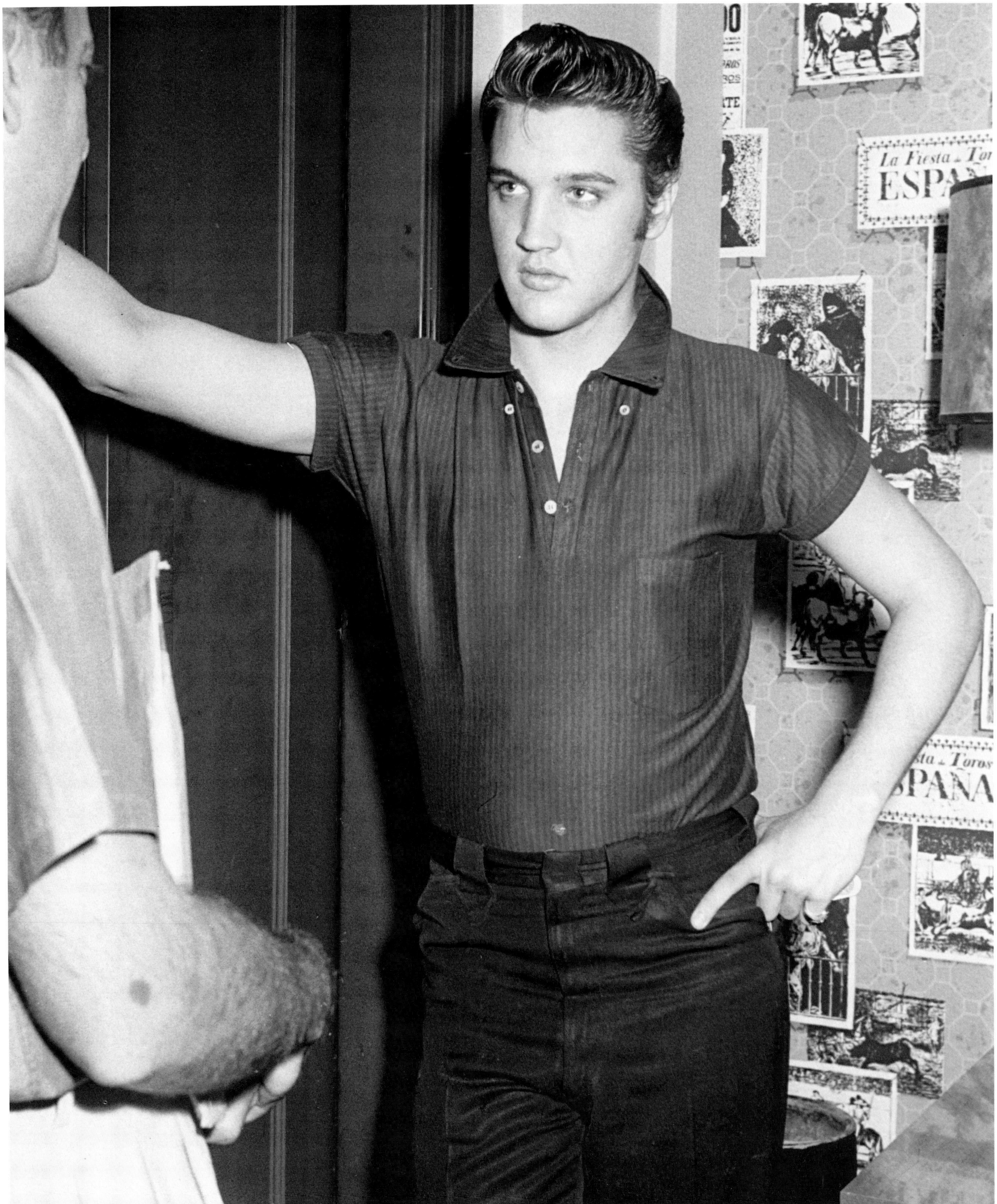
La Fiesta

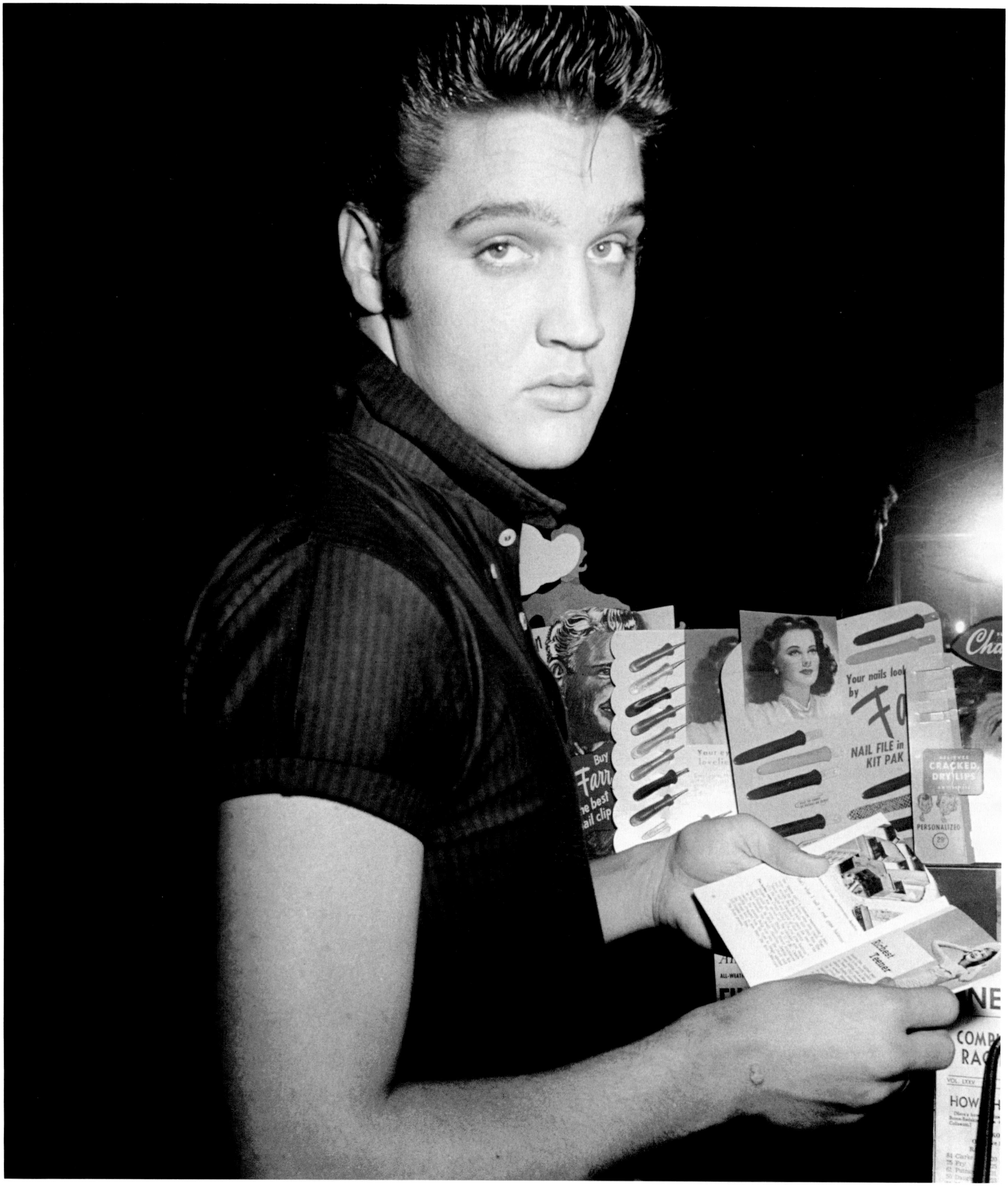
NAIL FILE in
KIT PAK
CRACKED, DRY LIPS
PERSONALIZED

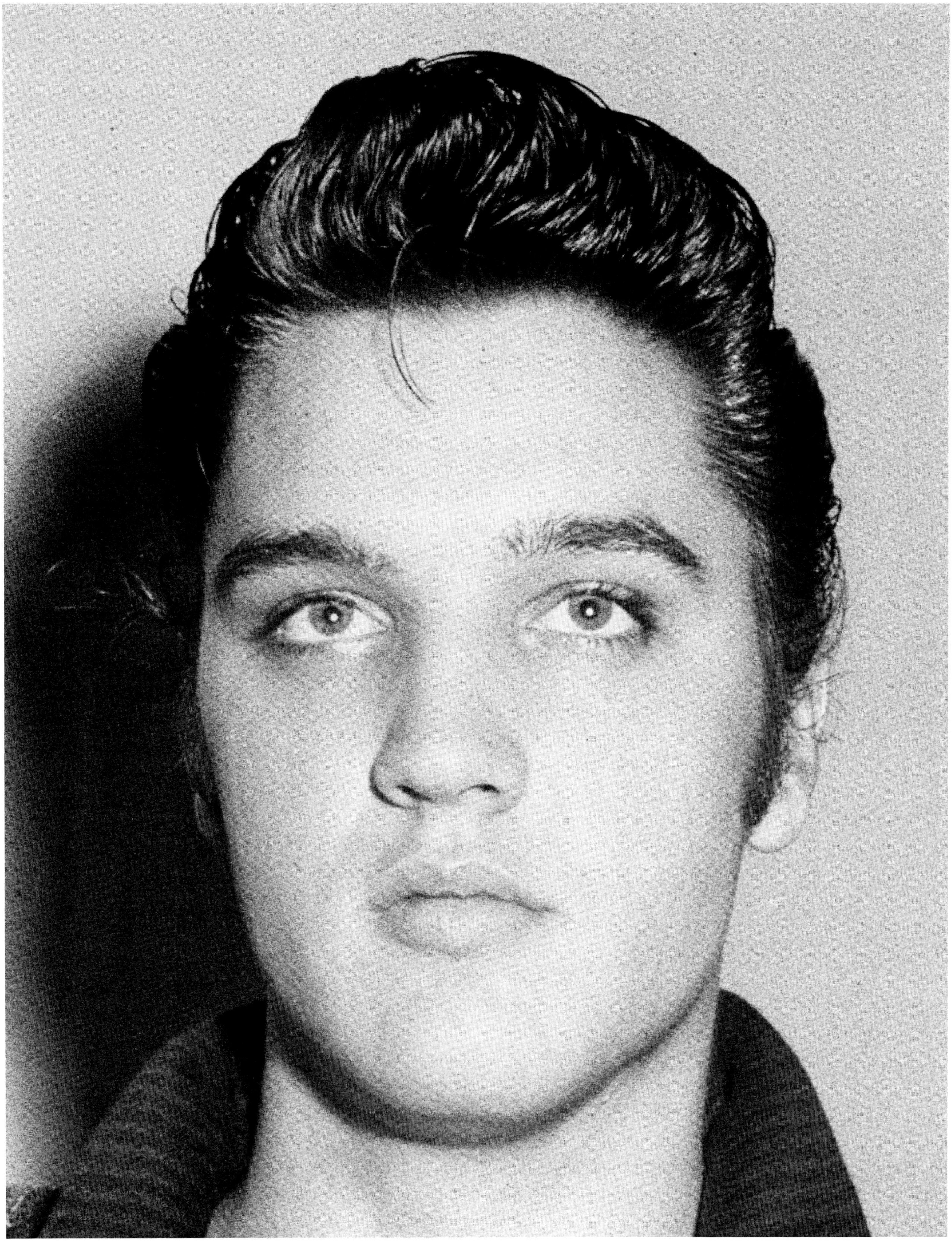

The essential conditions of everything you do must be choice, love, passion.

Nadia Boulanger

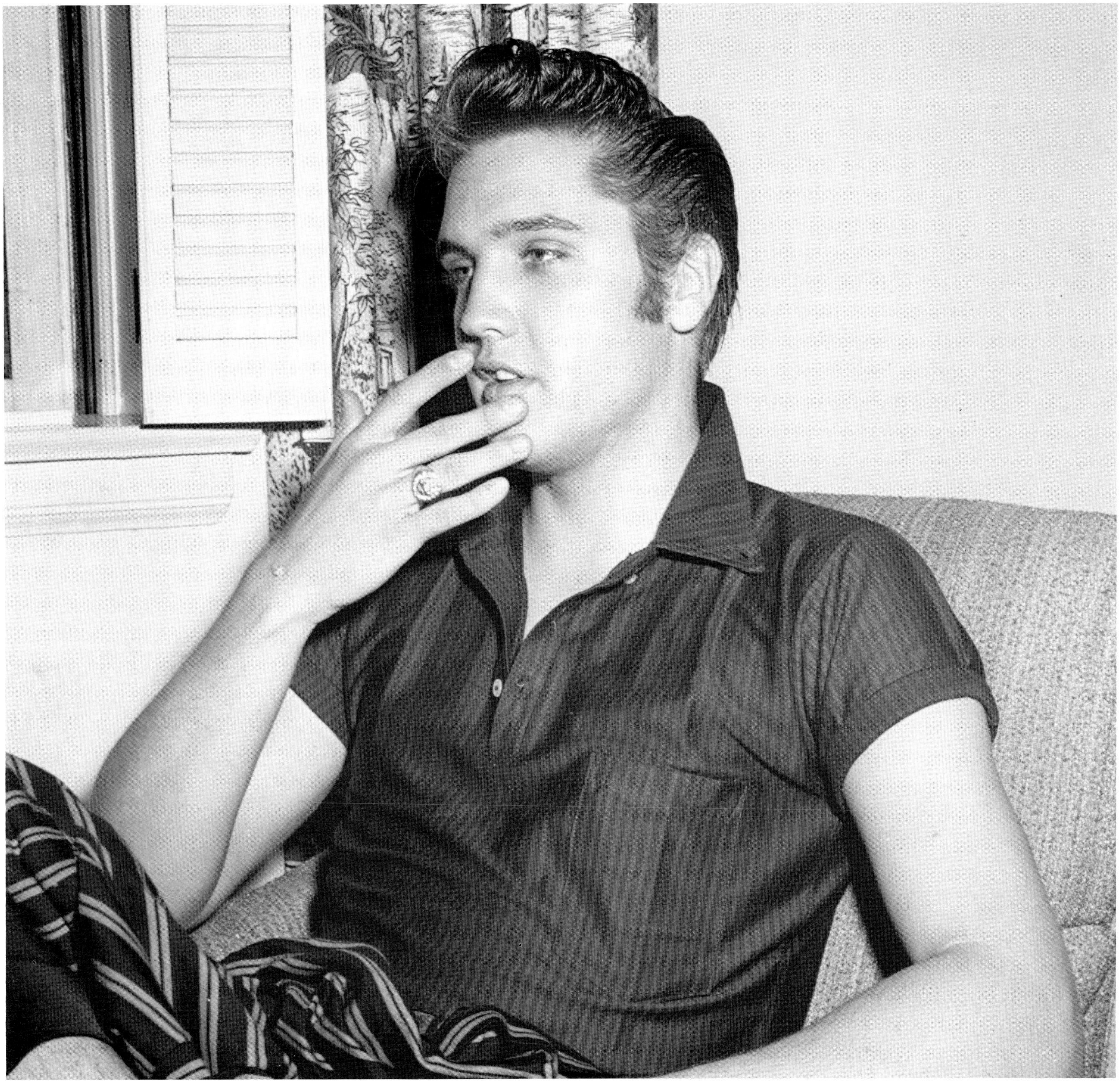

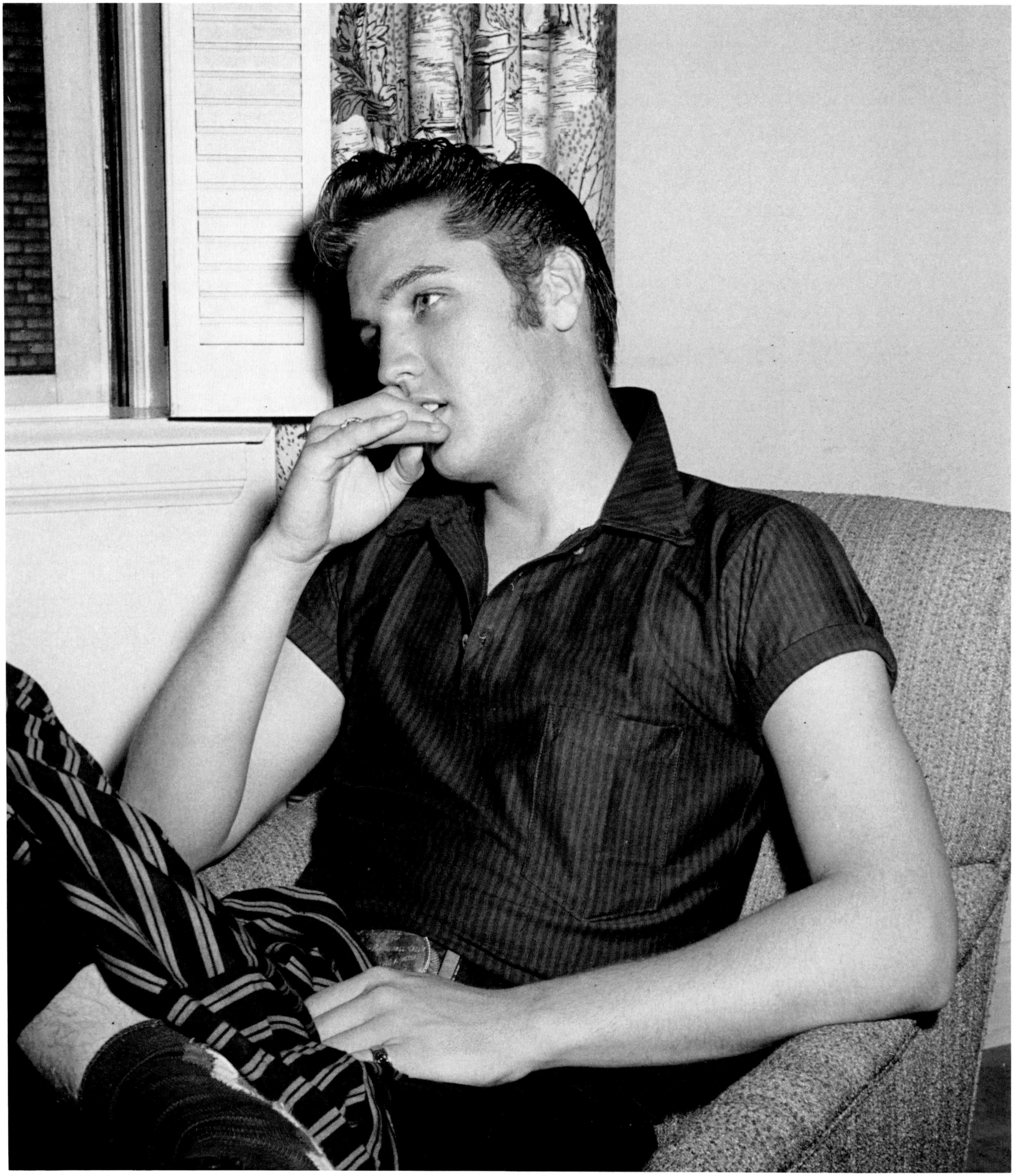

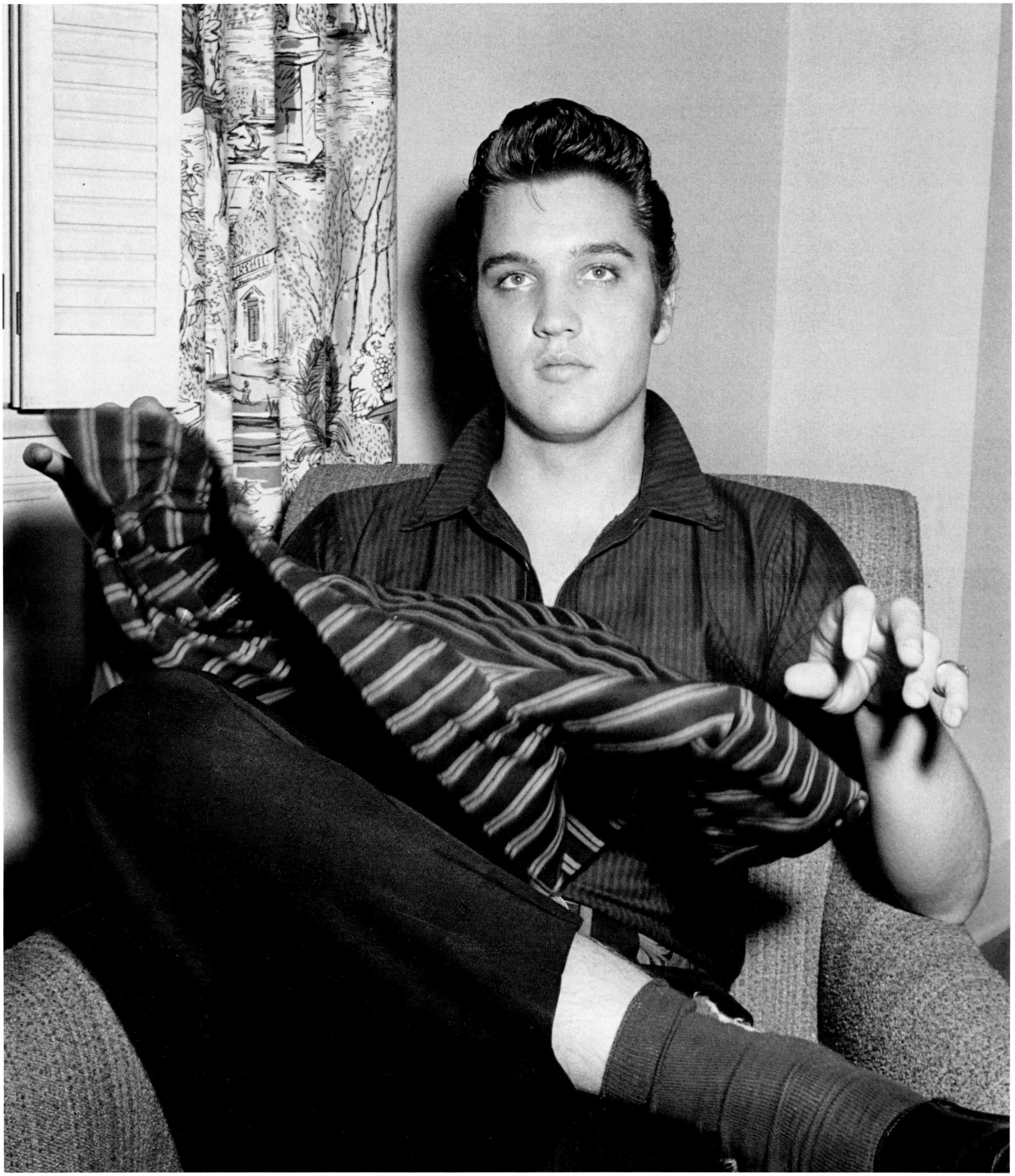

*Who is there that, in logical words,
can express the effect music has
on us? A kind of inarticulate
unfathomable speech, which leads
us to the edge of the Infinite,
and lets us for moments
gaze into that!*

Thomas Carlyle

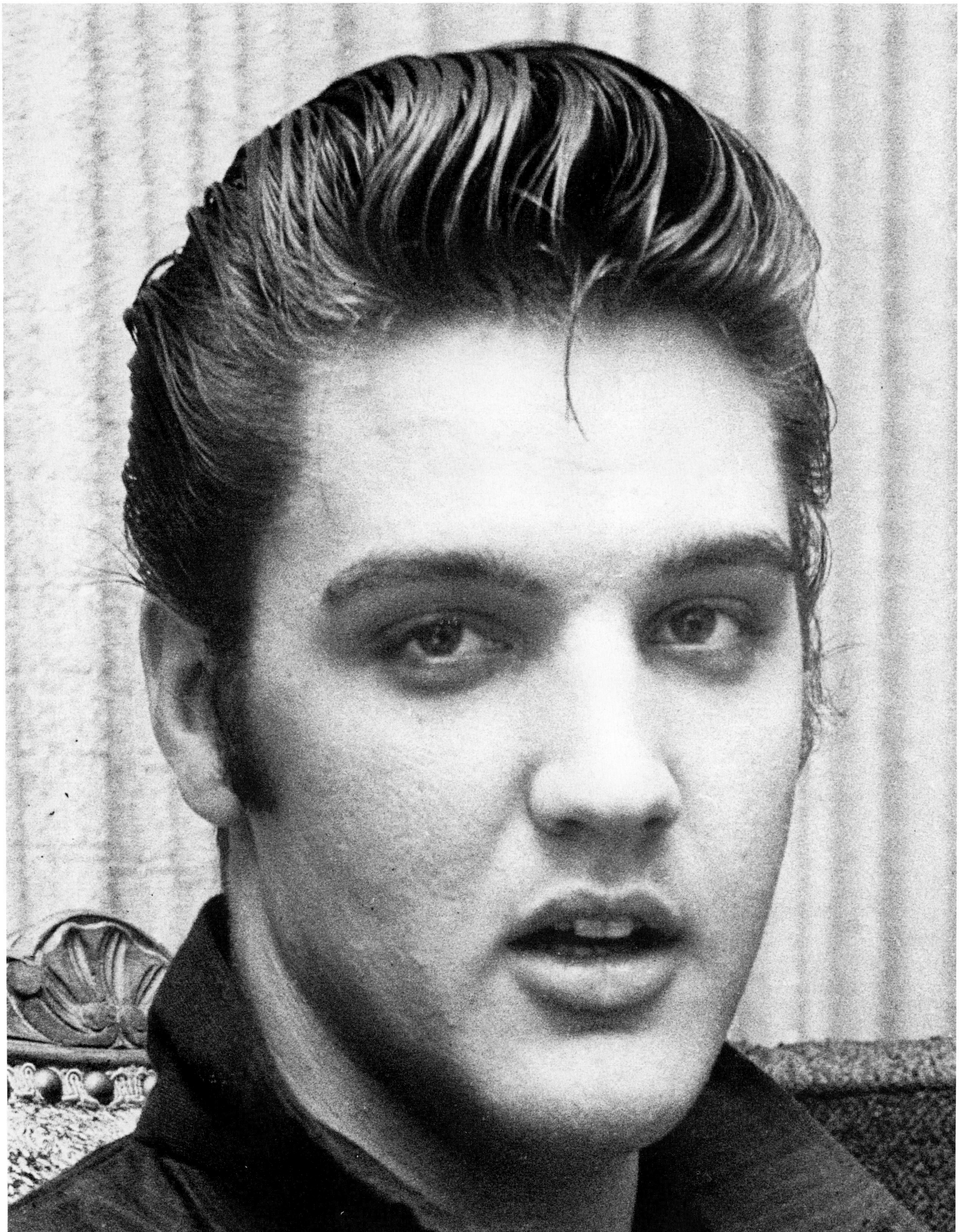

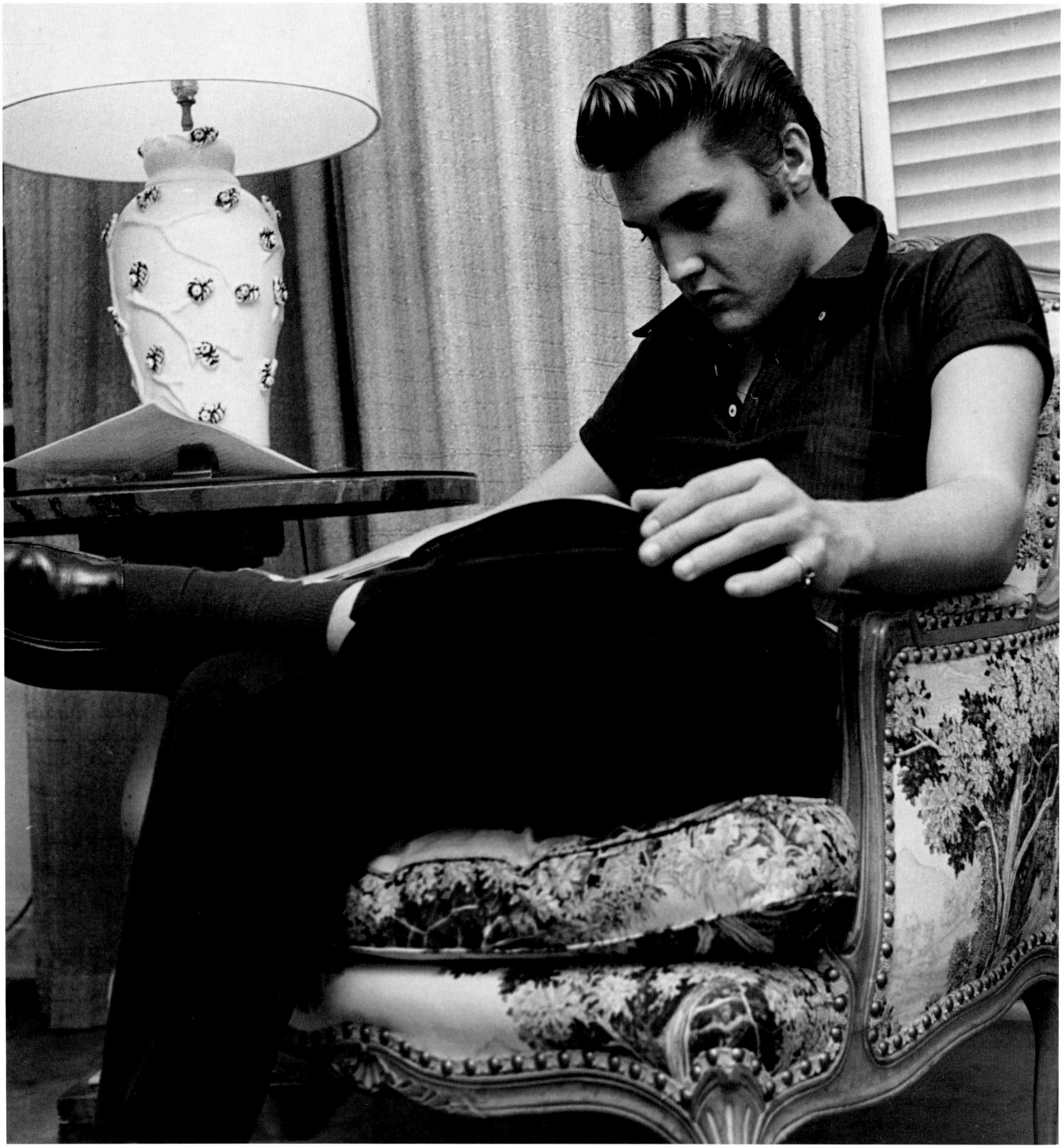

*Where there's music
there can be no evil.*

Miguel De Cervantes

The trouble with music appreciation in general is that people are taught to have too much respect for music; they should be taught to love it instead.

Igor Stravinsky

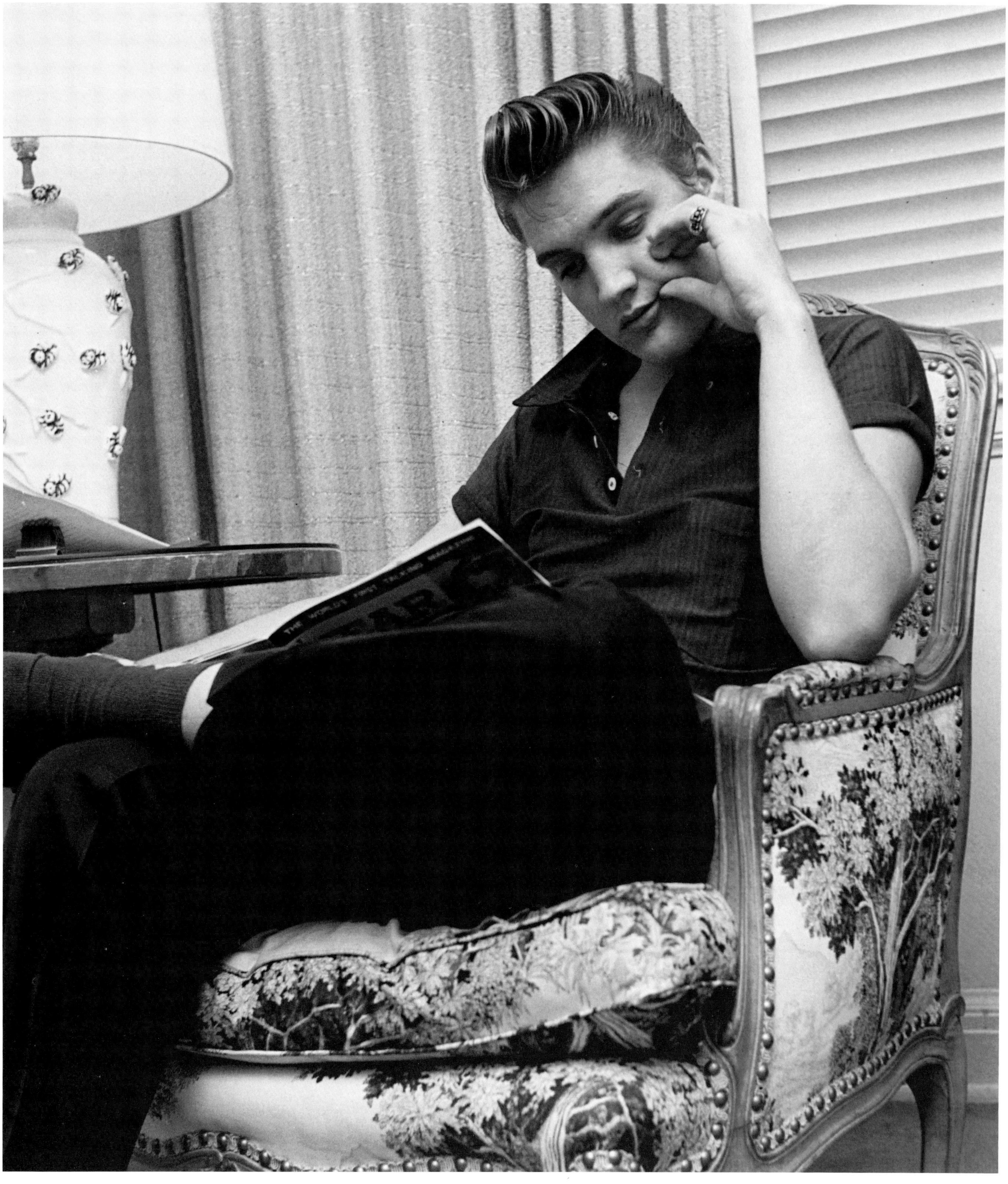
THE WORLD'S FIRST TALKING MAGAZINE

THE WORLD'S FIRST TALKING MAGAZINE!
HEAR
HEAR TAB HUNTER!
WILLIAMS
HUDSON

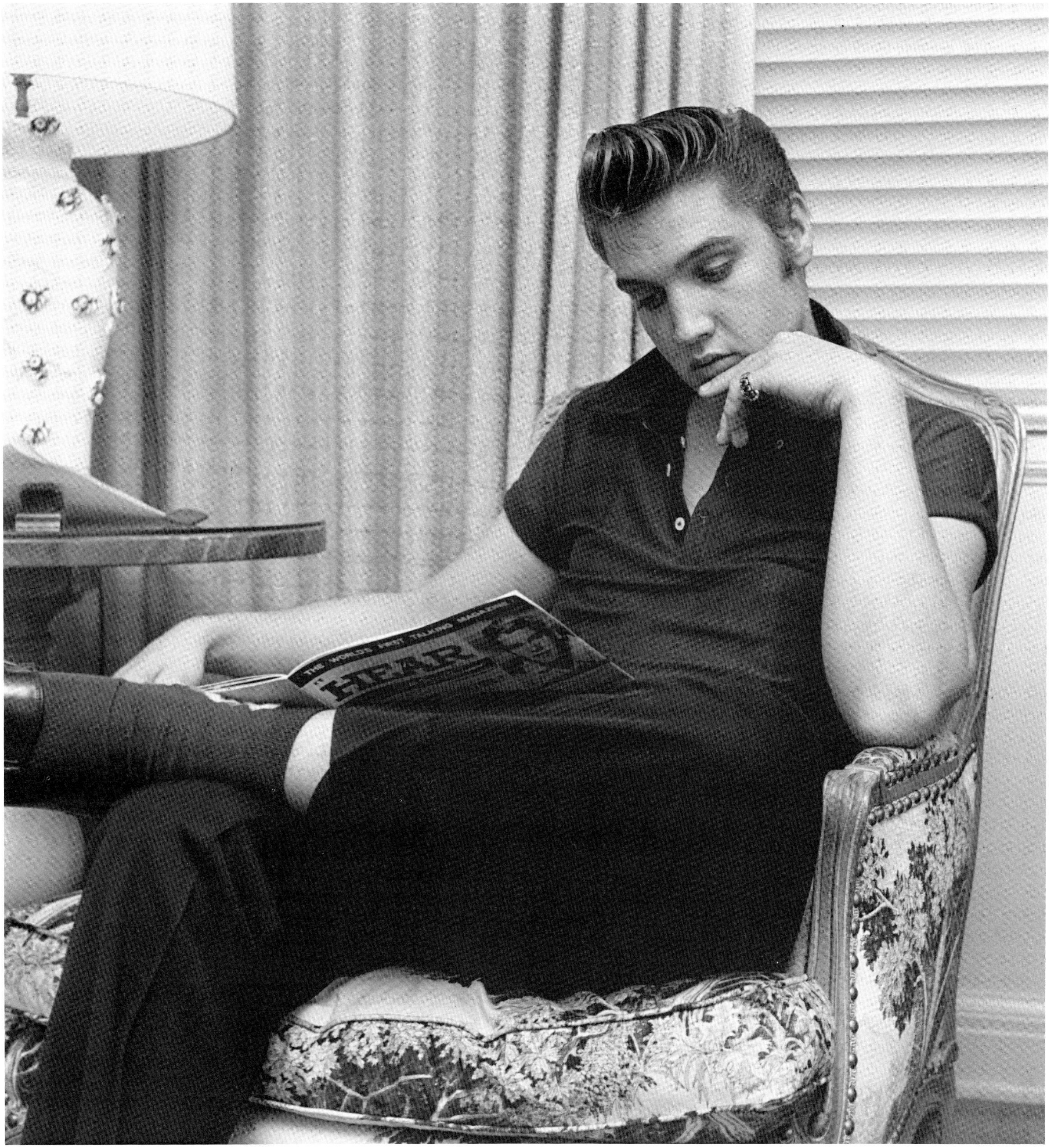
THE WORLD'S FIRST TALKING MAGAZINE
HEAR

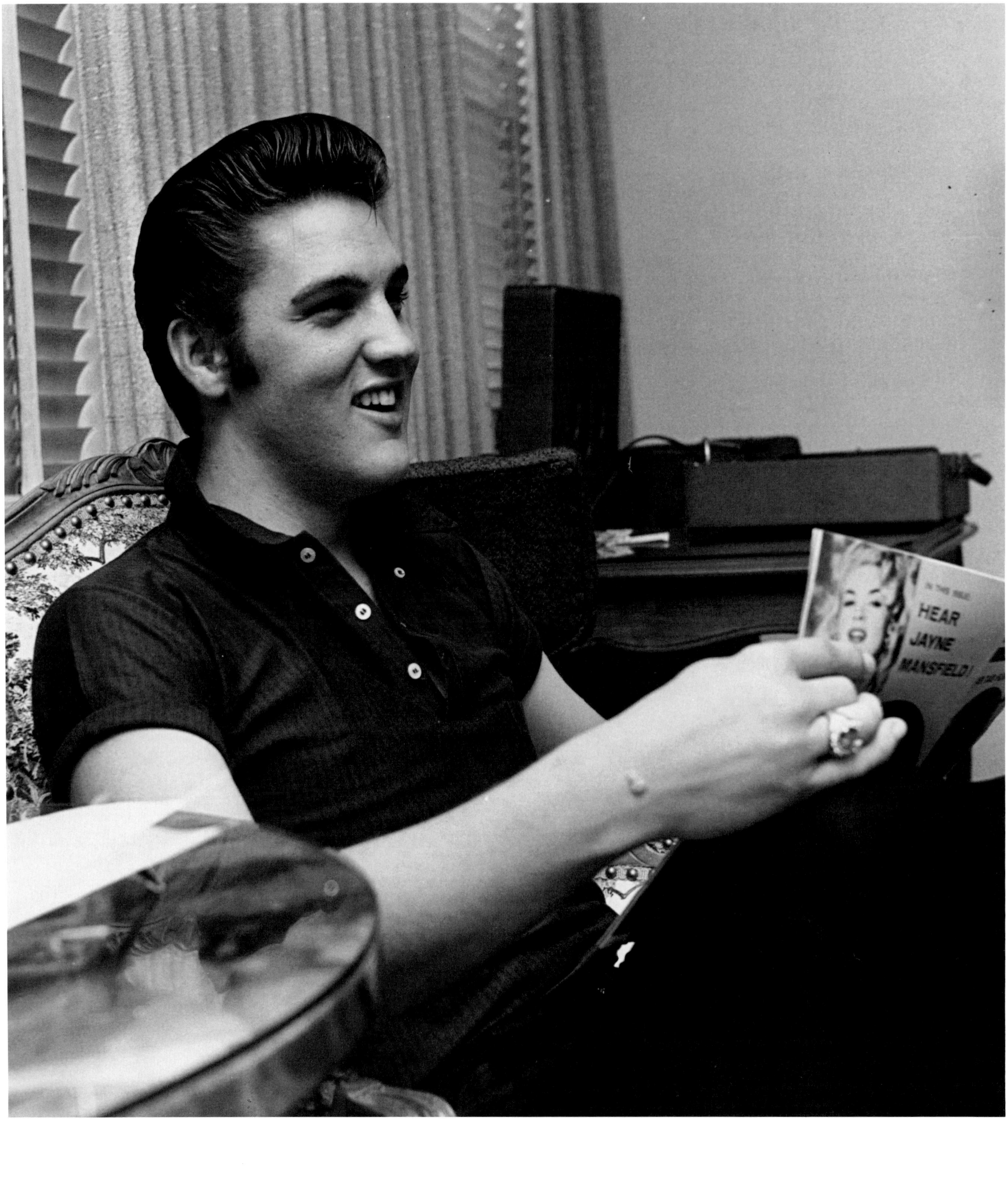
HEAR
JAYNE
MANSFIELD!

*When people hear good music,
it makes them homesick for
something they never had,
and never will have.*

Edgar Watson Howe

*Music is well said to be the speech
of angels; in fact, nothing among the
utterances allowed to man is felt
to be so divine. It brings us
near to the Infinite.*

Thomas Carlyle

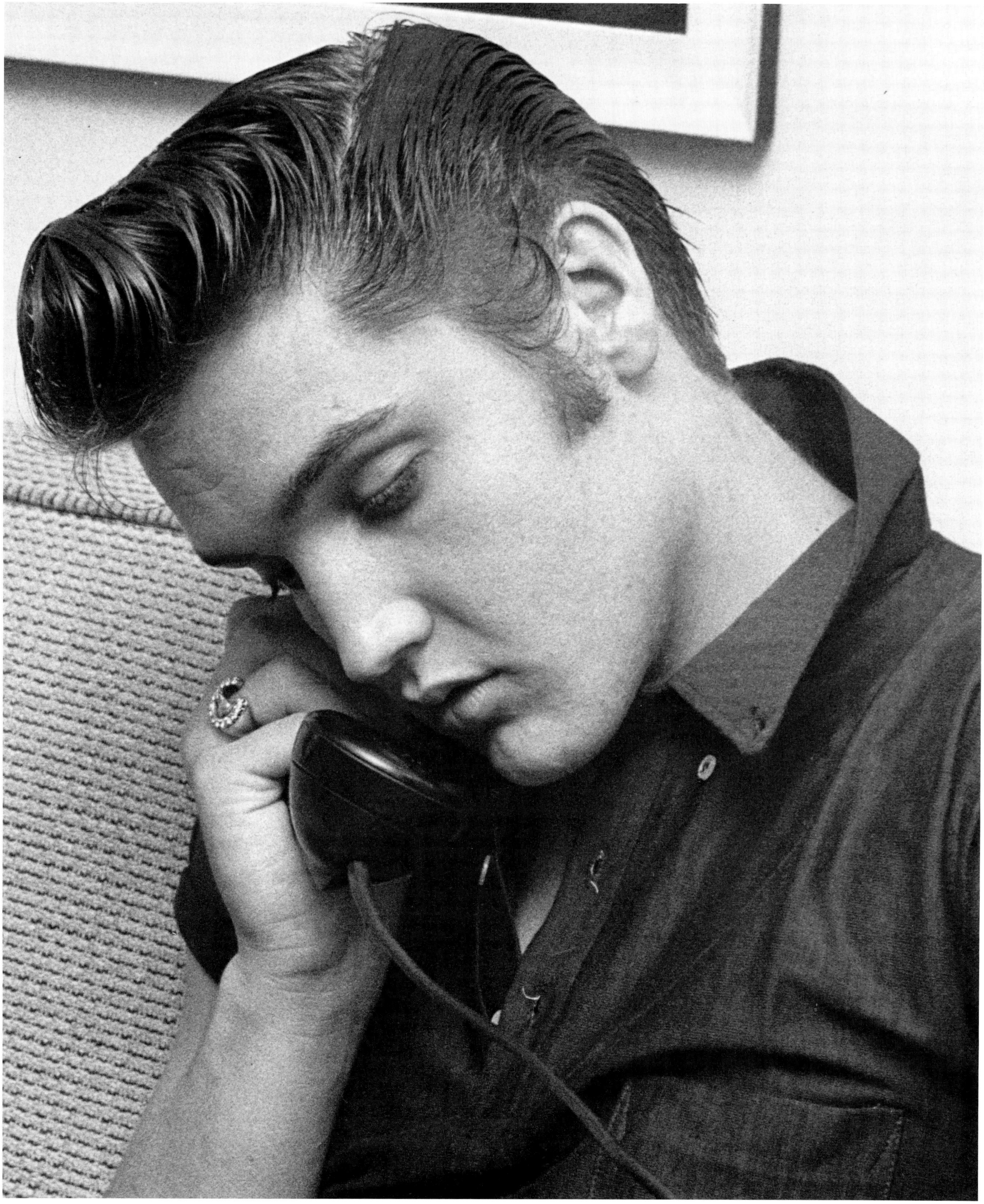

*A just conception of life
is too large a thing to grasp
during the short interval
of passing through it.*

Thomas Hardy

*A verbal art like poetry is reflective;
it stops to think. Music is immediate,
it goes on to become.*

W.H. Auden

*When love and skill work together,
expect a masterpiece.*

John Ruskin

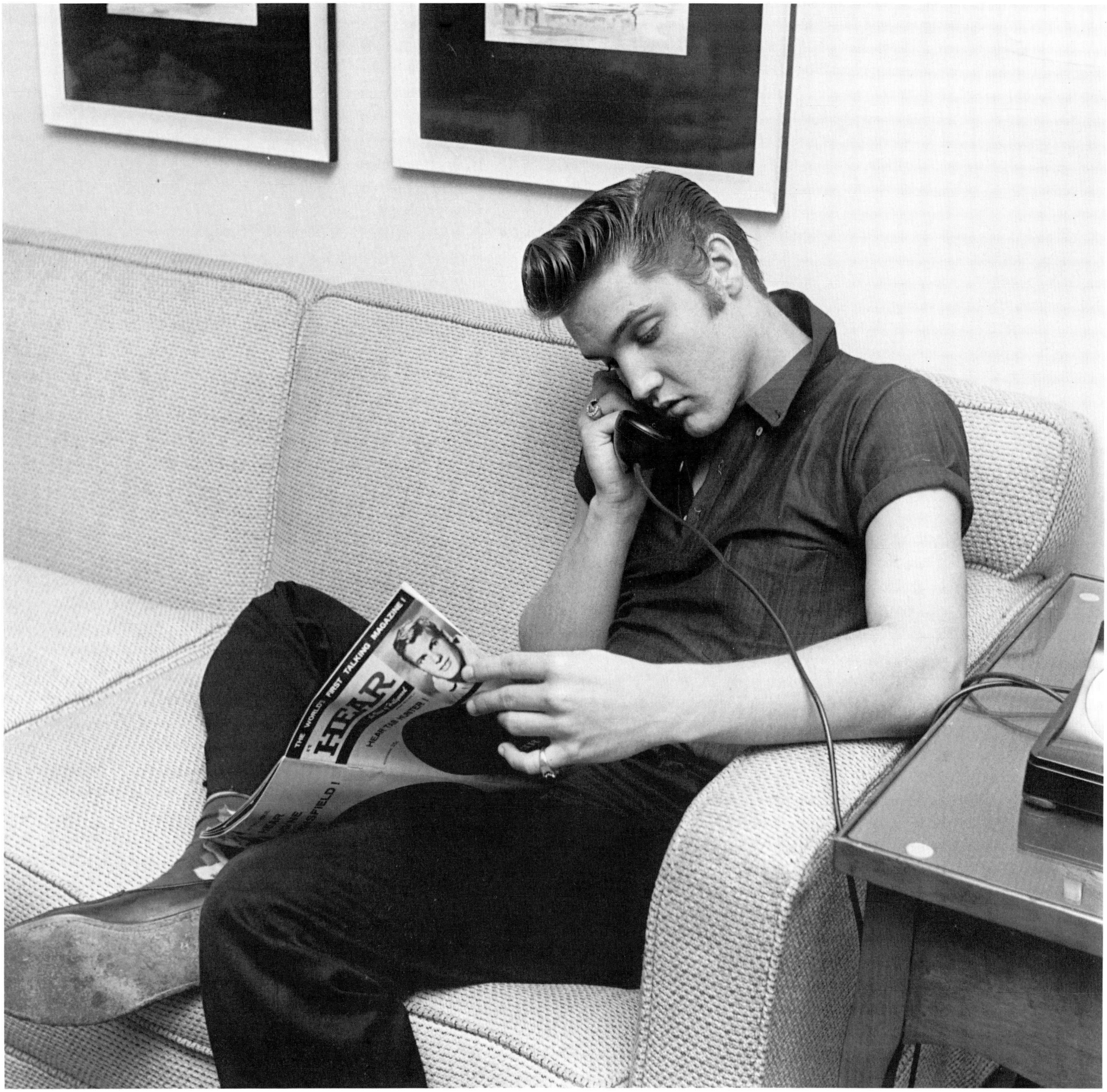
THE WORLD'S FIRST TALKING MAGAZINE!
HEAR

True worth is in being, not seeming —
In doing, each day that goes by,
Some little good — not in dreaming
Of great things to do by and by,
For whatever men say in their blindness,
And spite of the fancies of youth,
There's nothing so kingly as kindness,
And nothing so royal as truth.

Alice Cary

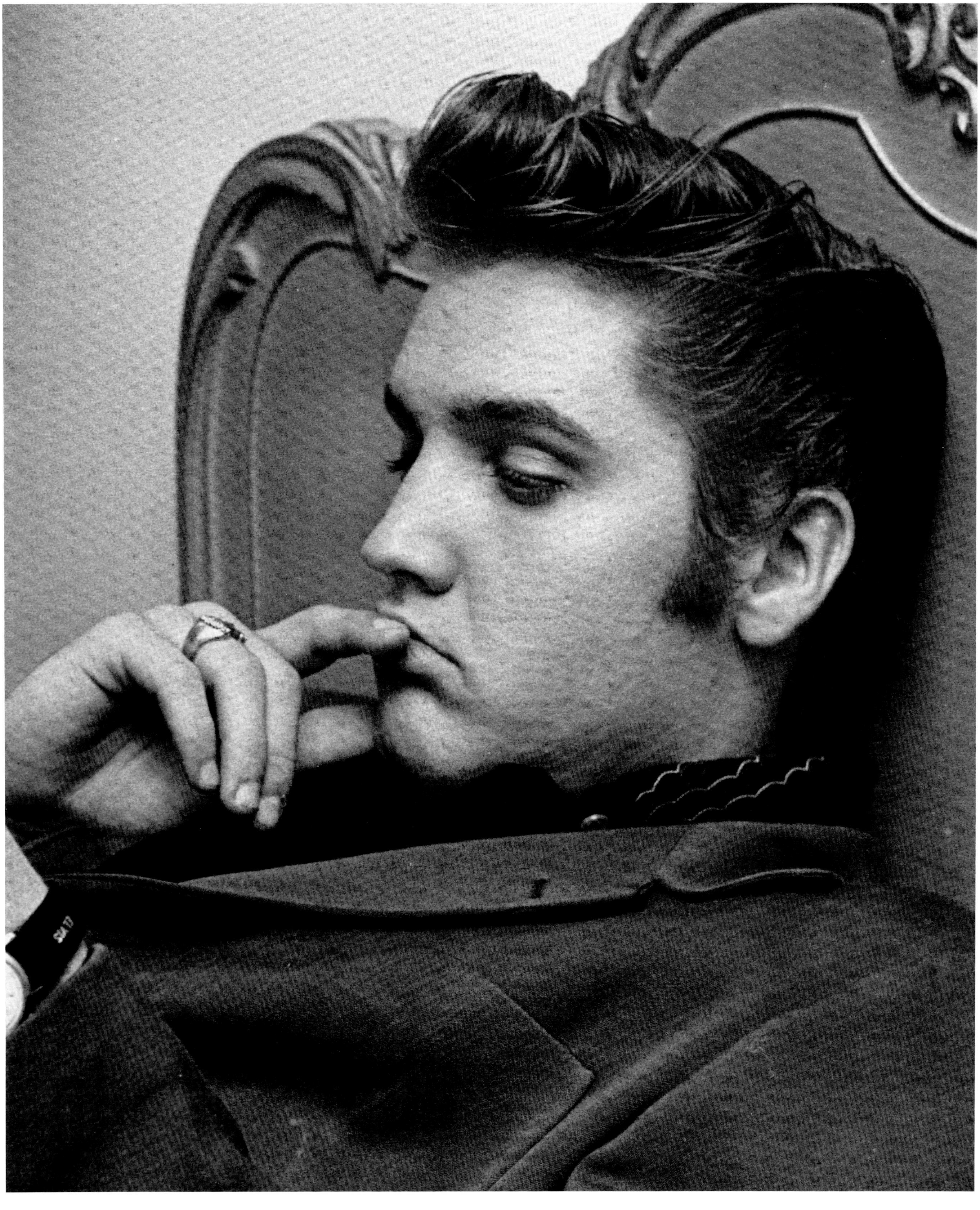

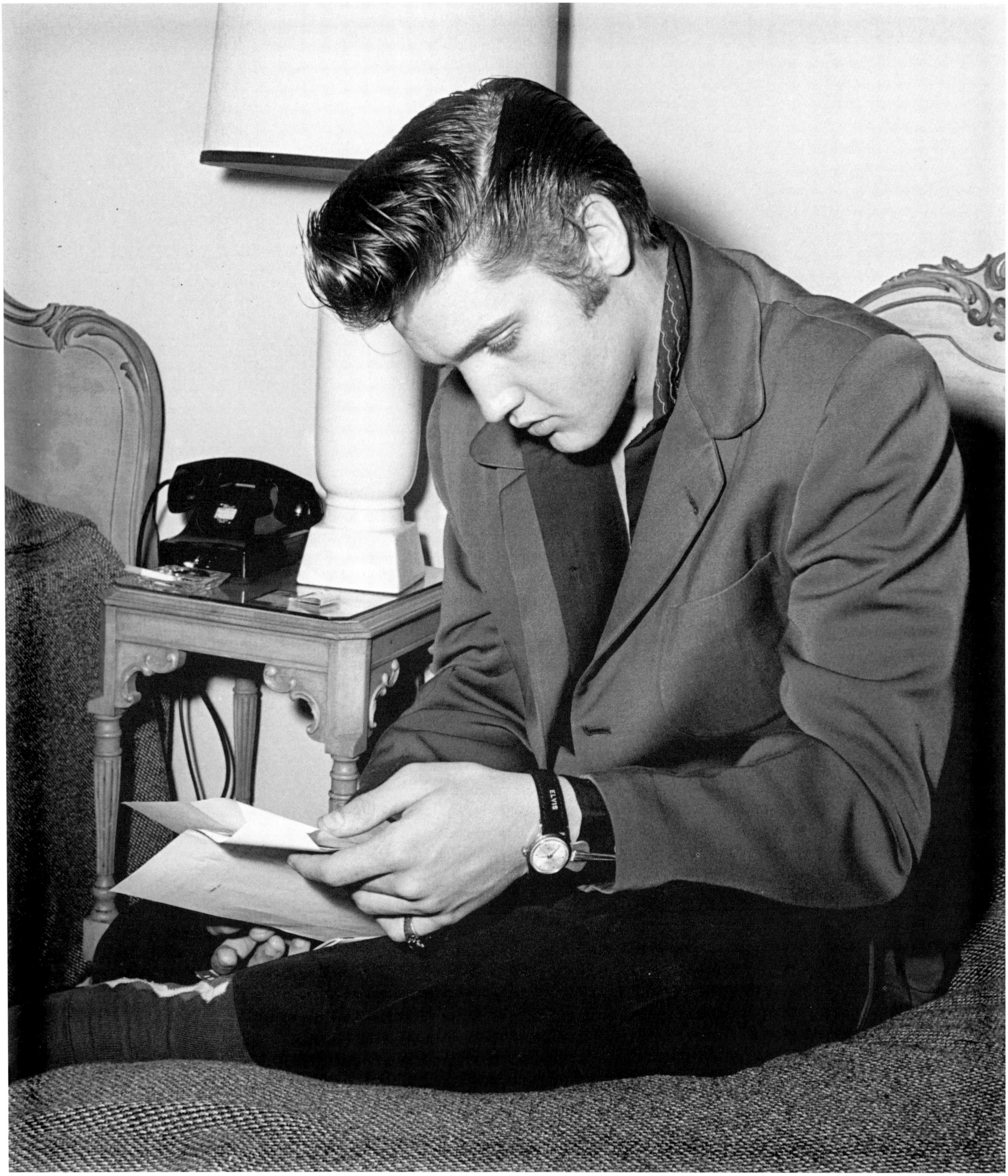
ELVIS

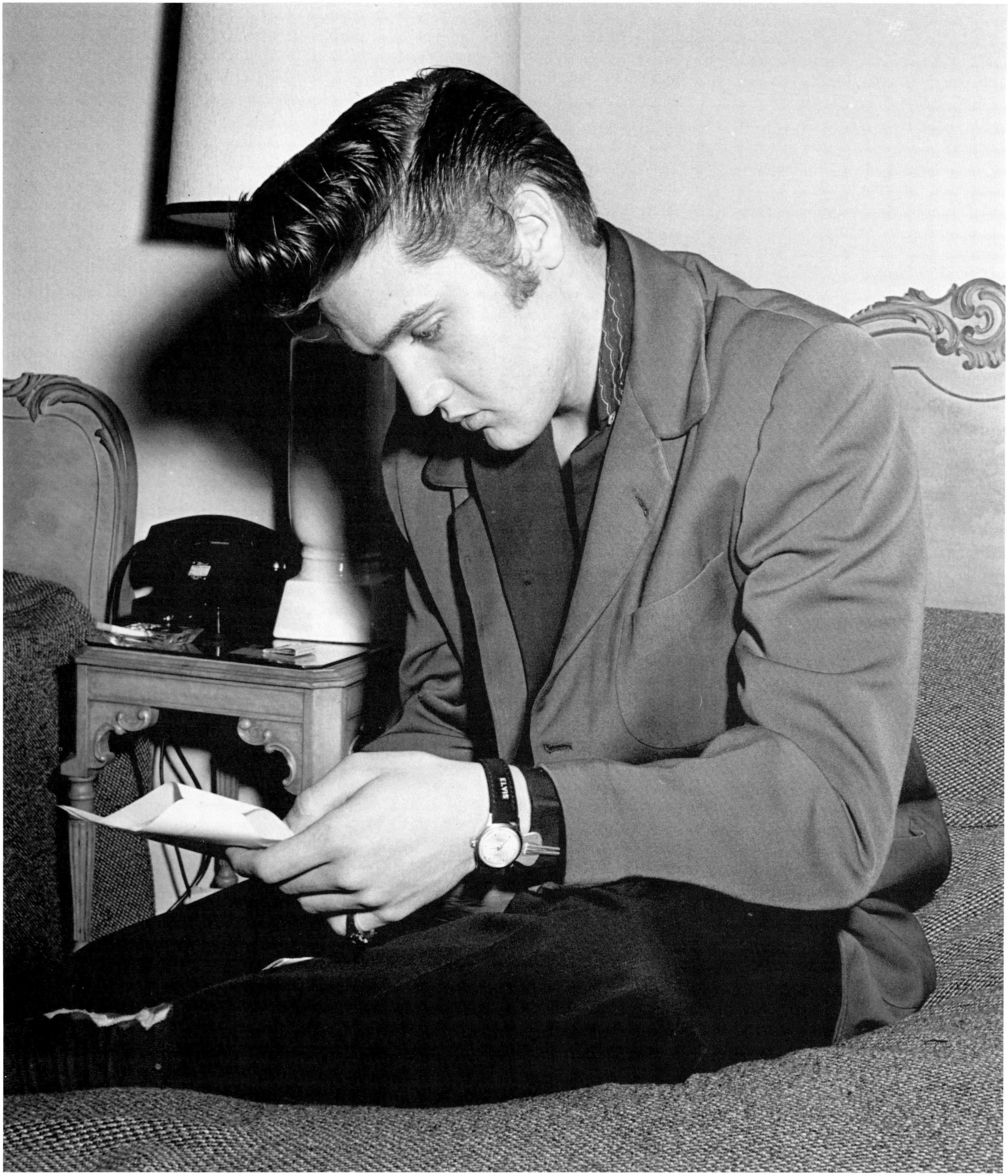

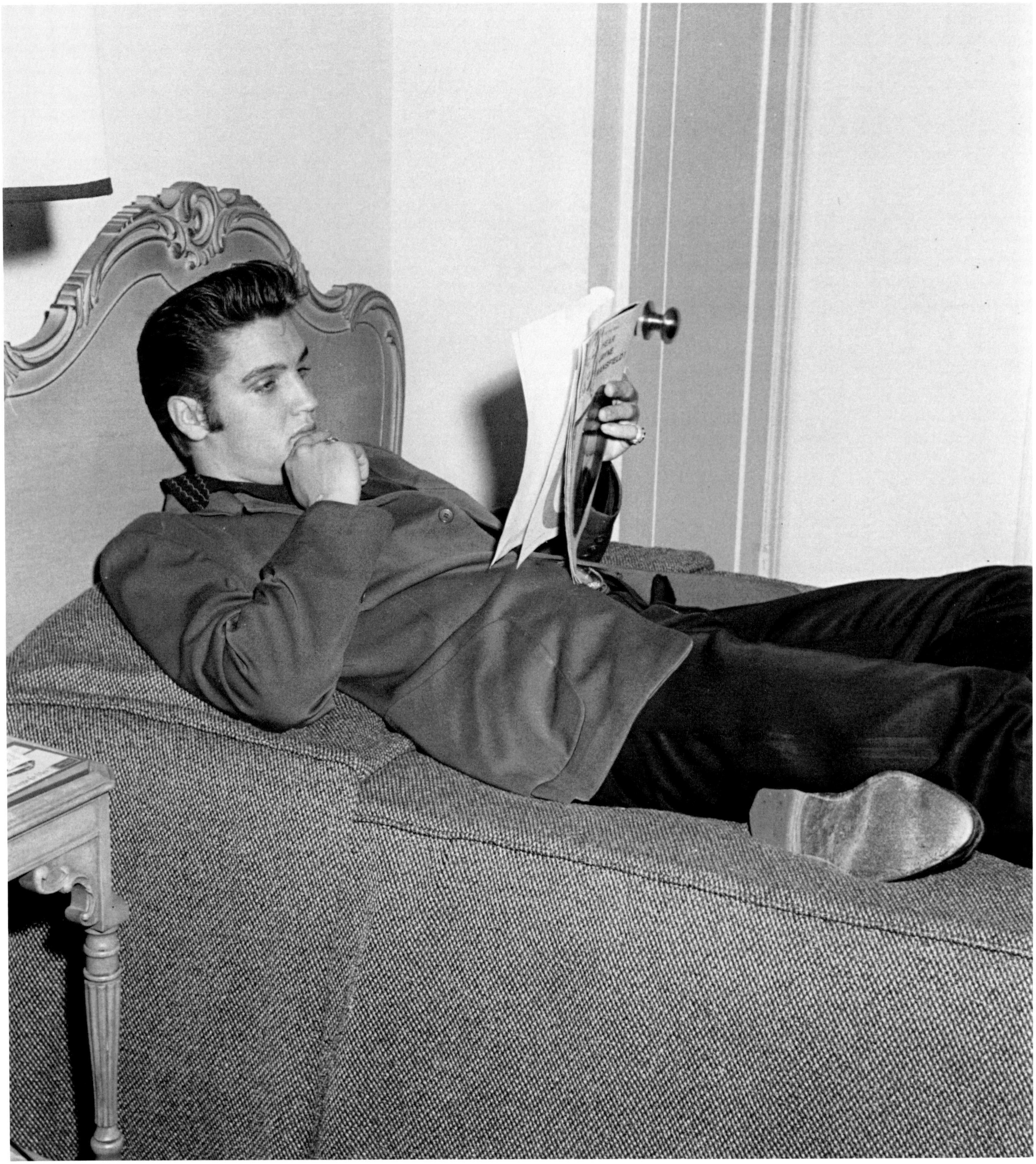

IN THIS ISSUE
HEAR
JAYNE
MANSFIELD!
THE WORLD'S FIRST TALKING MAGAZINE

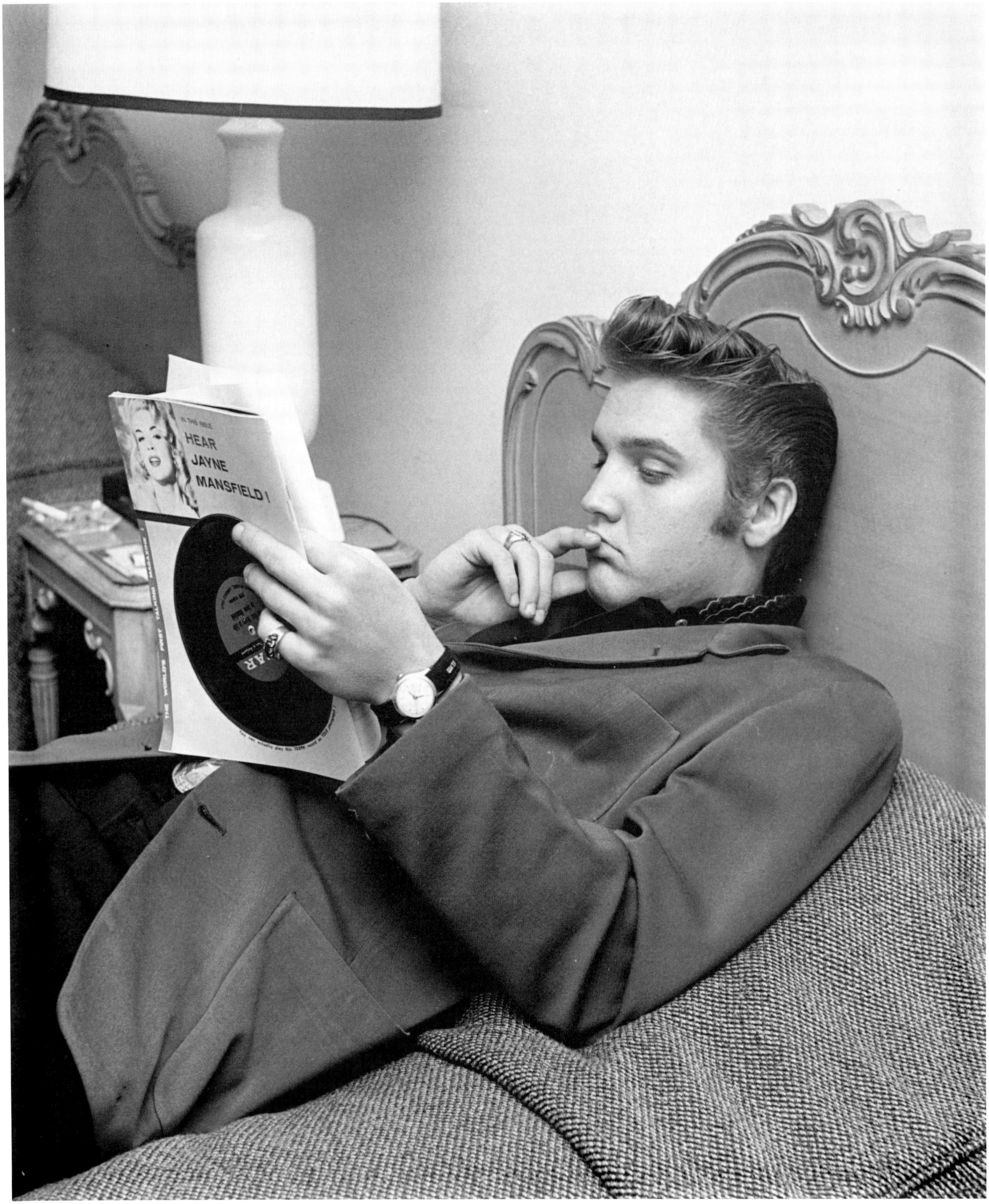
HEAR
JAYNE
MANSFIELD!
THE WORLD'S FIRST TALKING MAGAZINE

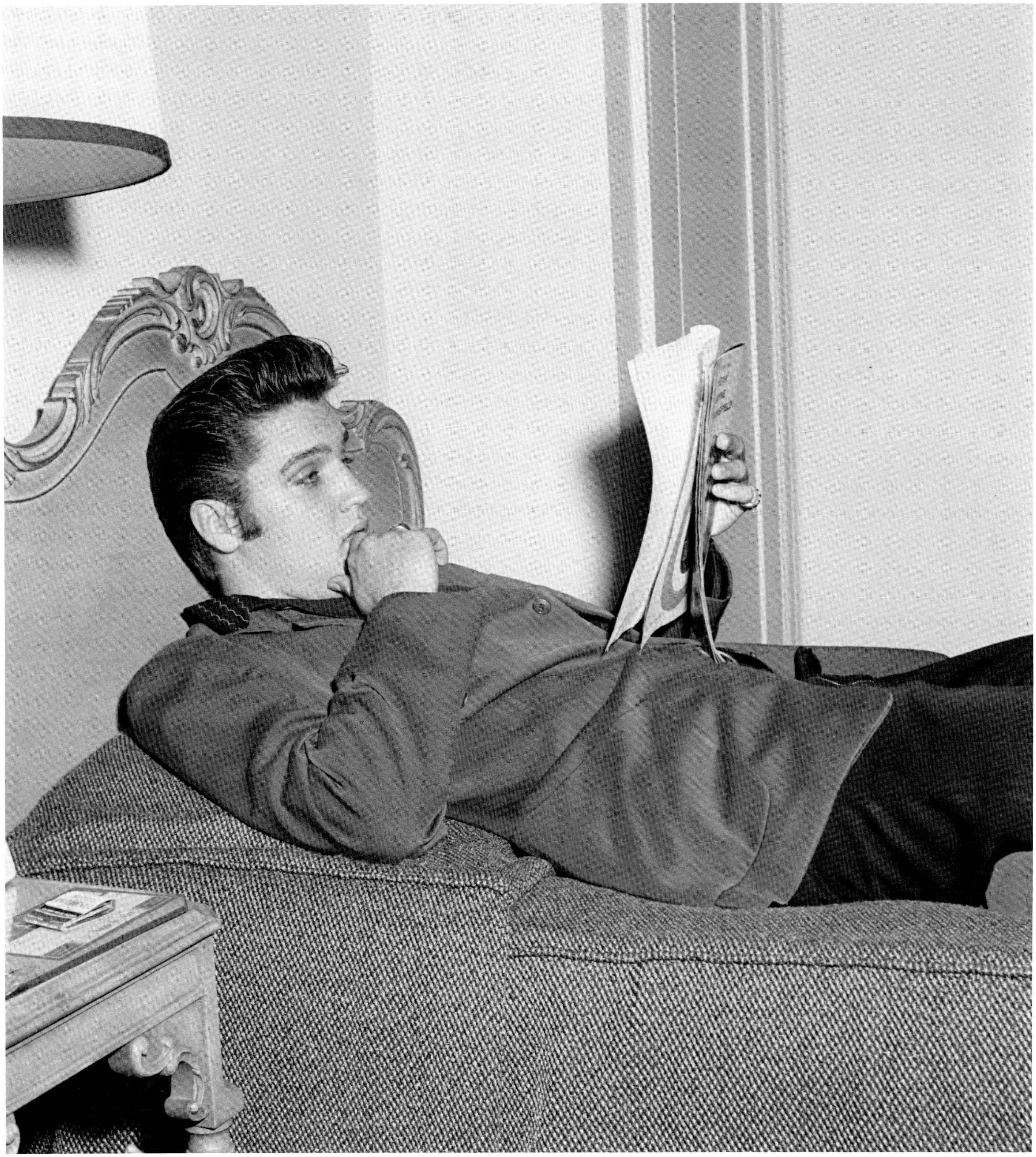

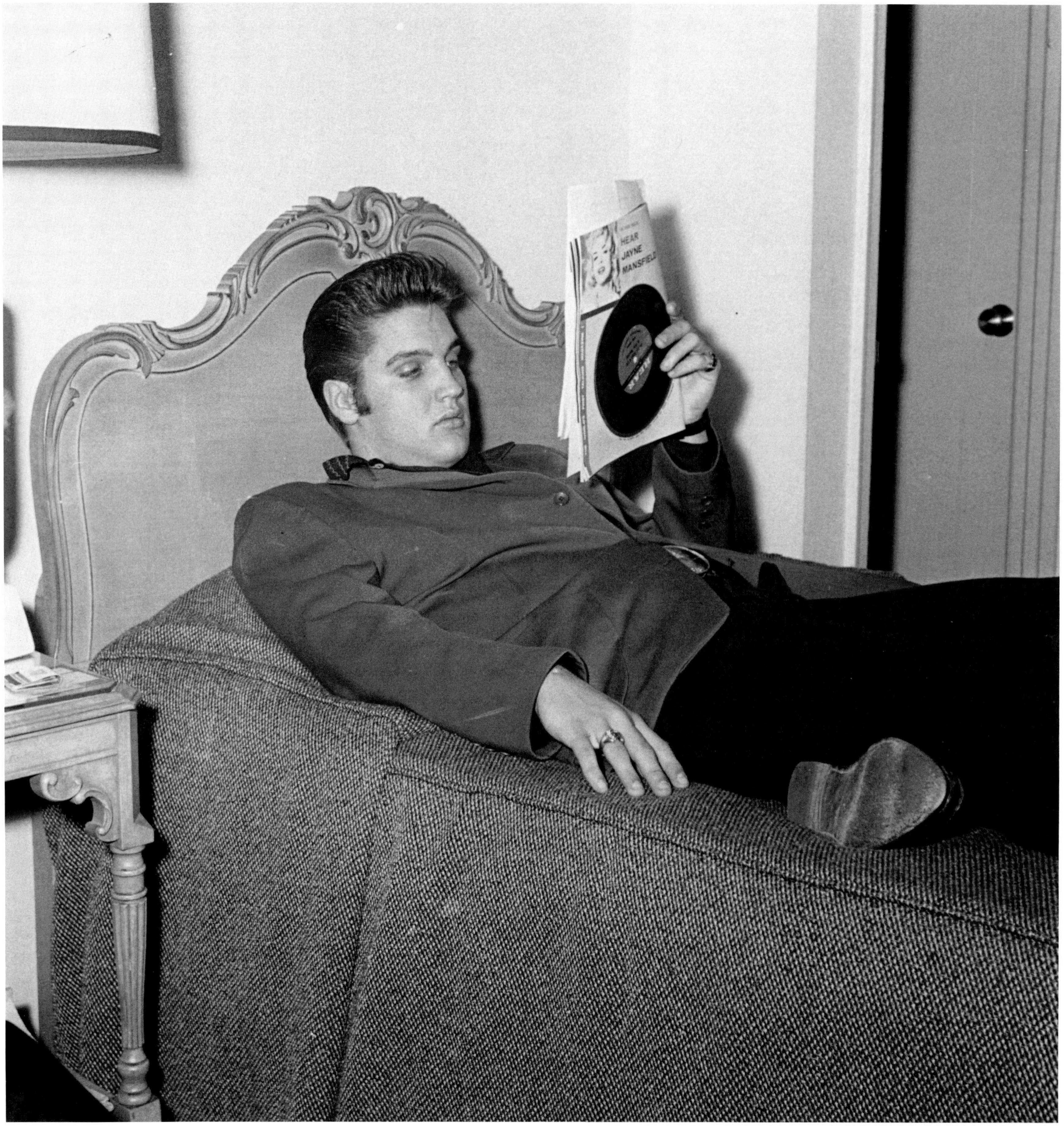
HEAR
JAYNE
MANSFIELD

A thing of beauty is a joy for ever:
Its loveliness increases;
it will never
Pass into nothingness; . . .

John Keats

*It is not sufficient
to see and to know the beauty of a work.
We must feel and be affected by it.*

François Voltaire

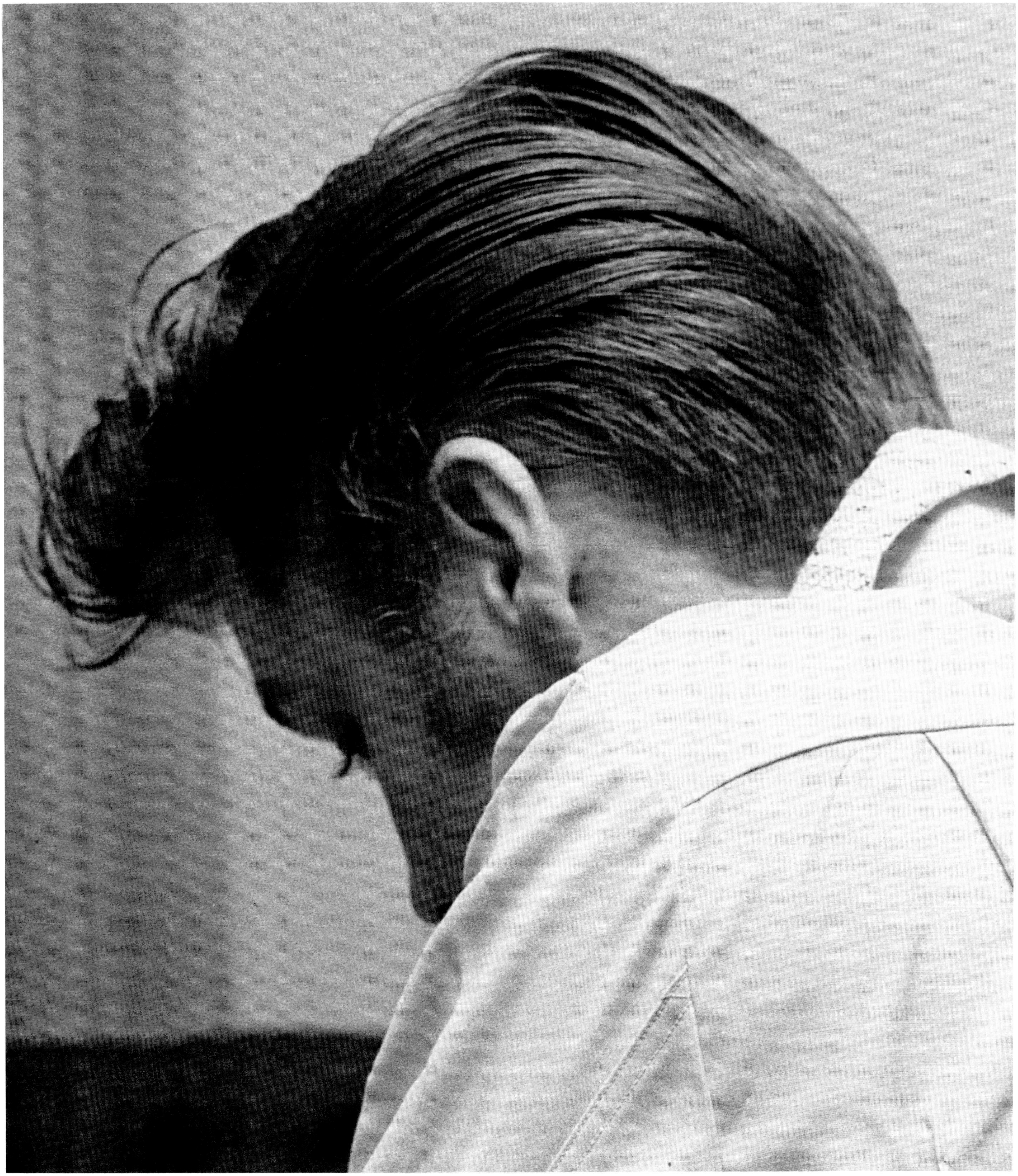

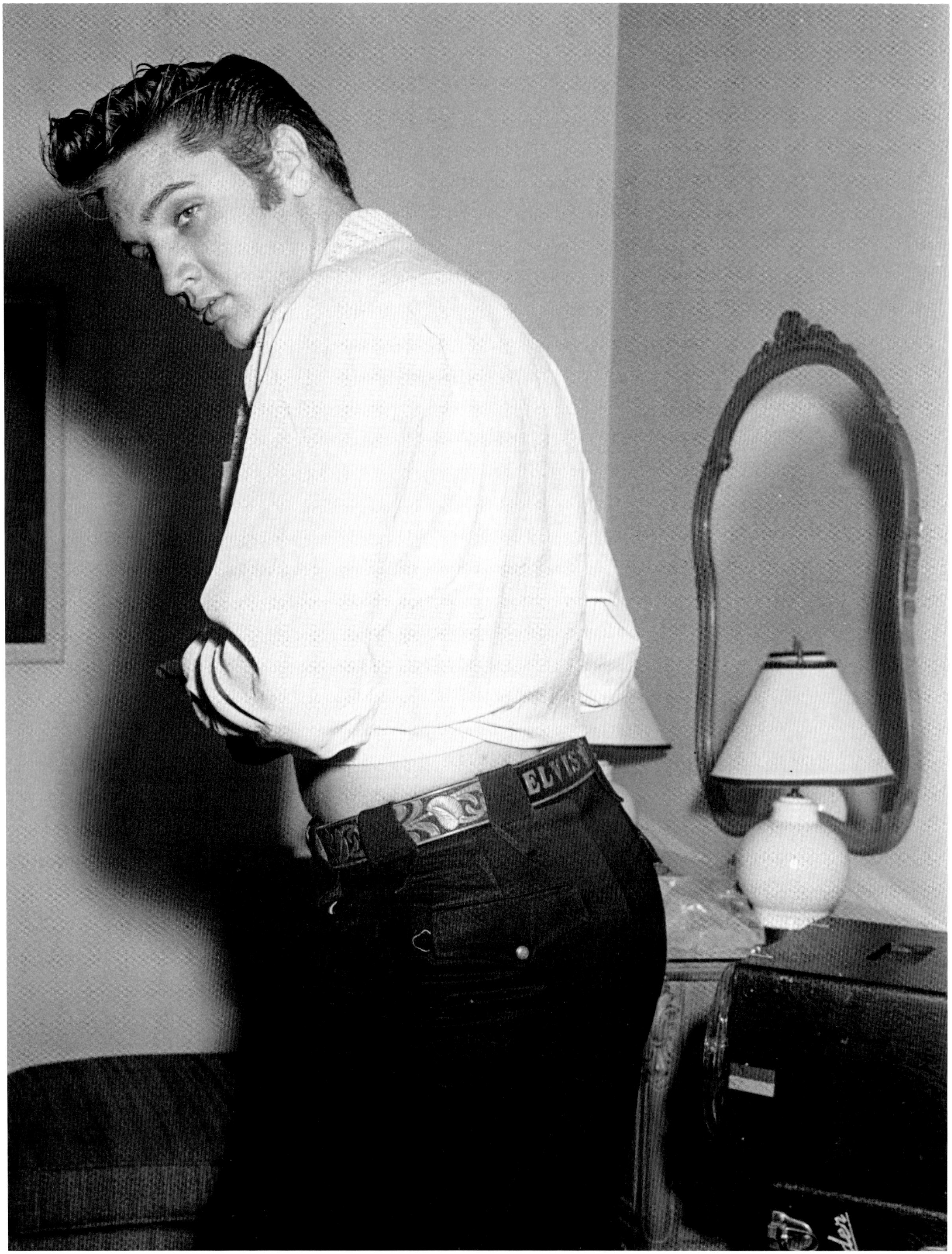
ELVIS

Music is edifying,
for from time to time it sets souls in operation.

John Cage

Music, when soft voices die,
Vibrates in the memory; . . .

Percy Bysshe Shelley

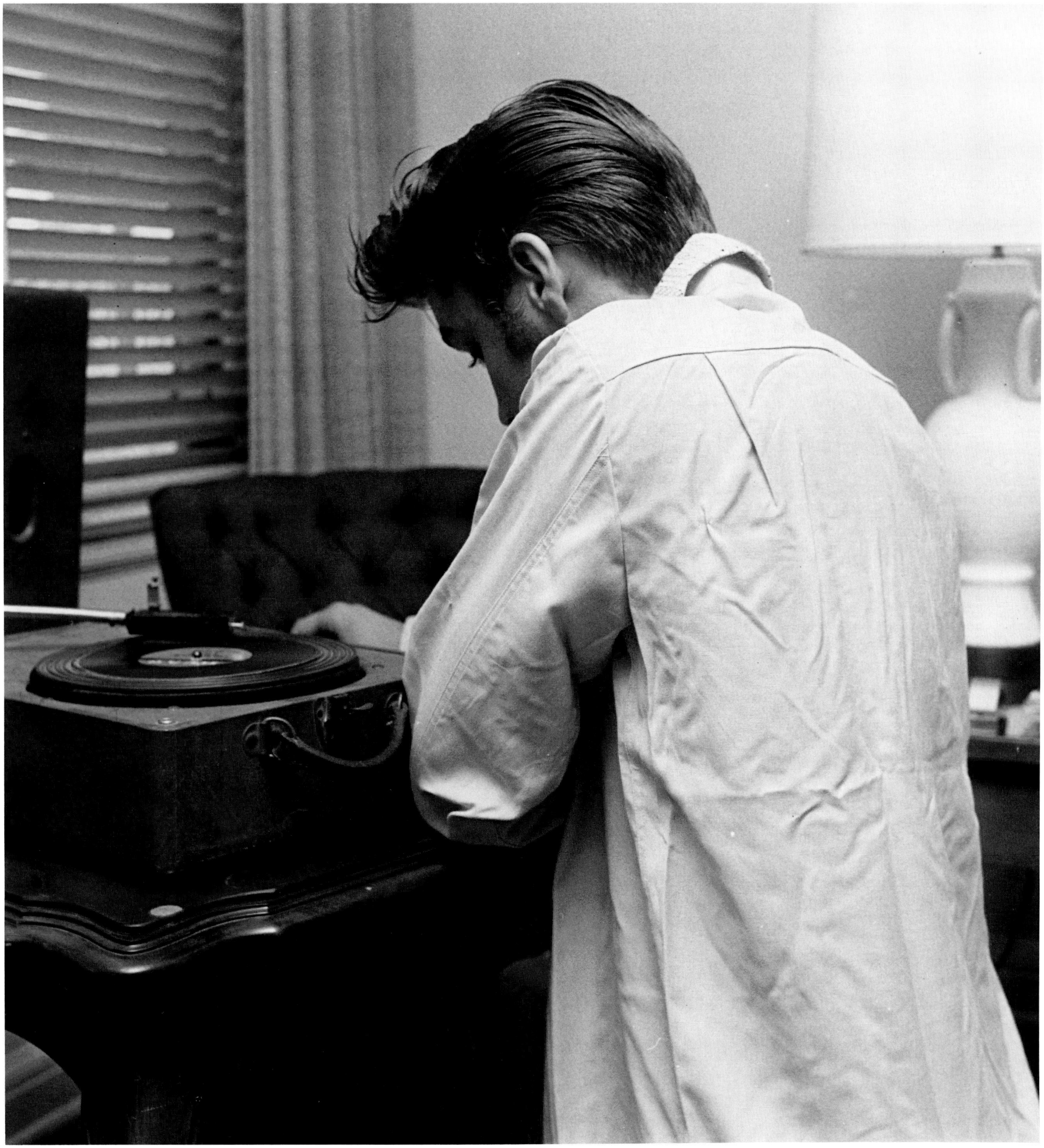

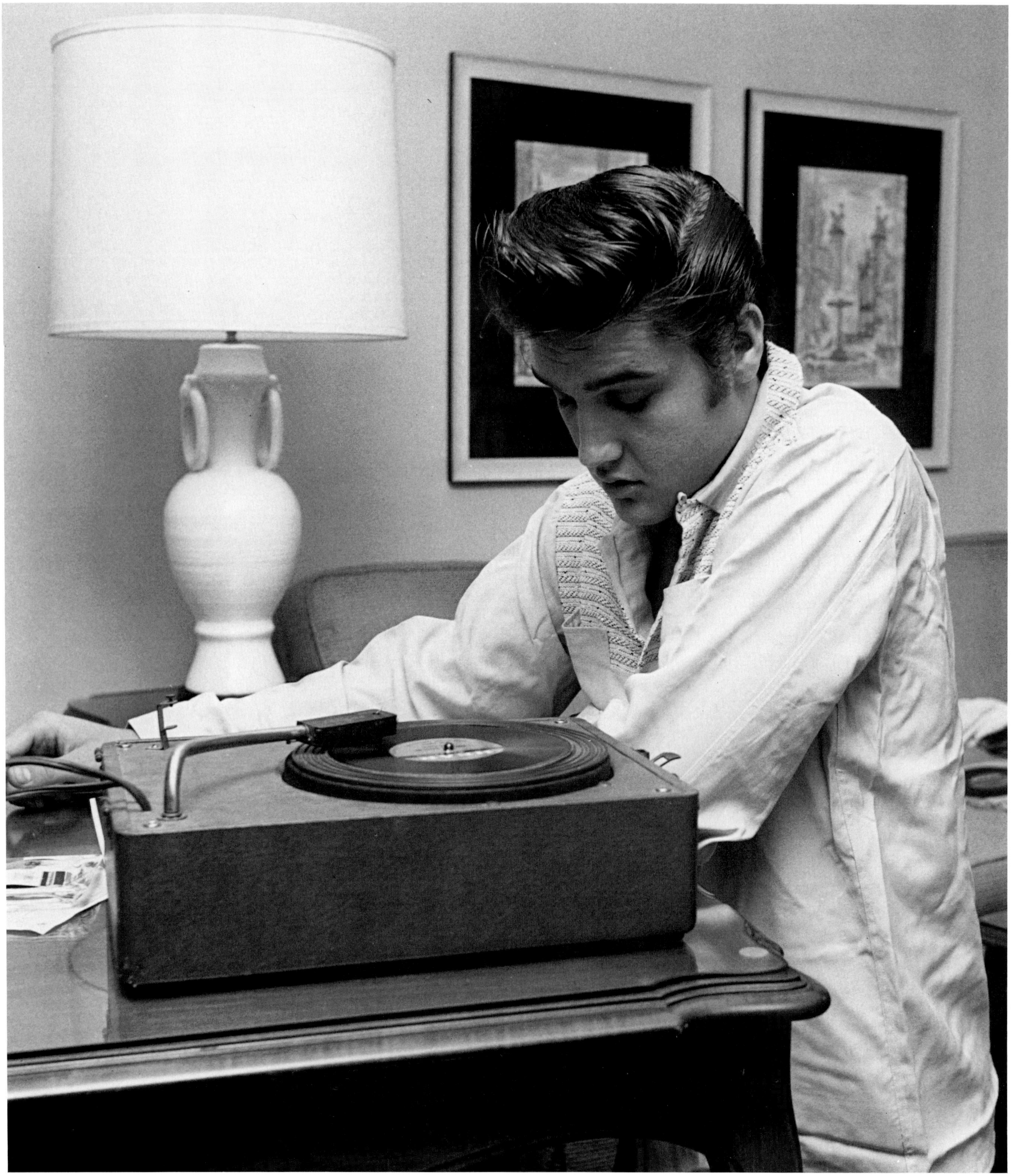

Every creator painfully experiences the chasm between his inner vision and its ultimate expression.

Isaac Bashevis Singer

[Music] takes us out of the actual and whispers to us dim secrets that startle our wonder as to who we are, and for what, whence, and whereto.

Ralph Waldo Emerson

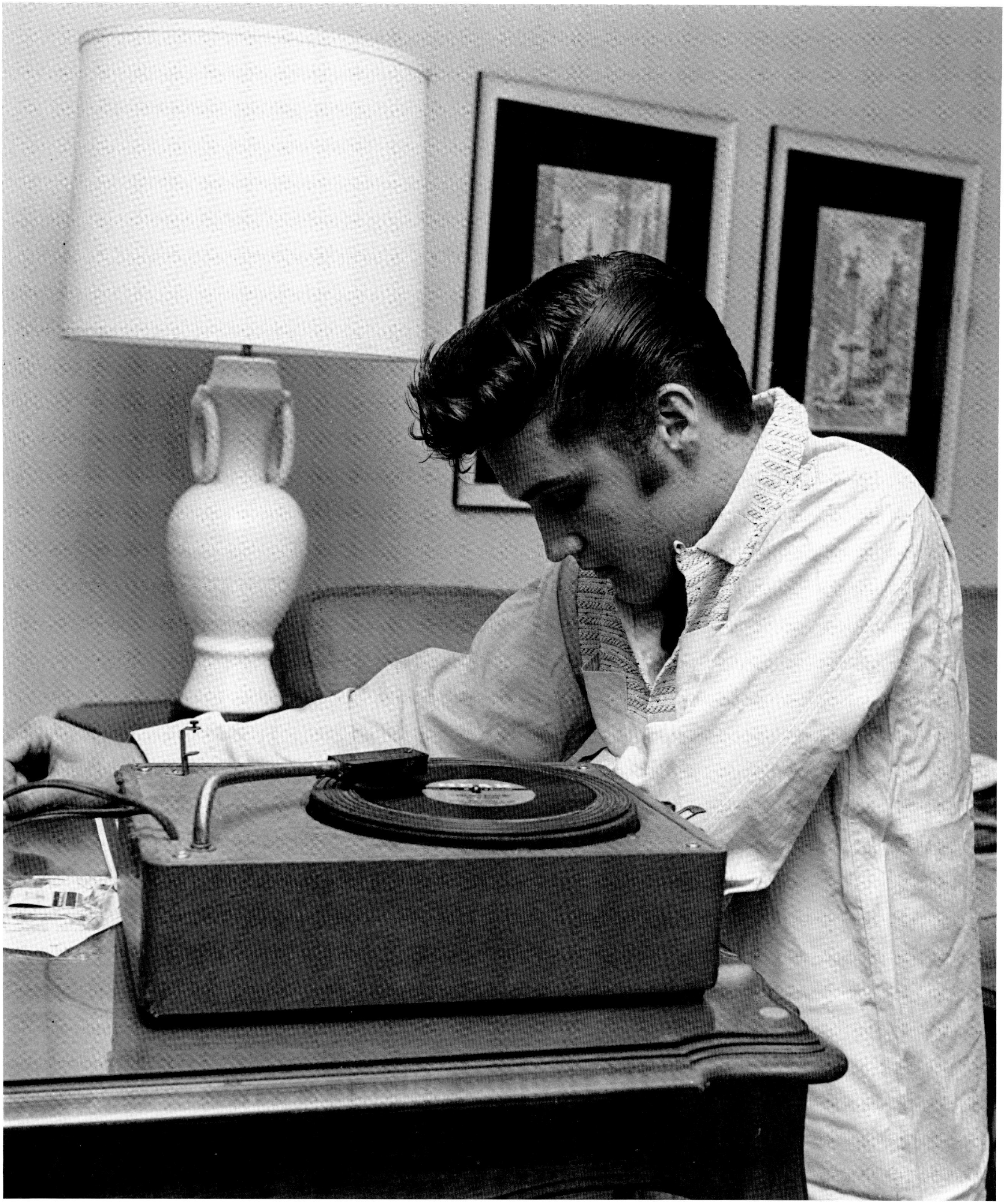

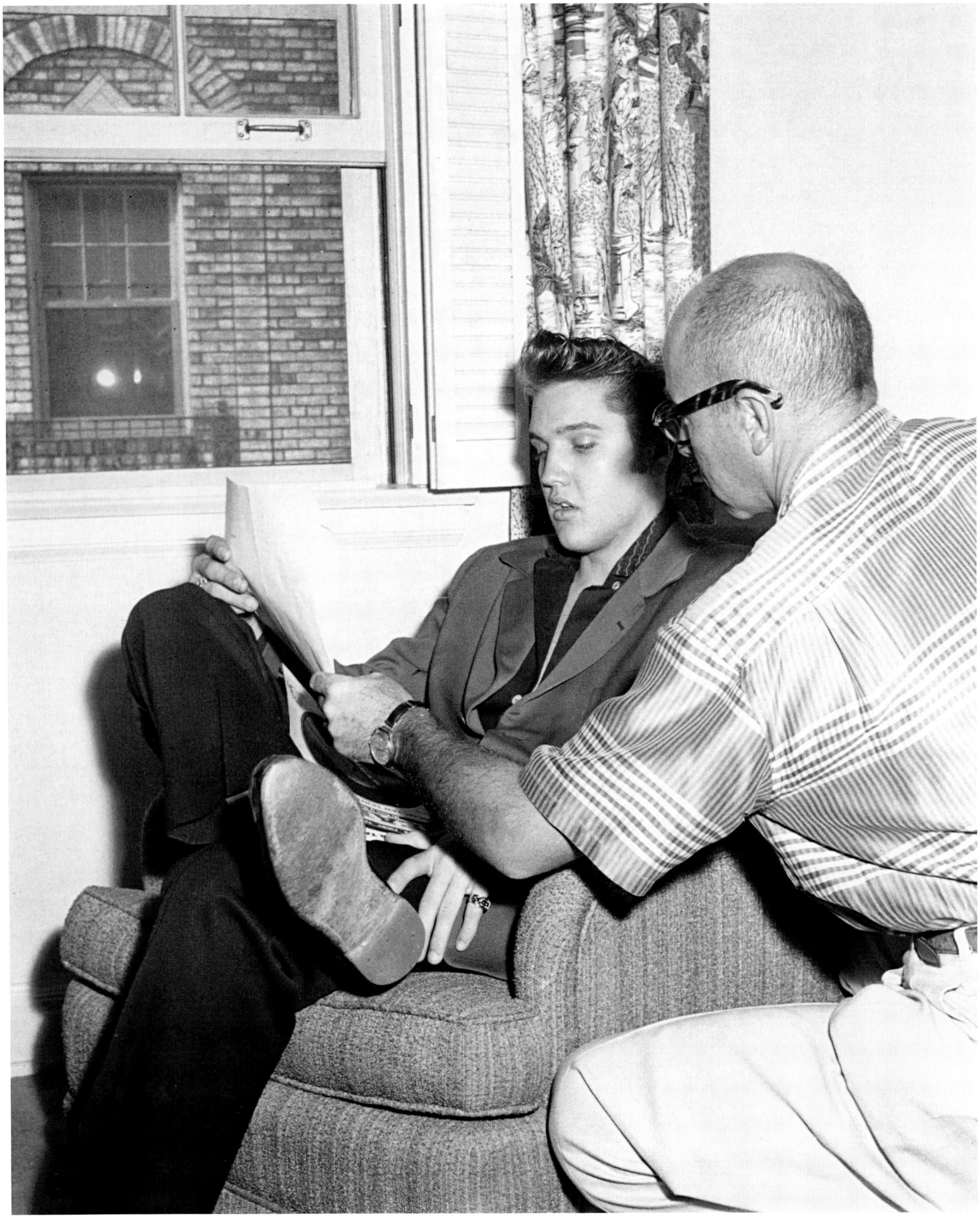

FLY
AME
WARNING
Do Not Put Drapes or Any Inflammable
Object Near Electric Heaters.
The Management

The eyes have one language everywhere.

George Herbert

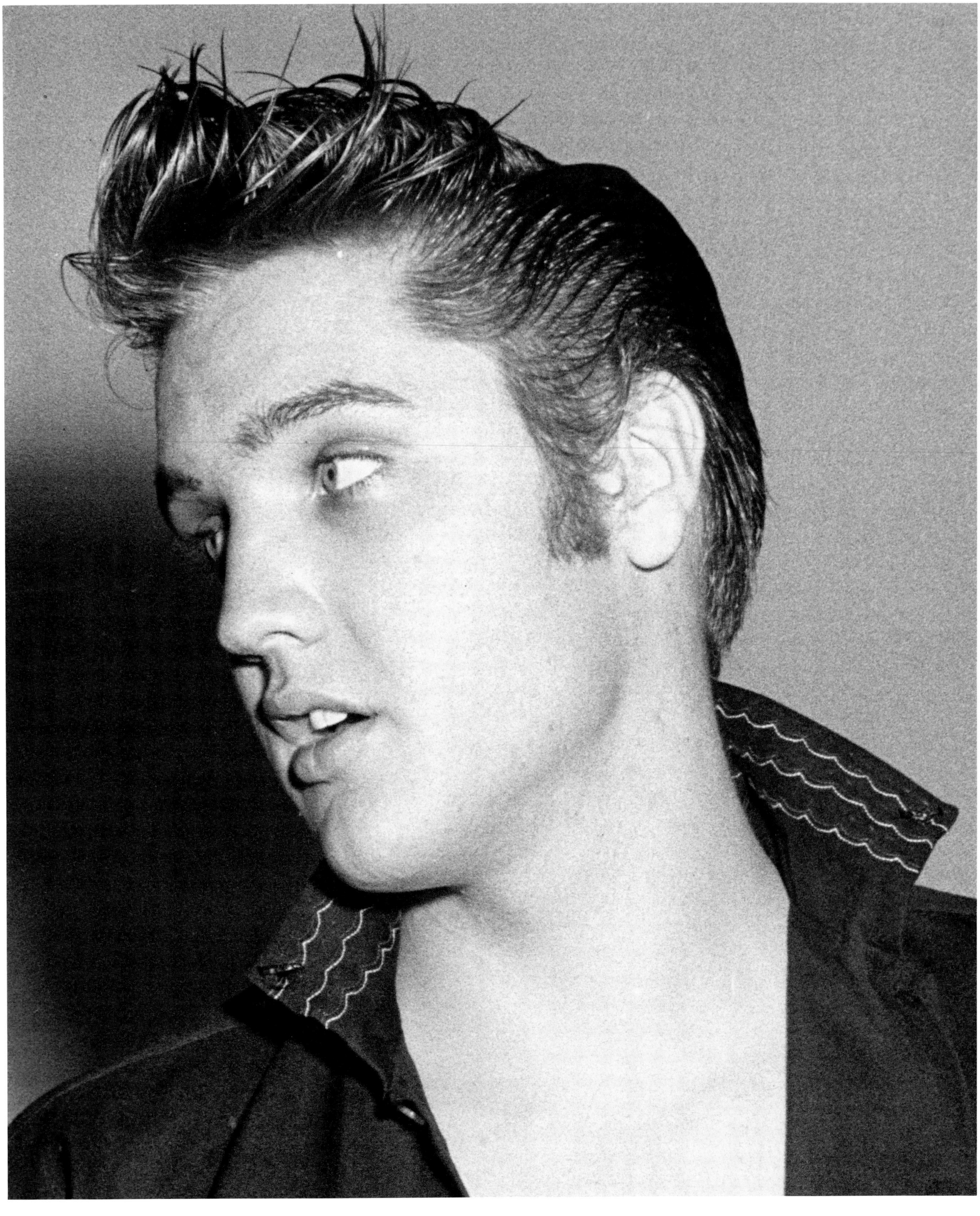

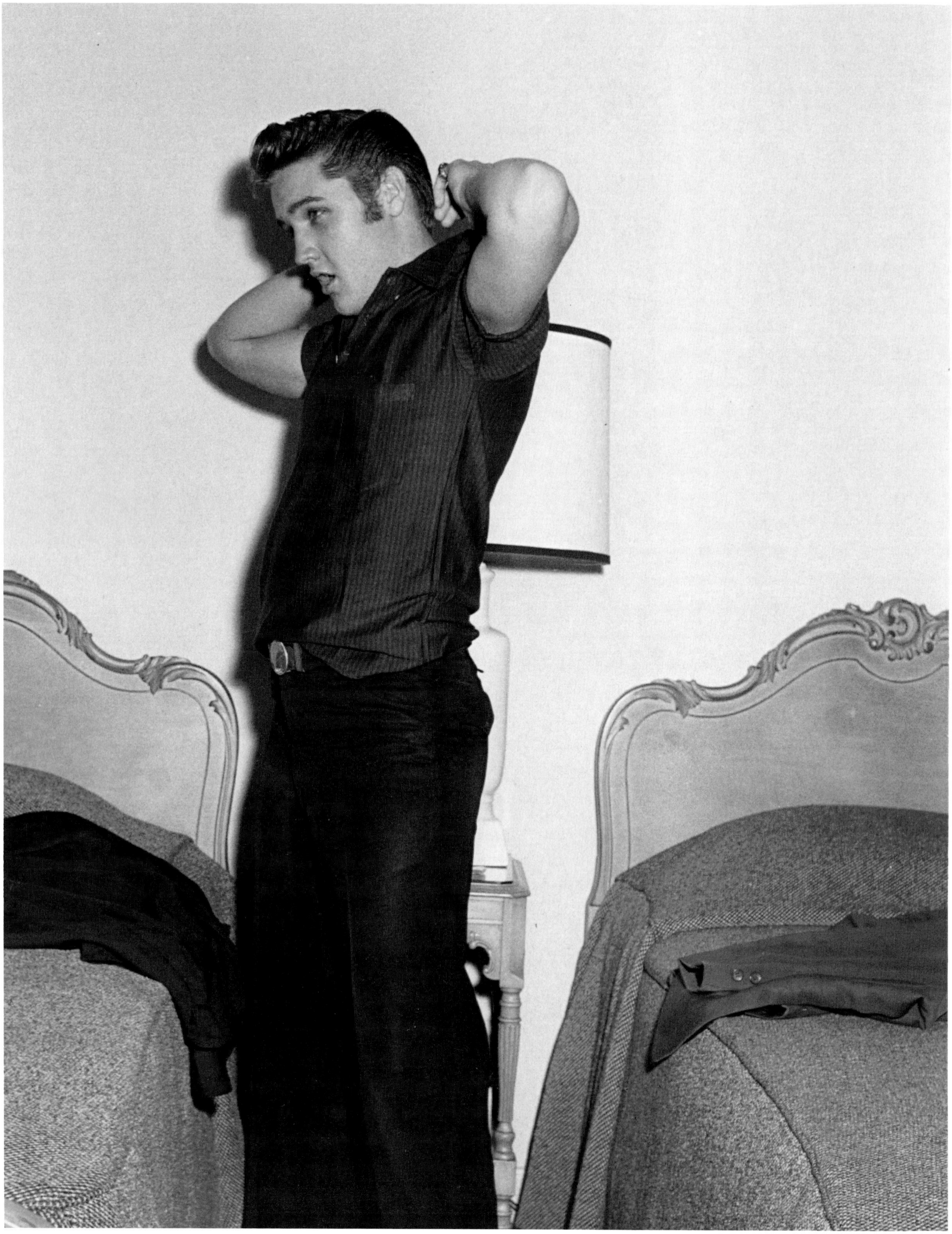

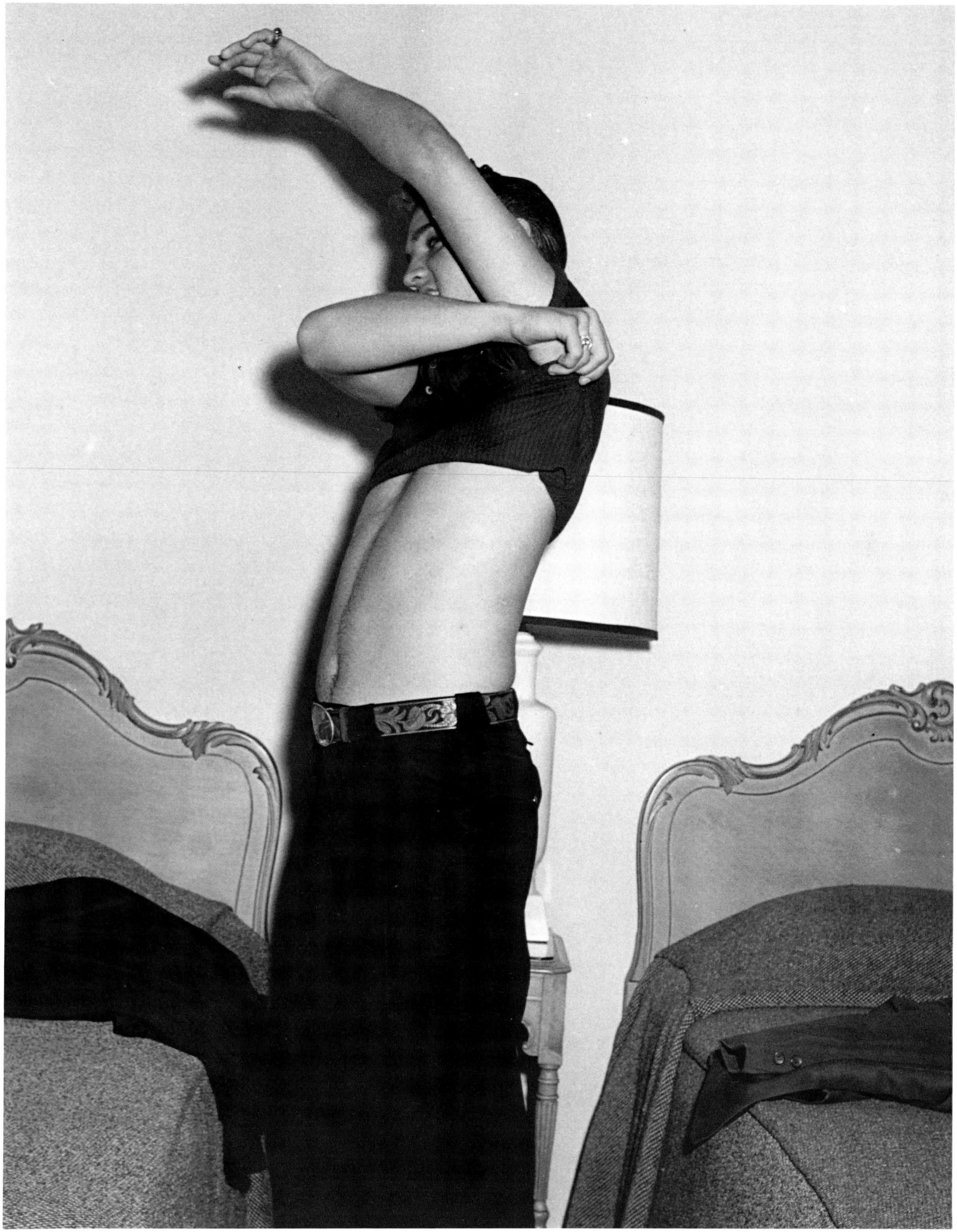

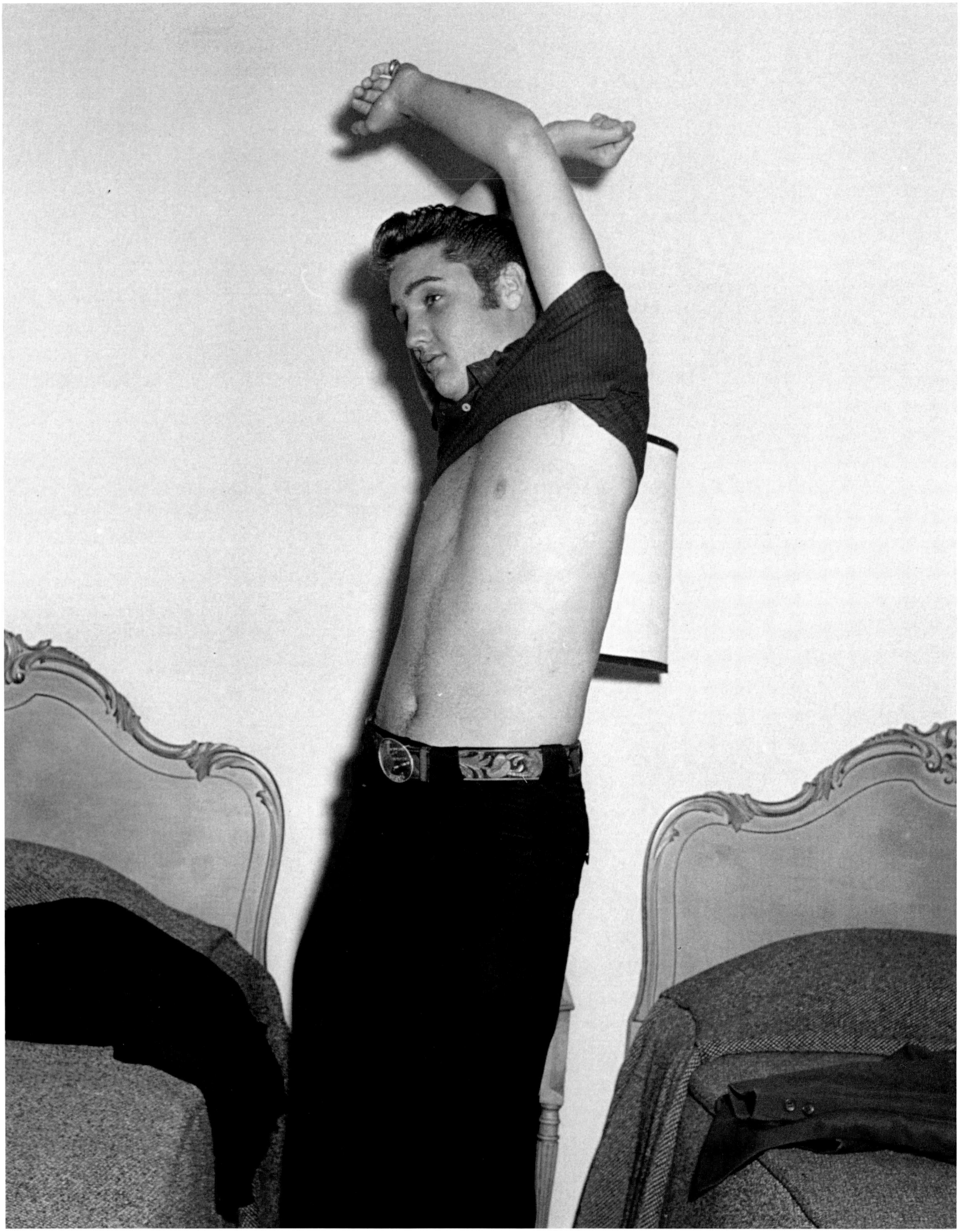

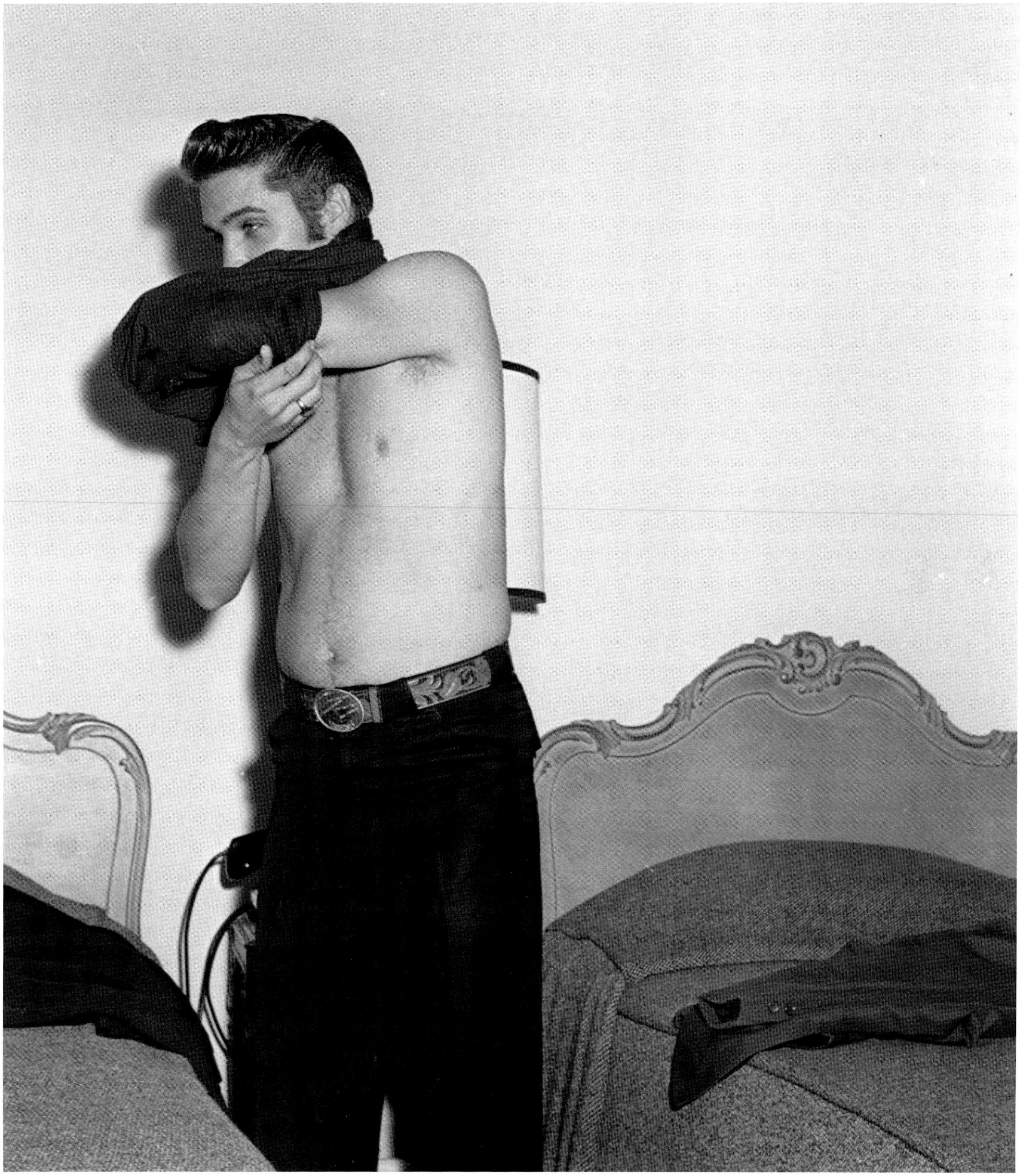

There are mystically in our faces certain characters which carry in them the motto of our souls, . . .

Sir Thomas Browne

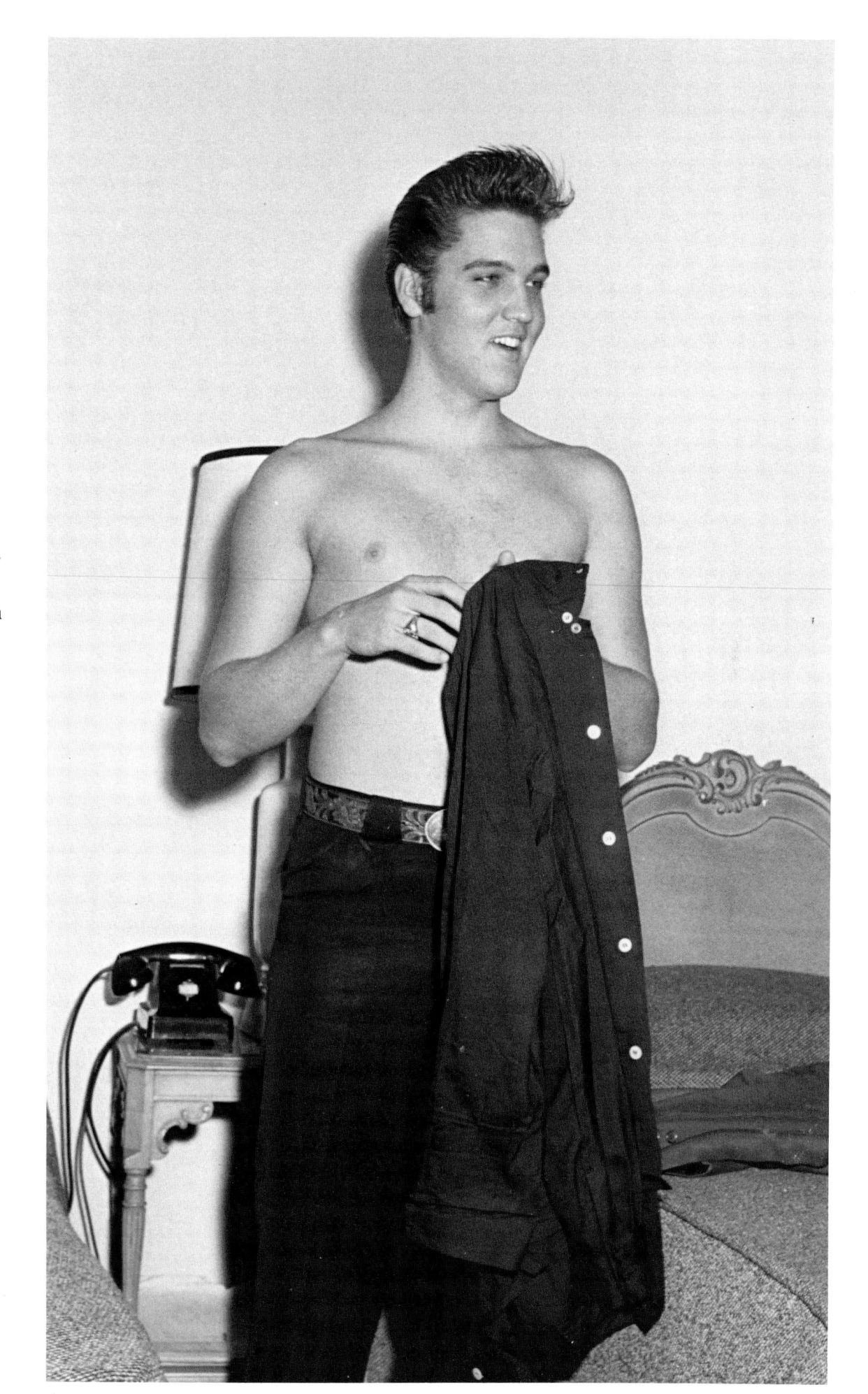

*The eyes
indicate the antiquity of the soul.*

Ralph Waldo Emerson

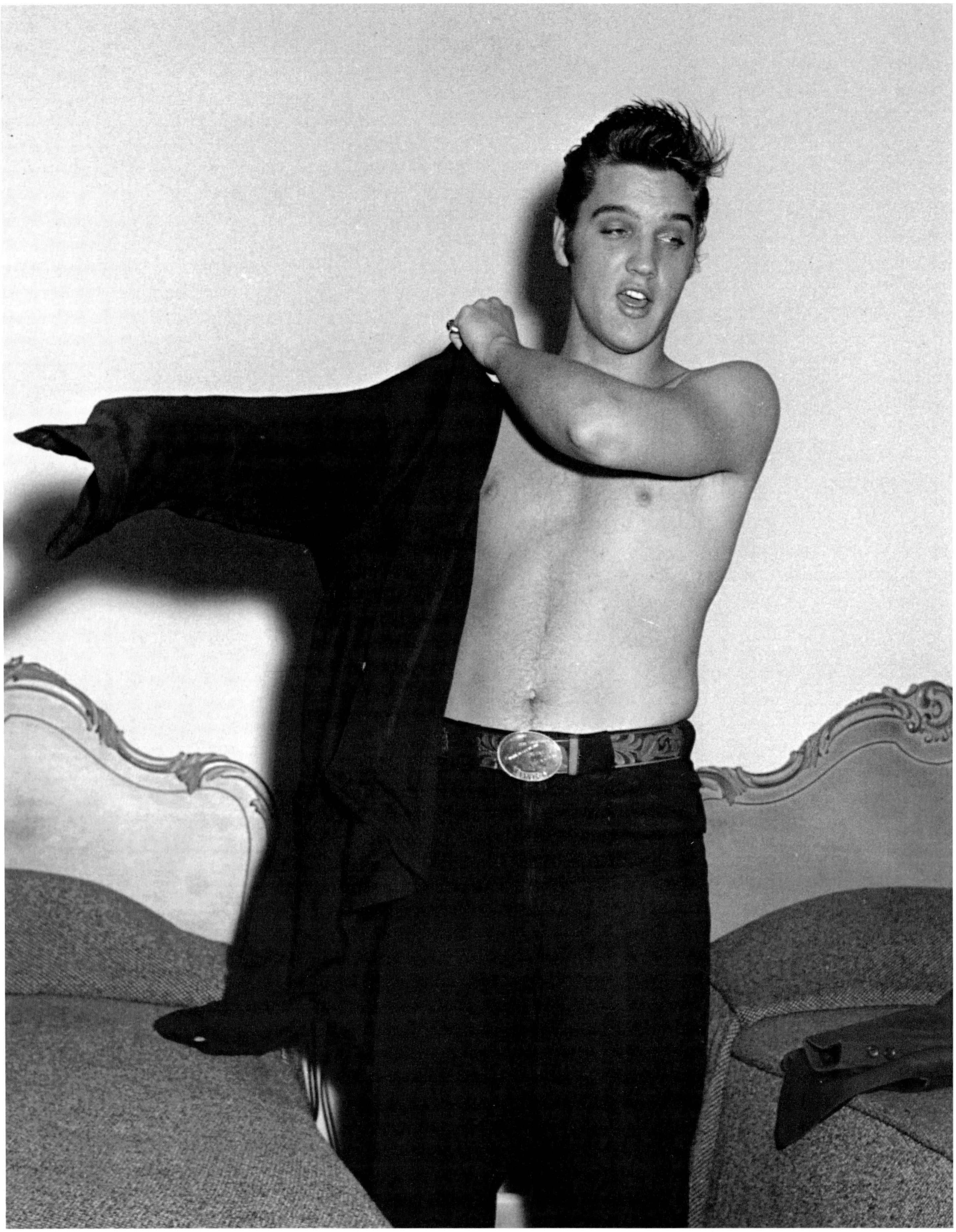

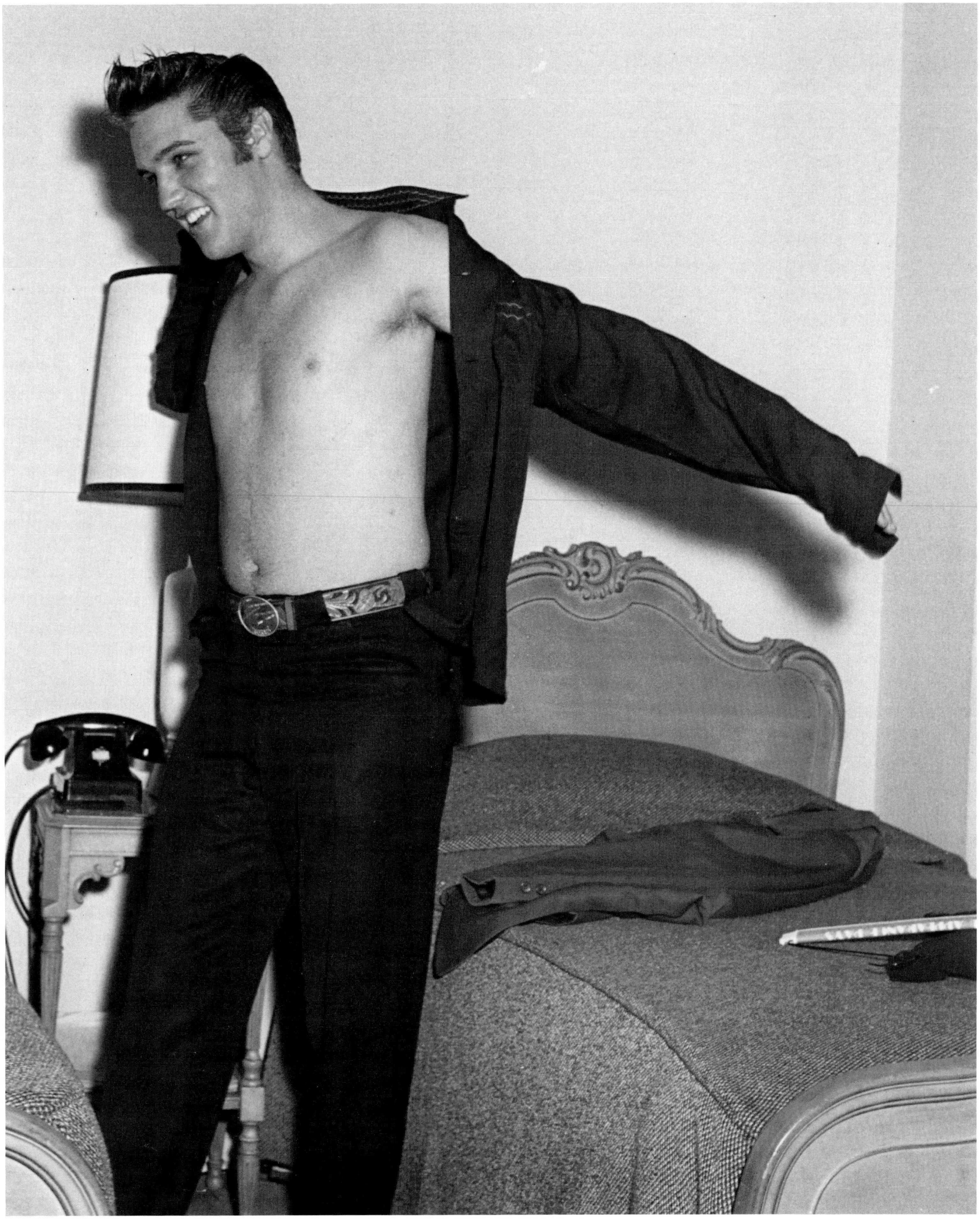

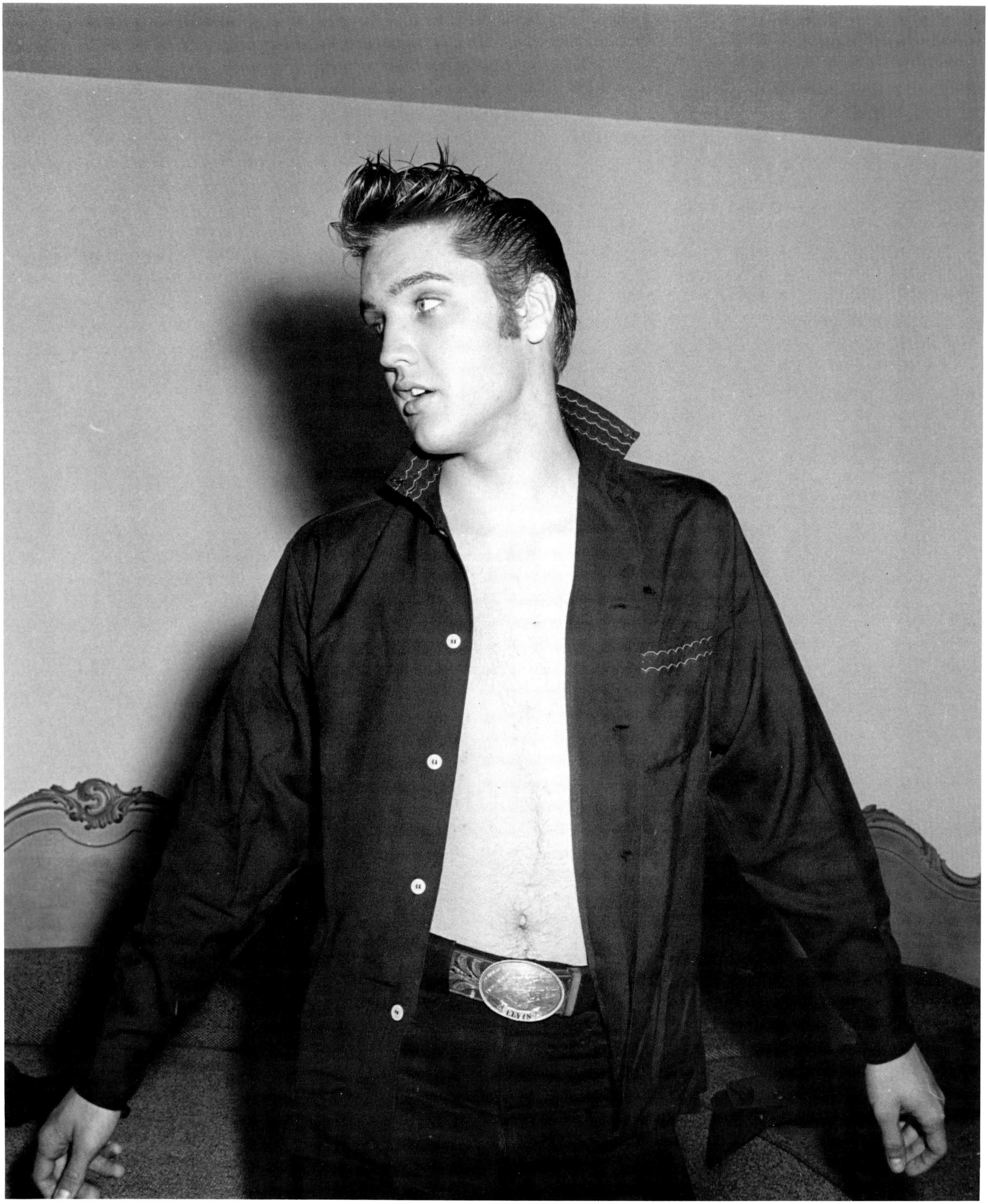
ELVIS

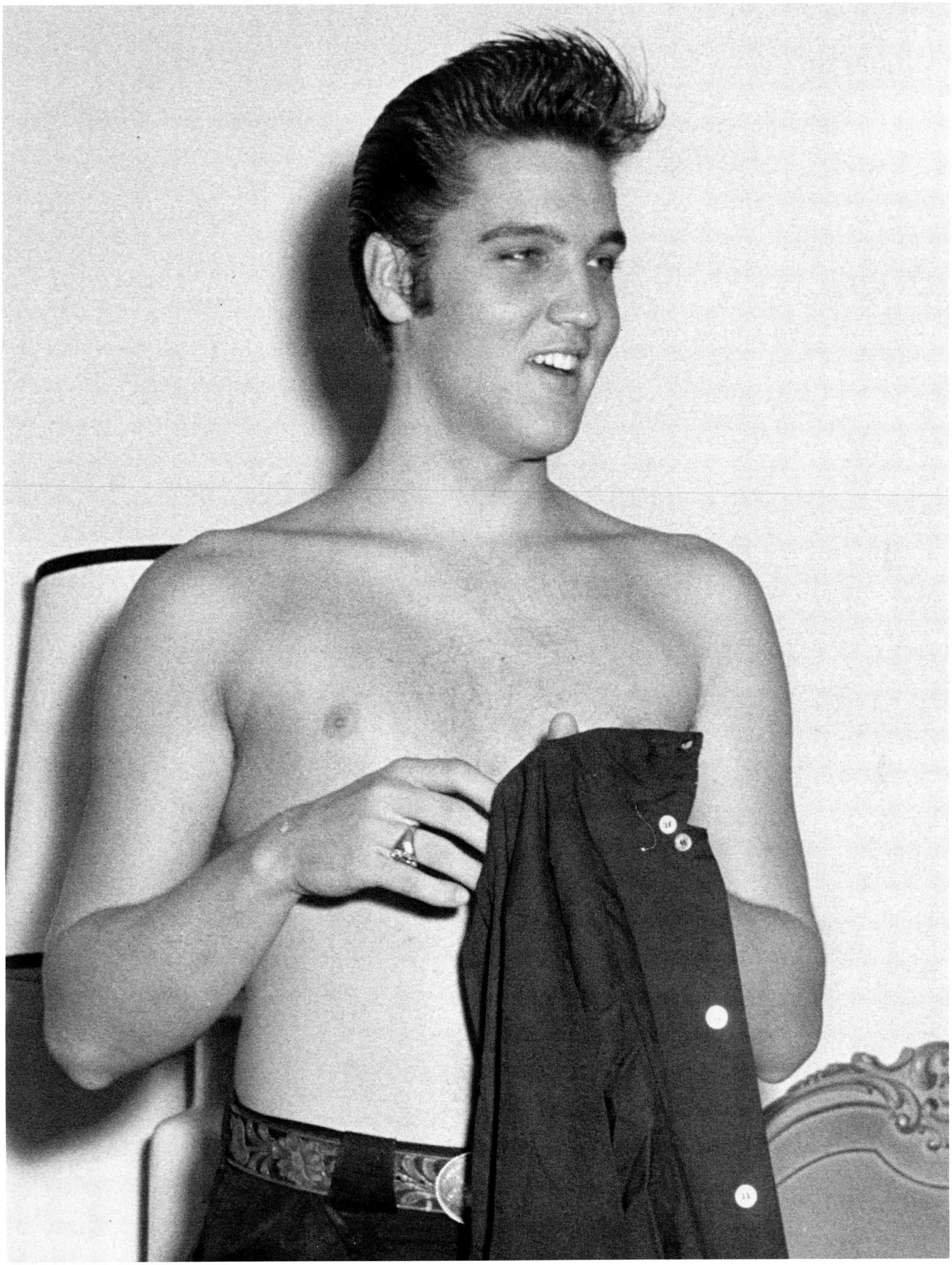

*Music is the sole domain
in which man realizes the present.*

Igor Stravinsky

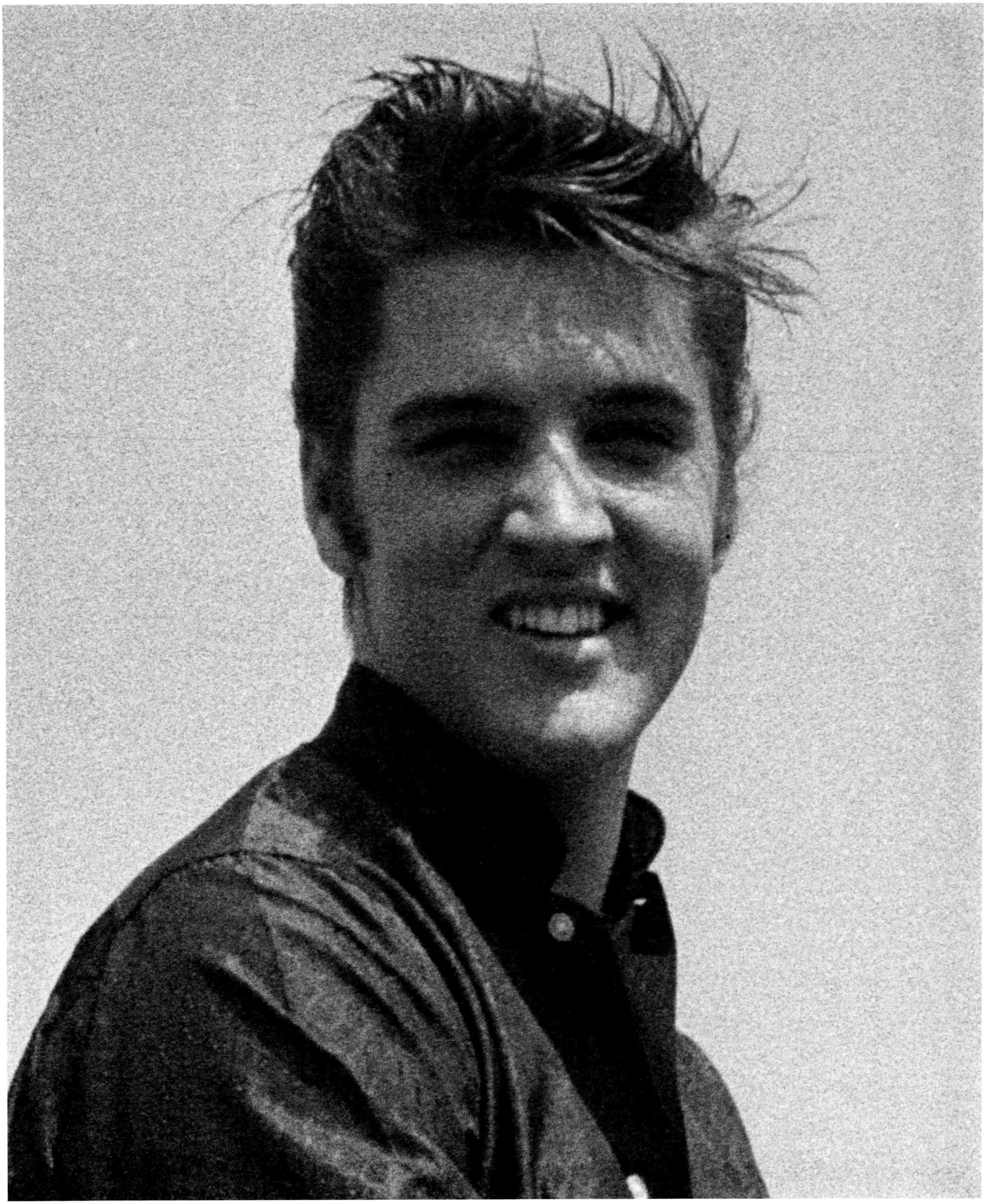

*Who hears music, feels his solitude
Peopled at once.*

Robert Browning

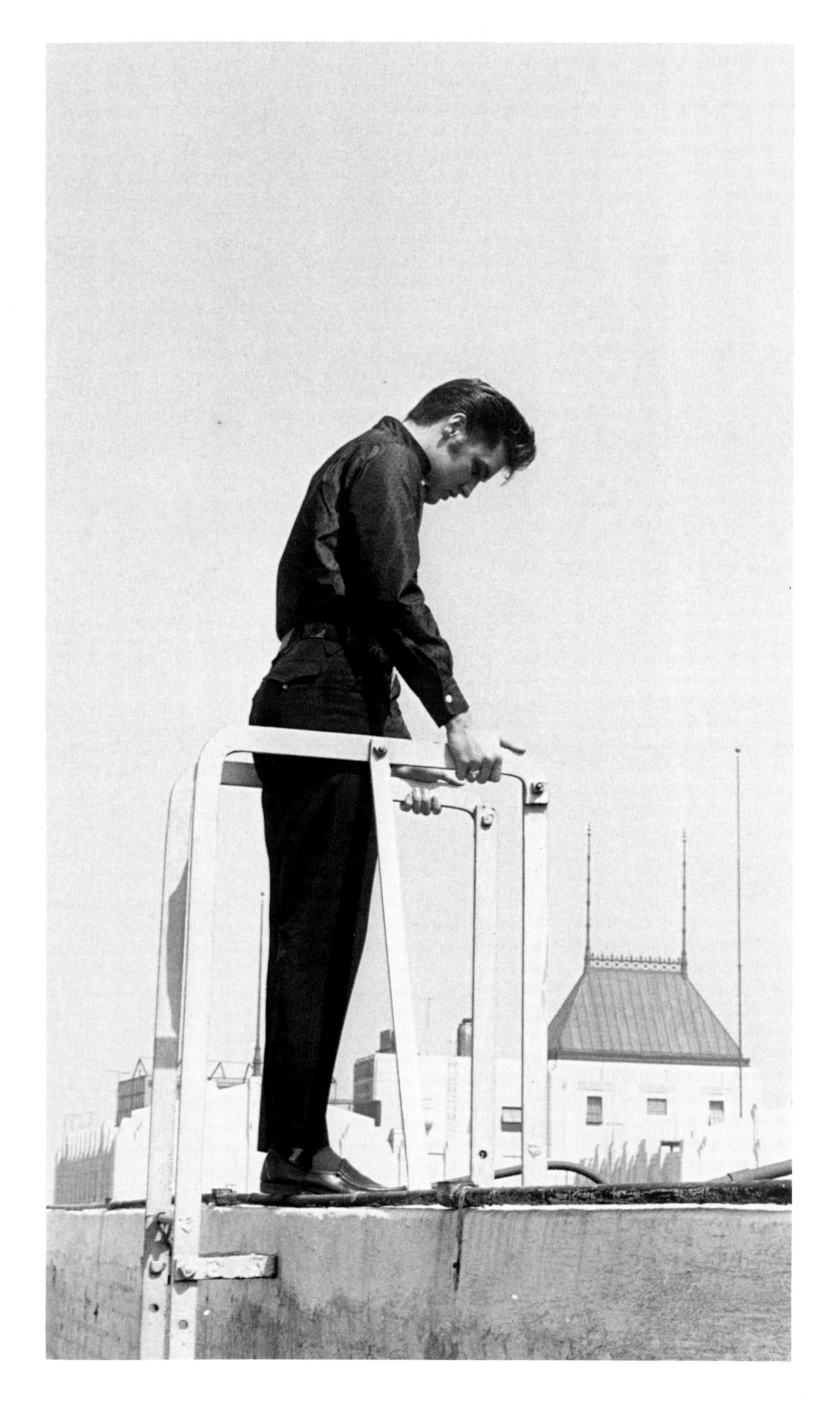

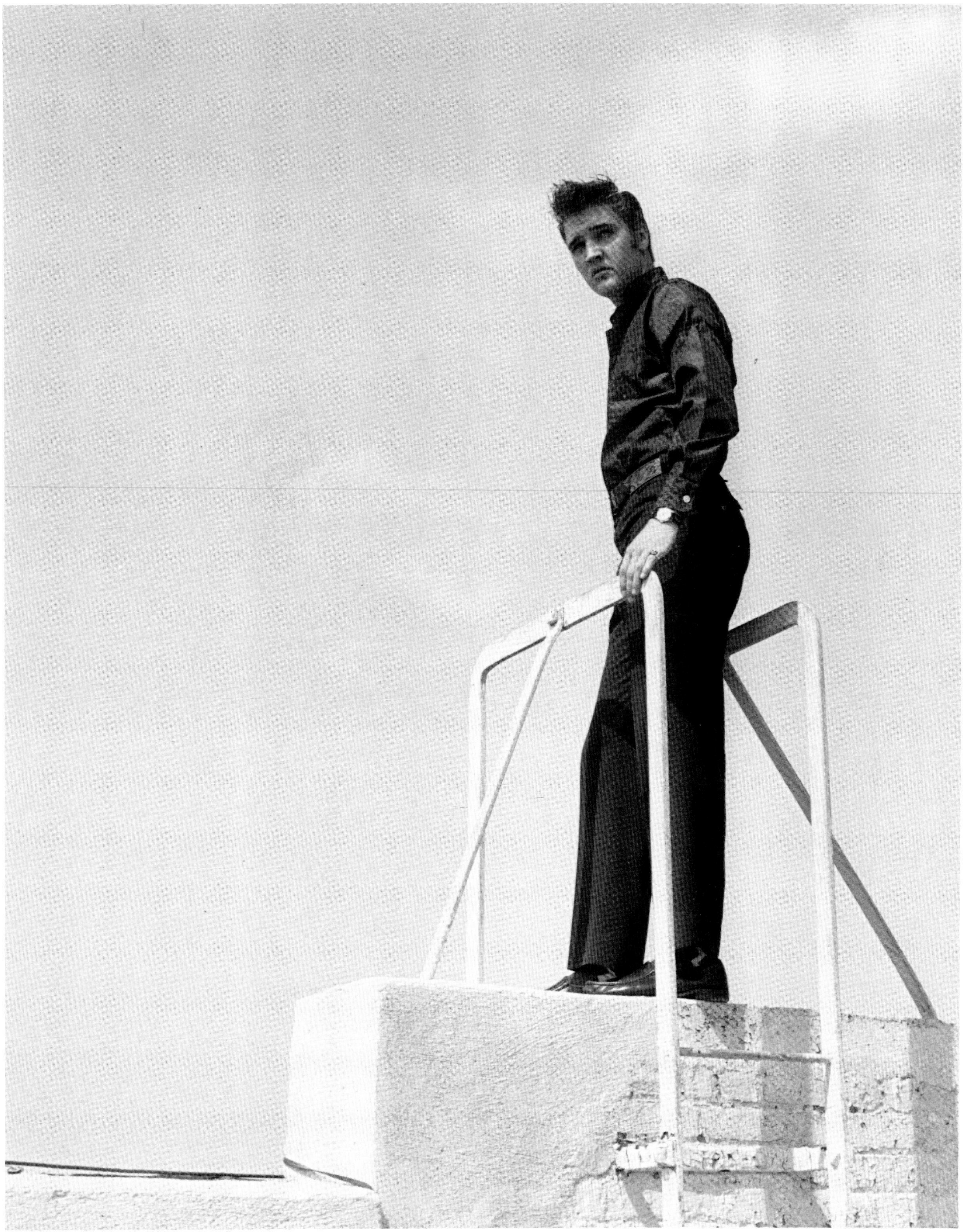

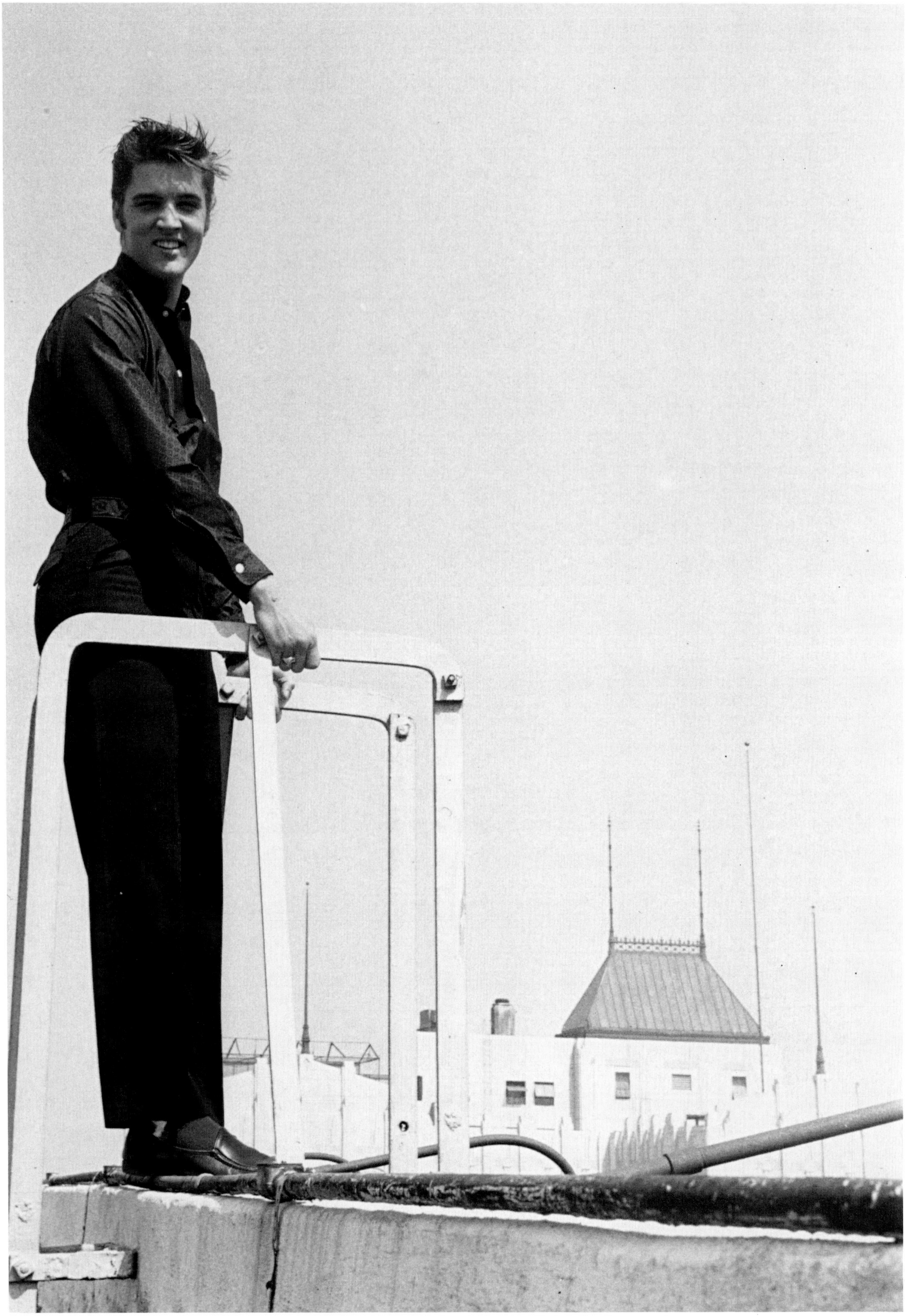

Living well and beautifully and justly are all one thing.

                    Socrates

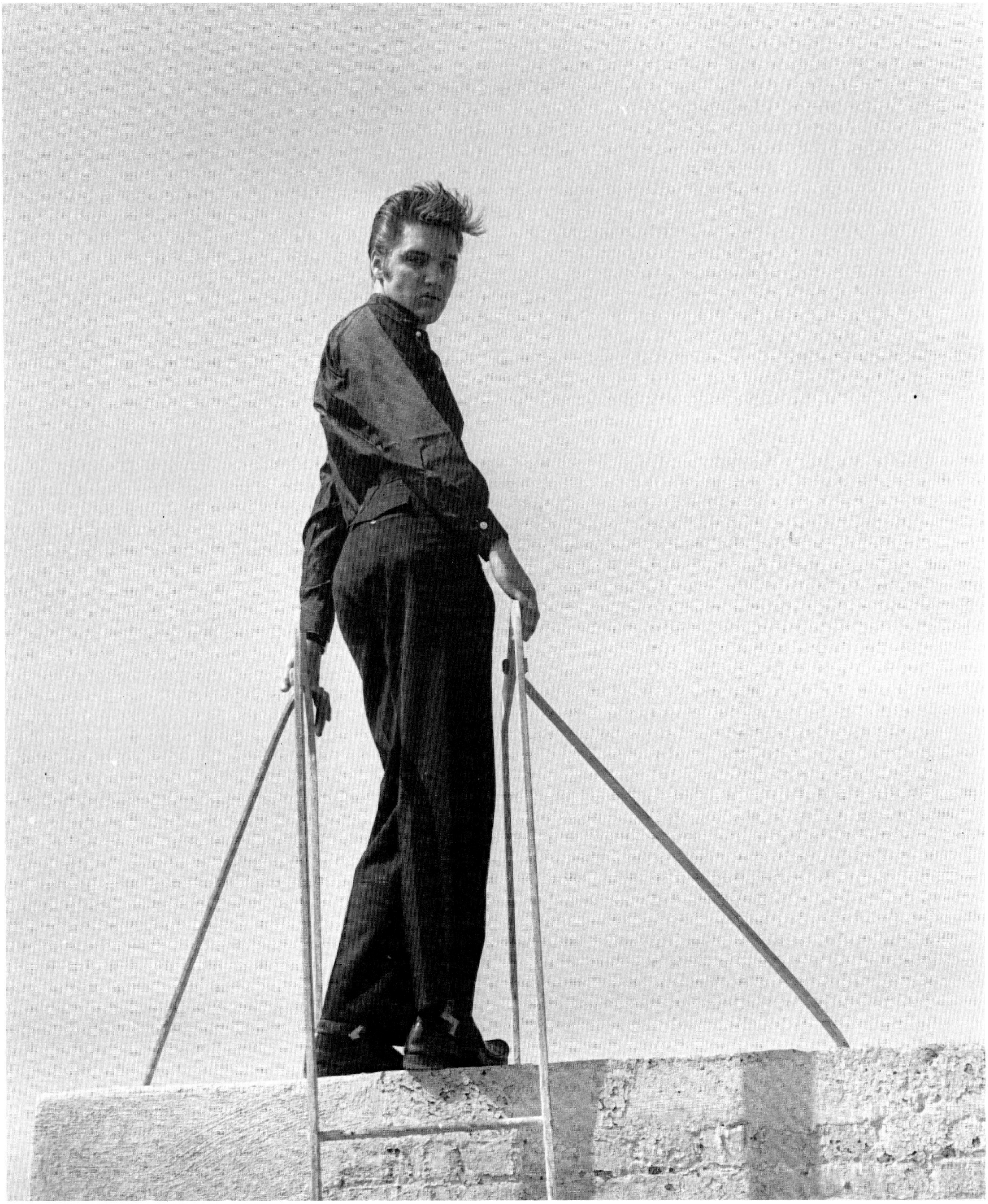

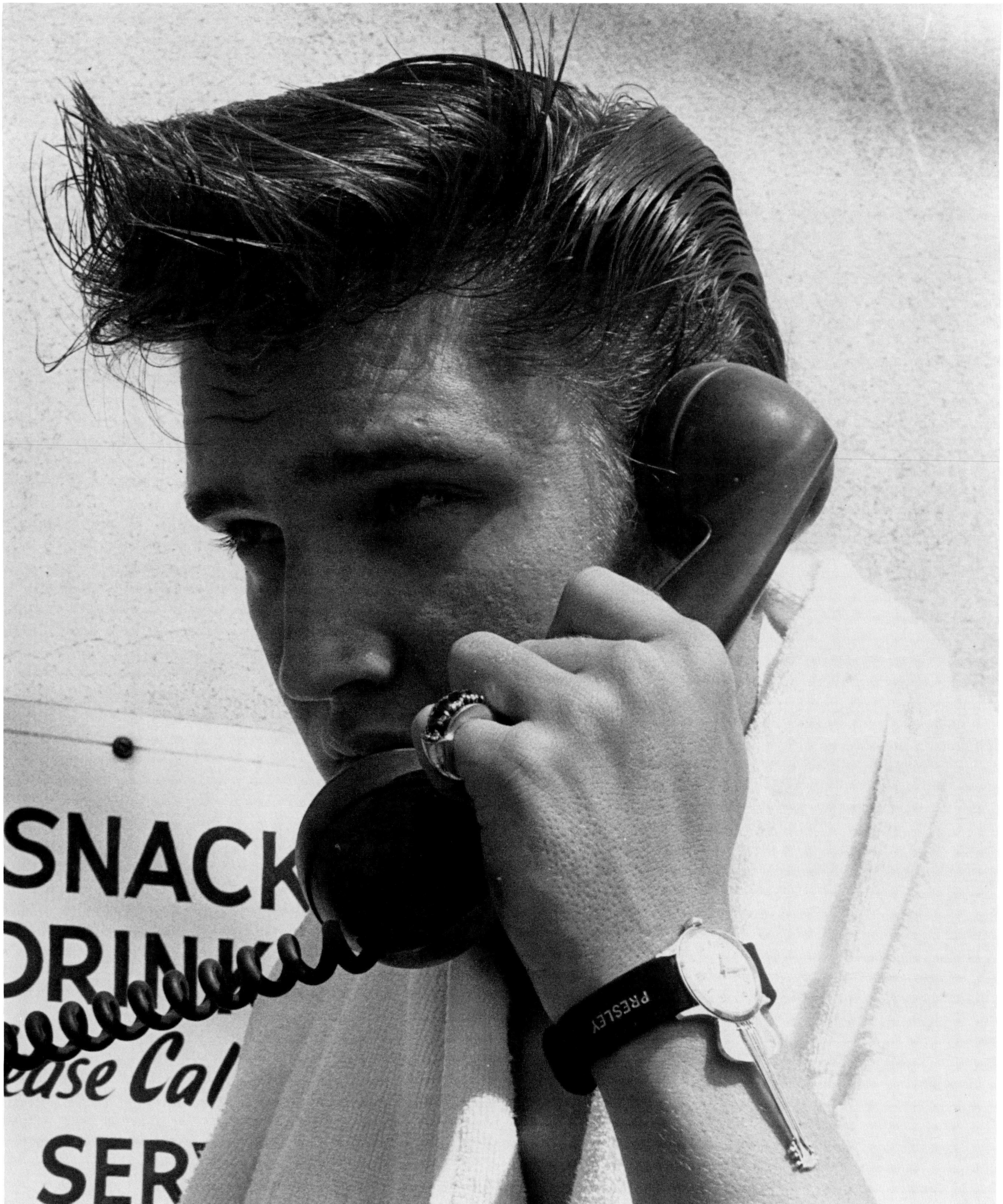
SNACK
DRIN
ease Cal
SER
PRESLEY

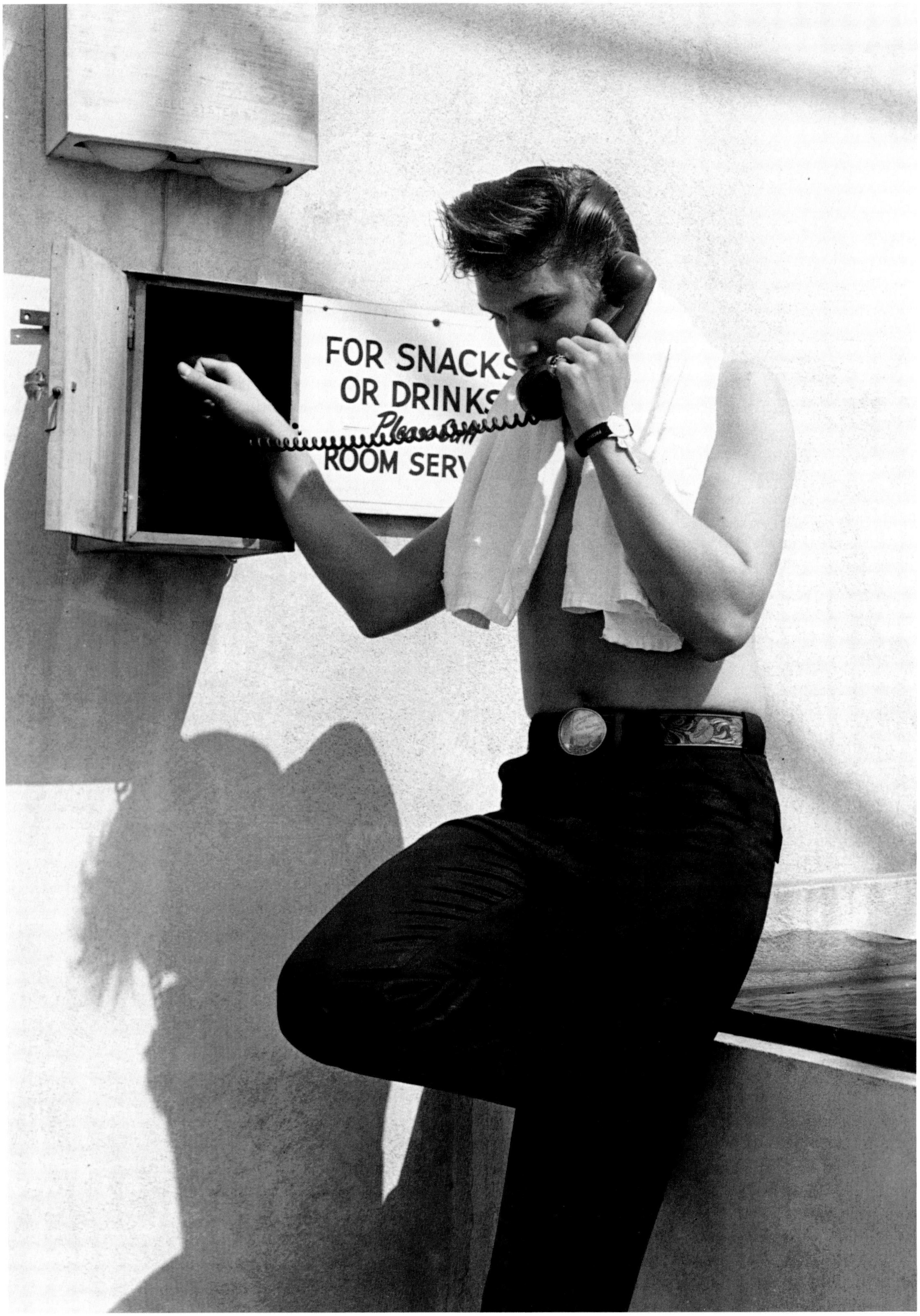
FOR SNACKS
OR DRINKS
ROOM SERV

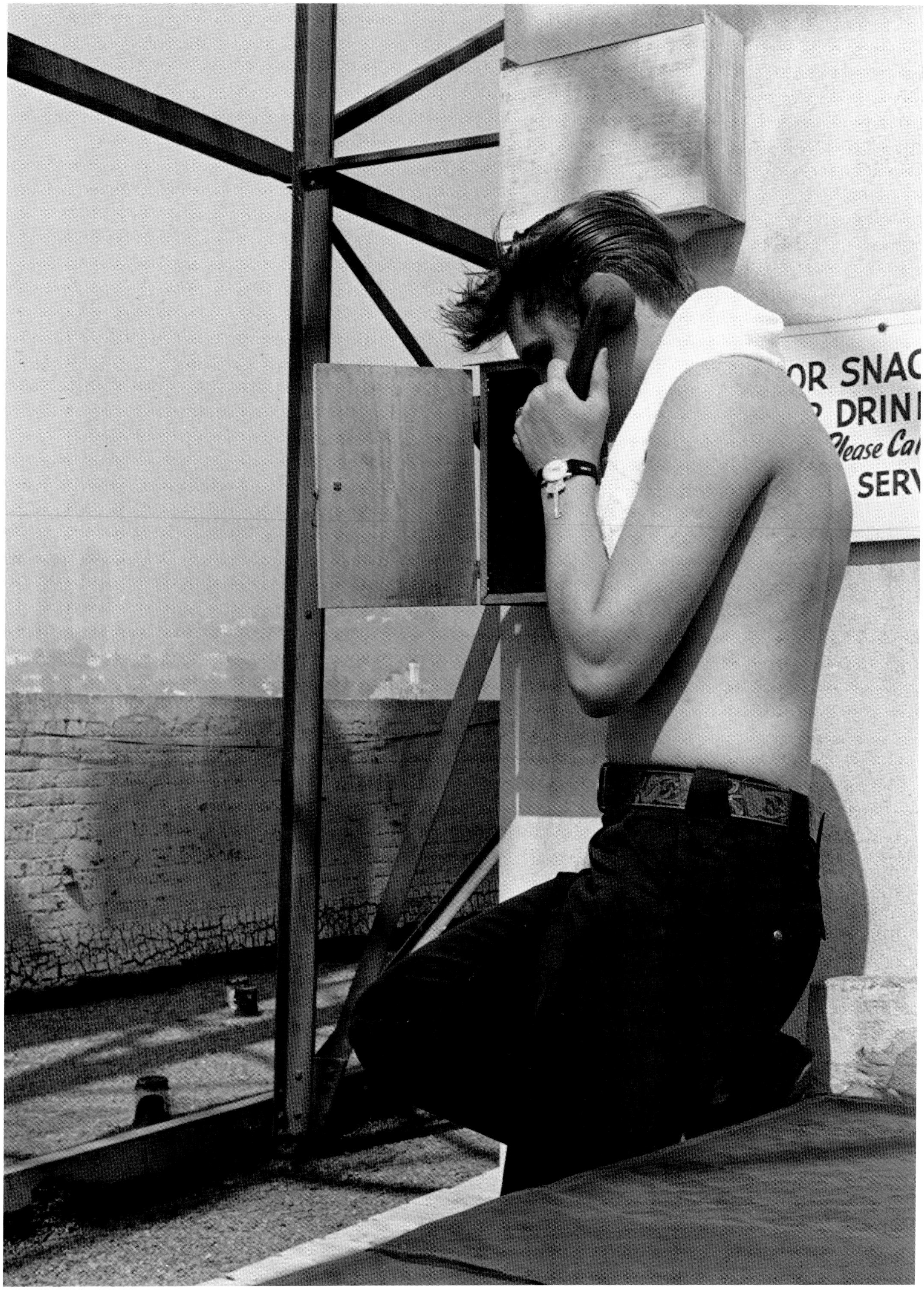
OR SNAC
R DRINI
Please Ca
SERV

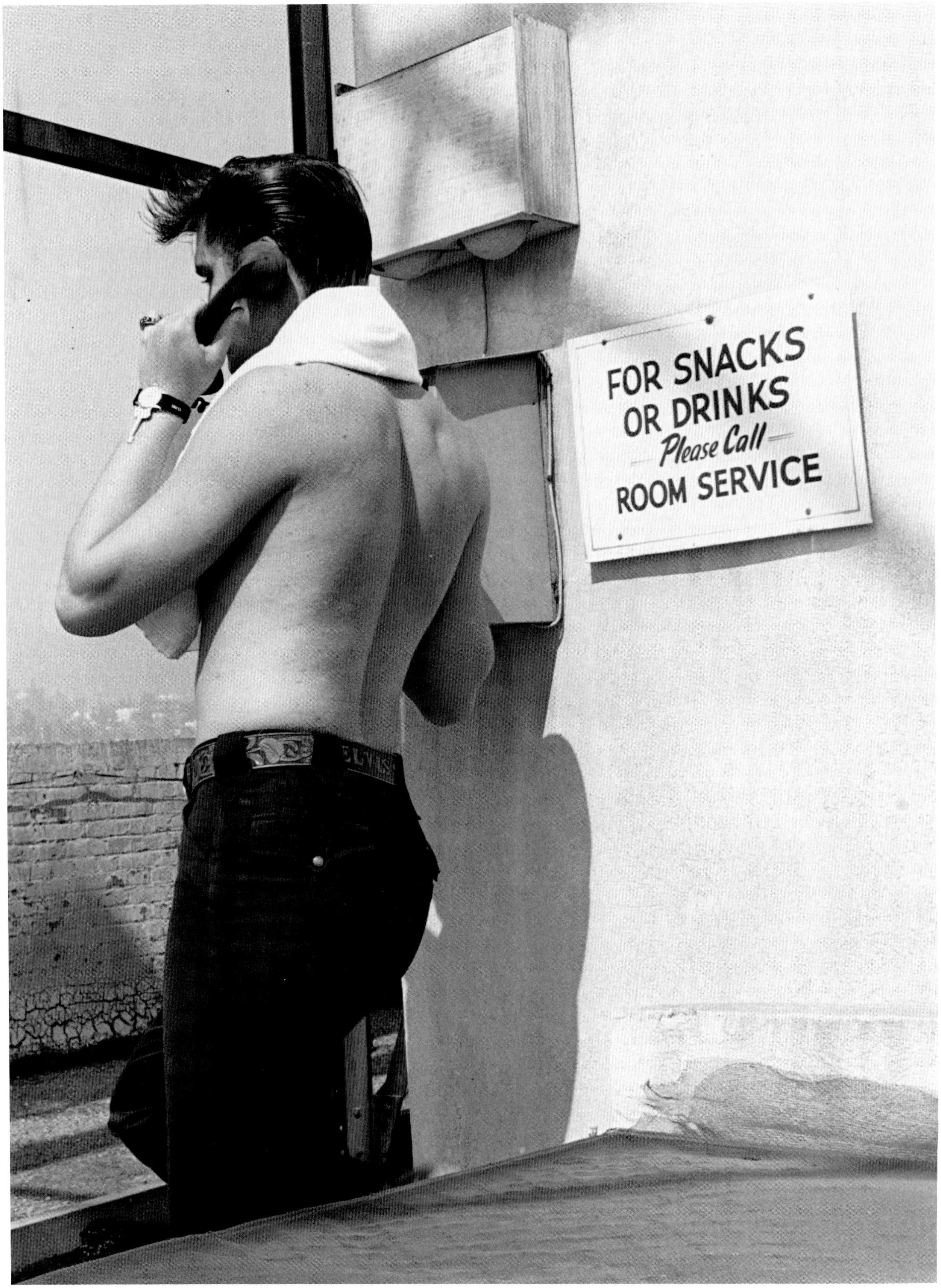
FOR SNACKS
OR DRINKS
Please Call
ROOM SERVICE

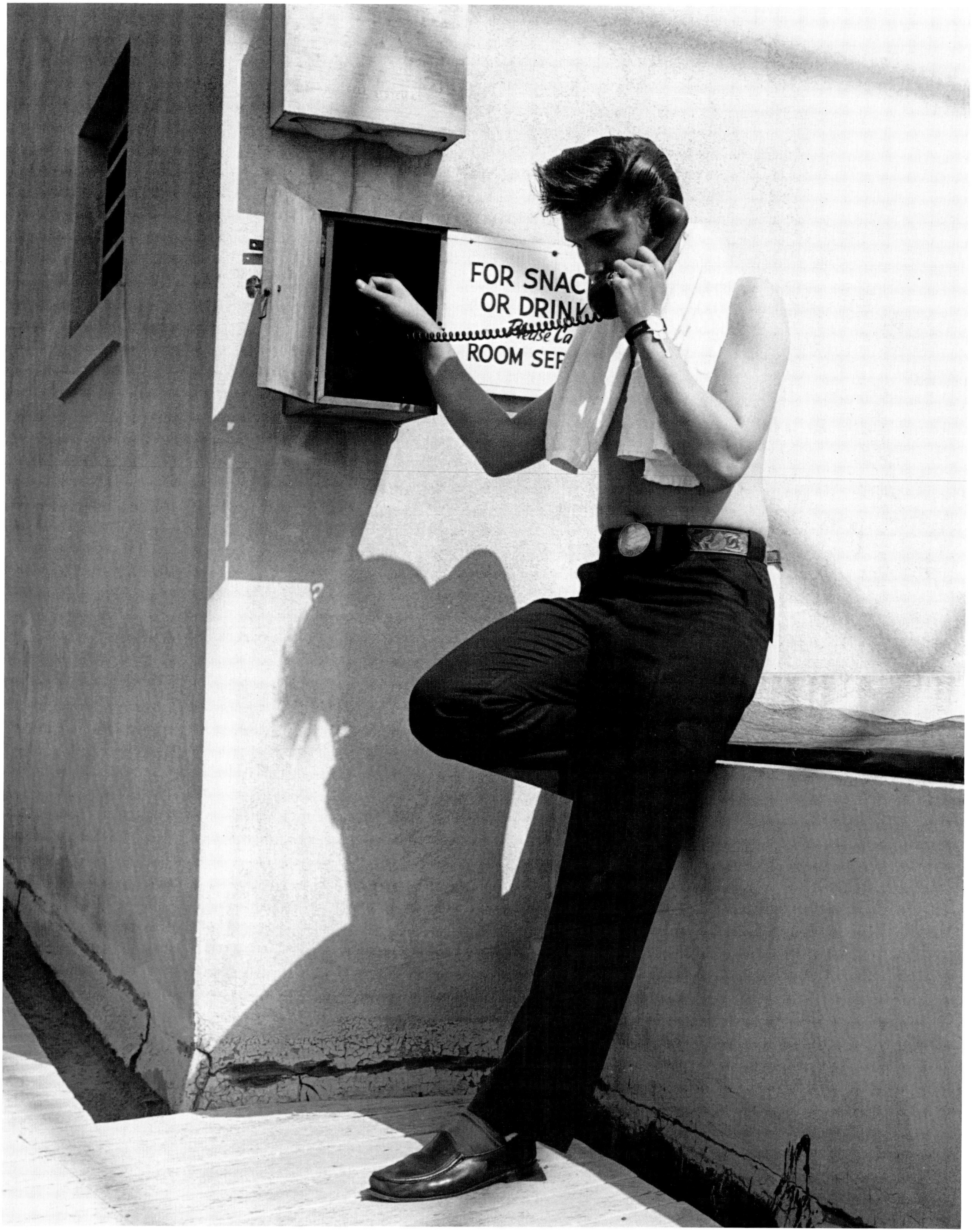
FOR SNAC
OR DRINK
ROOM SER

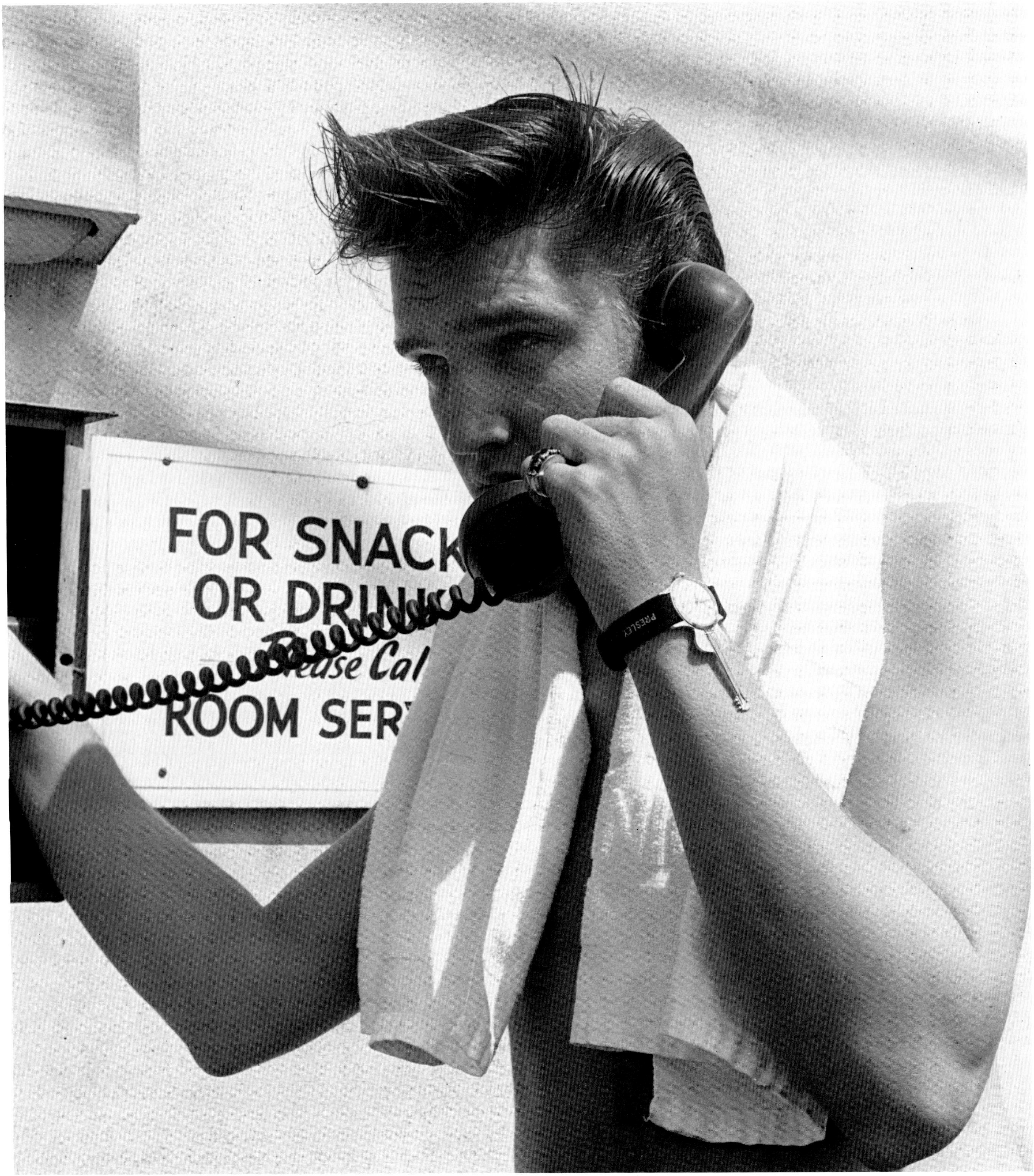
FOR SNACK
OR DRIN
ROOM SER
PRESLEY

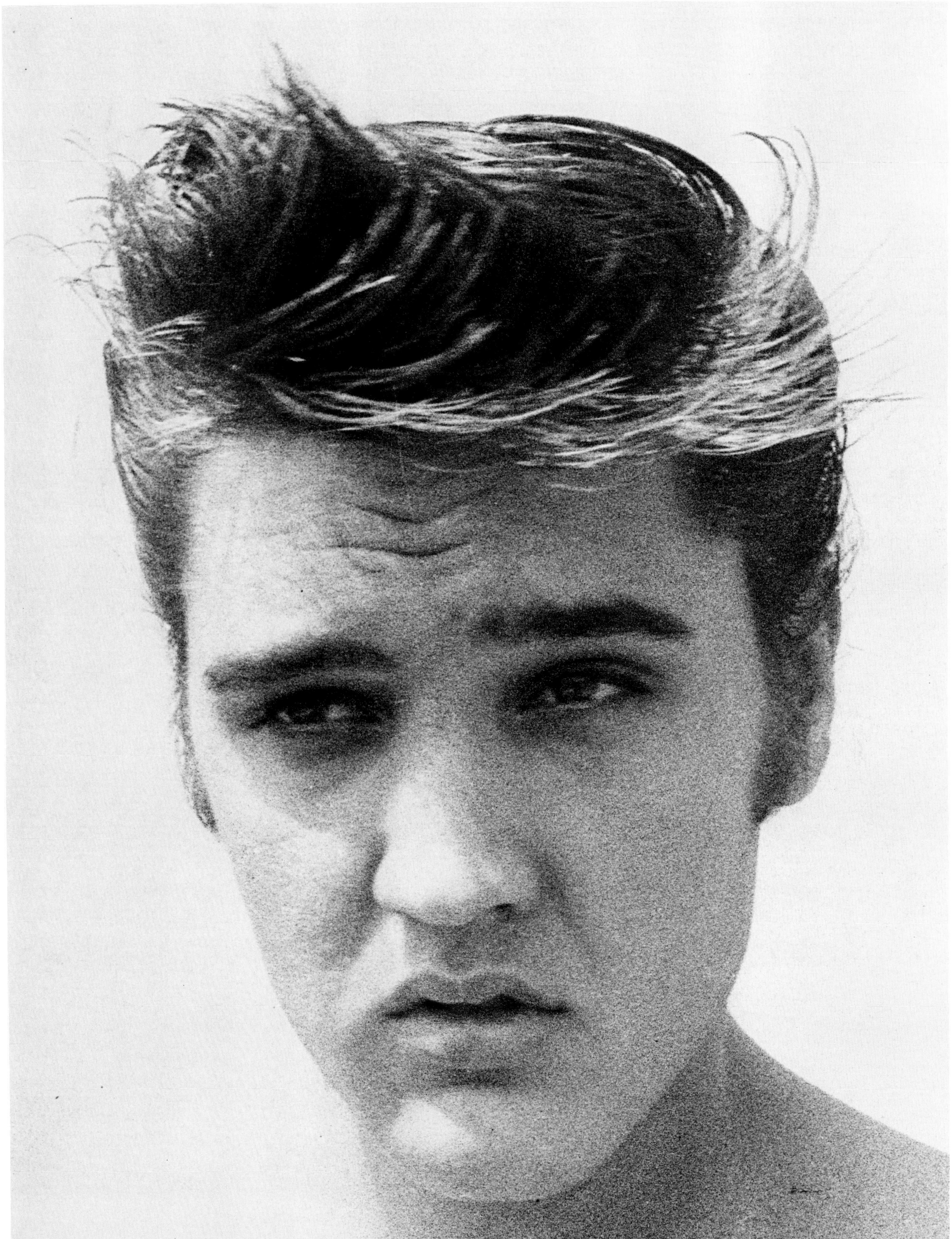

*Eyes, you know,
are the great intruders.*

Erving Goffman

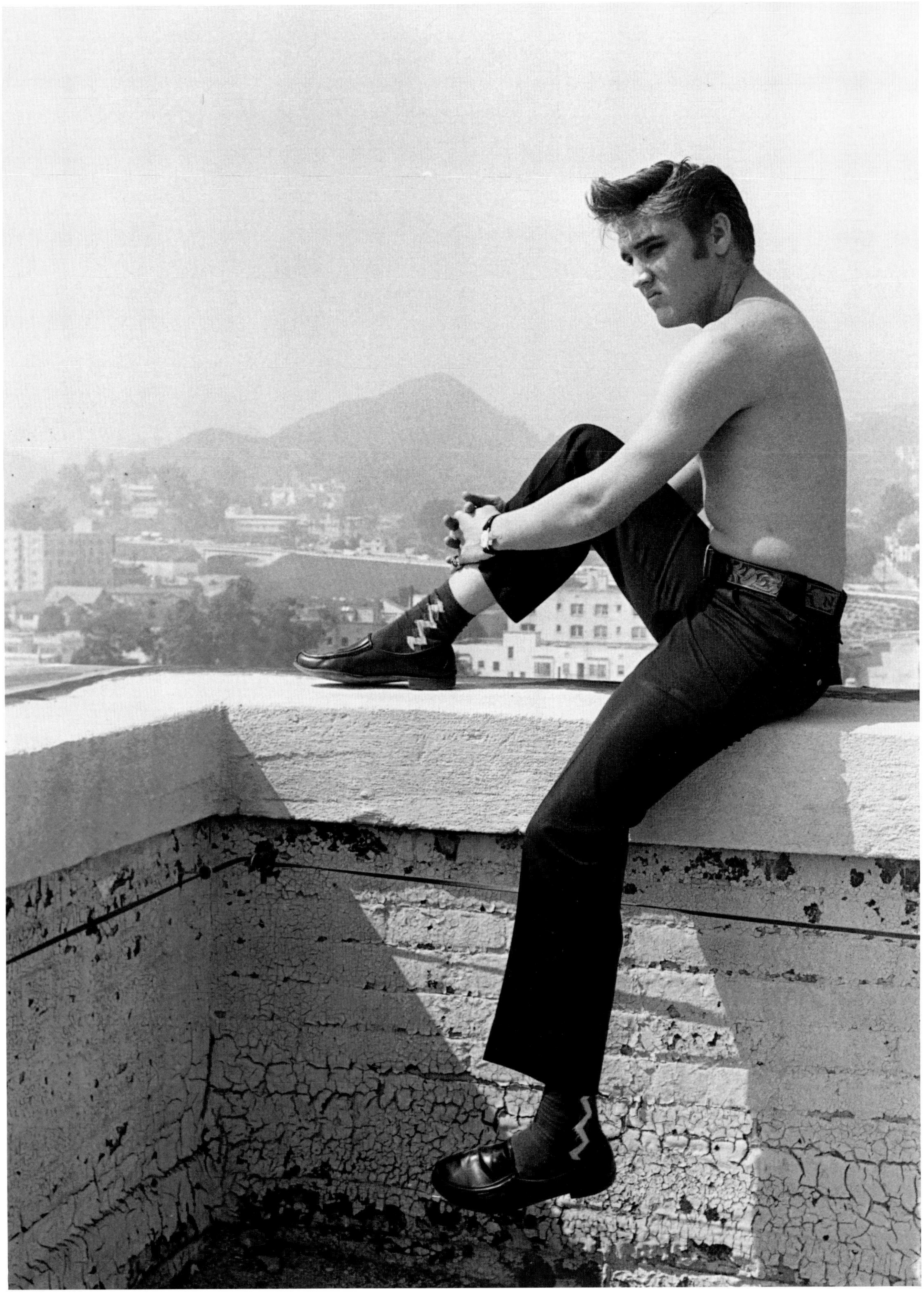

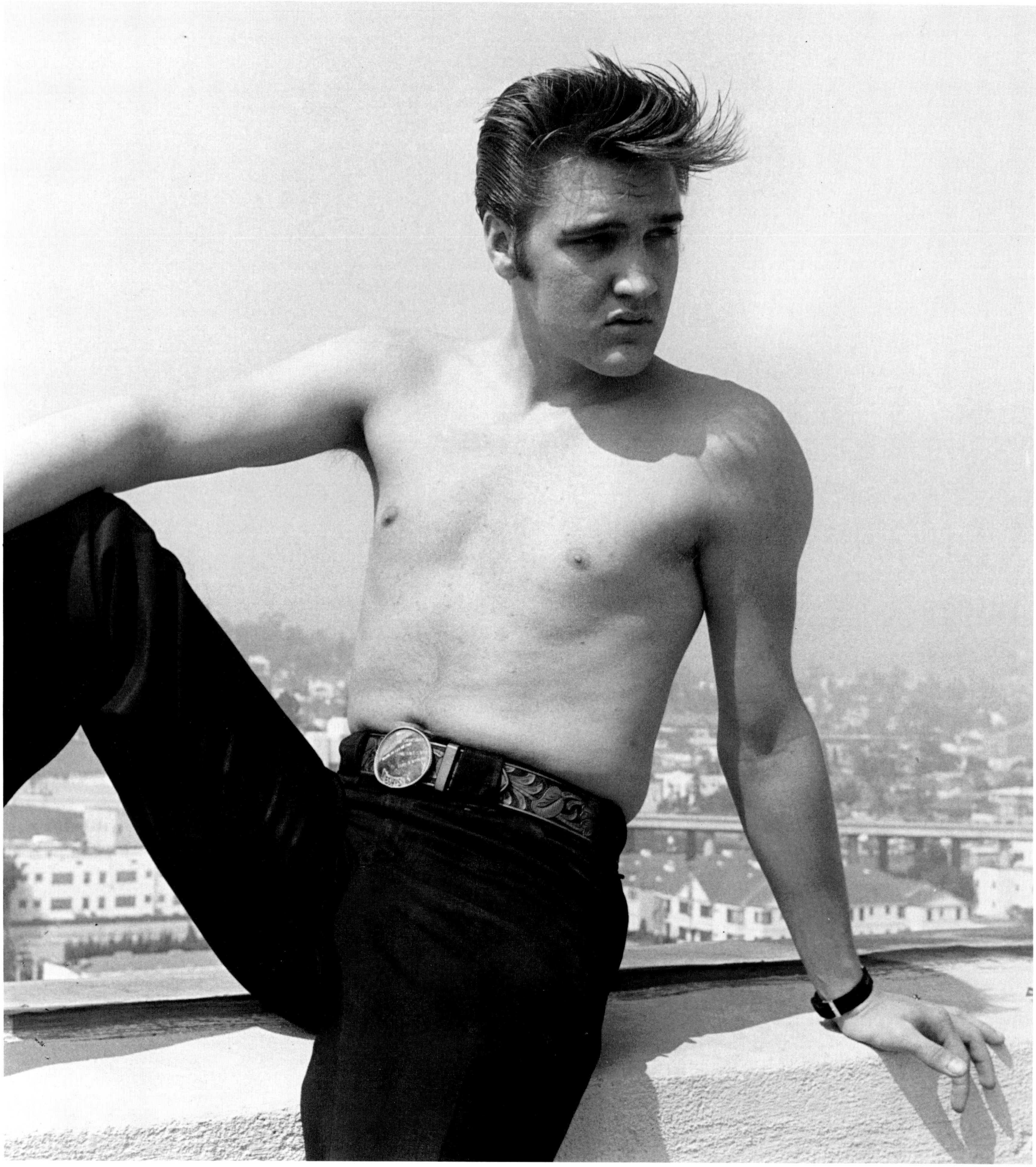

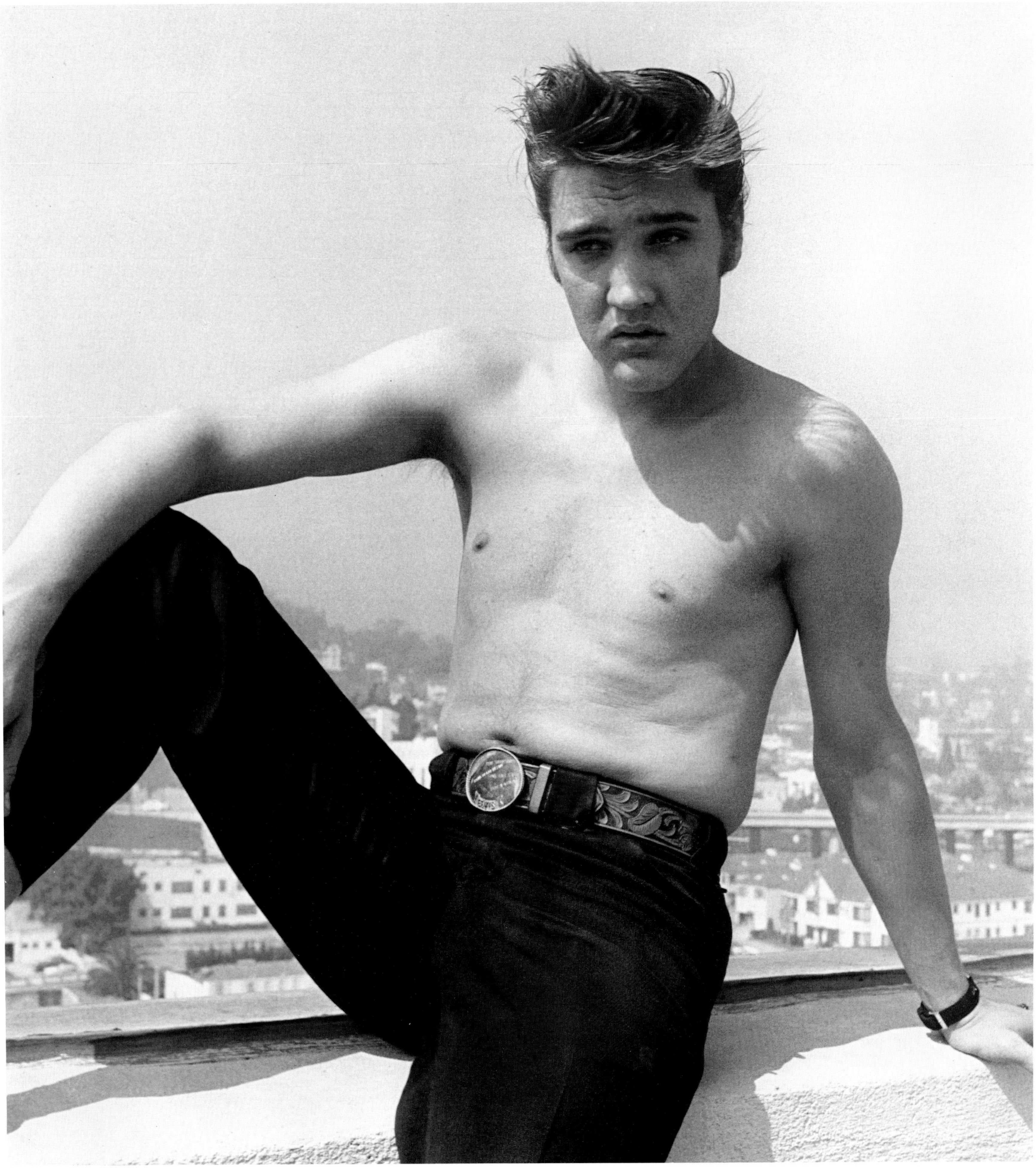

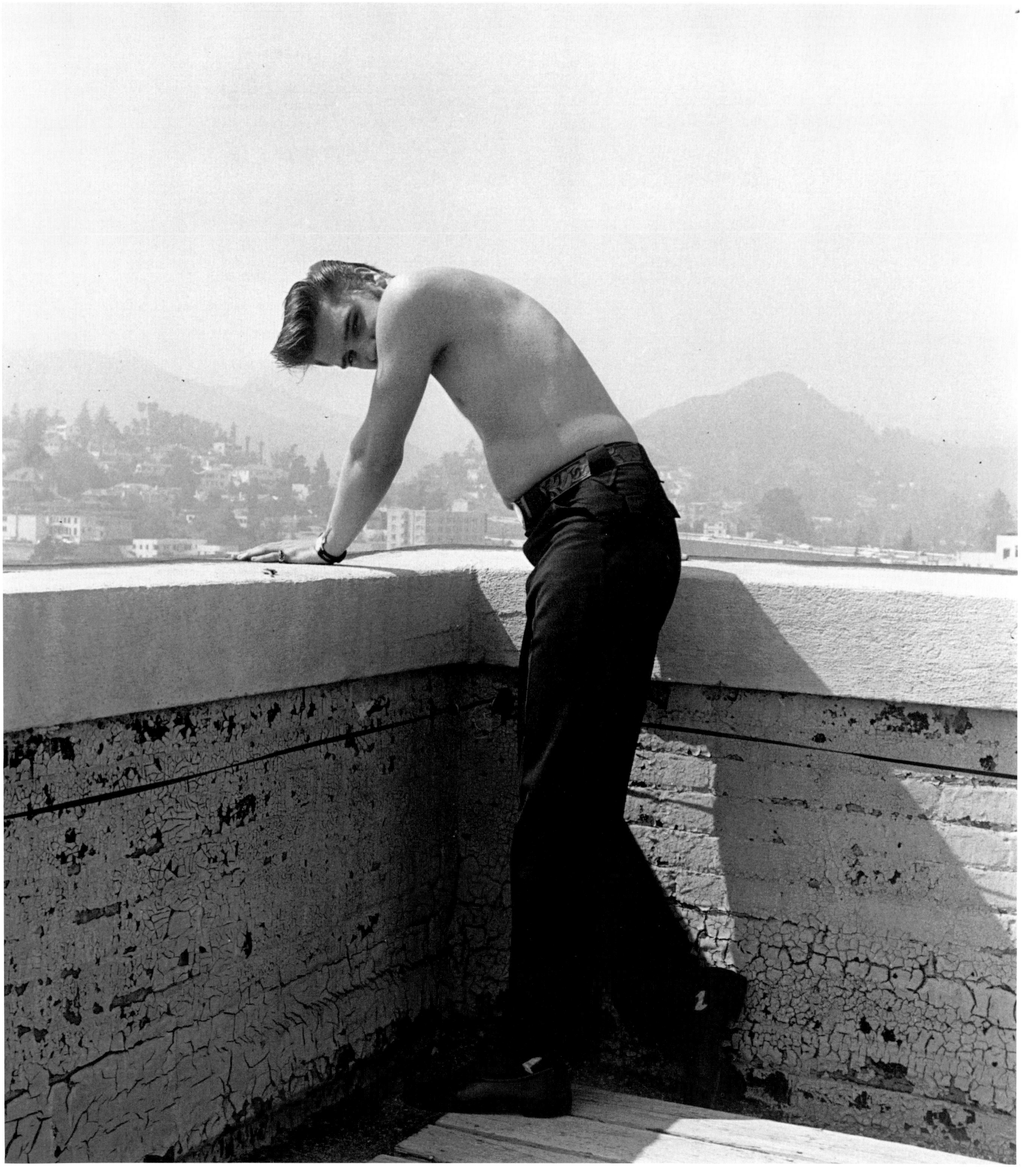

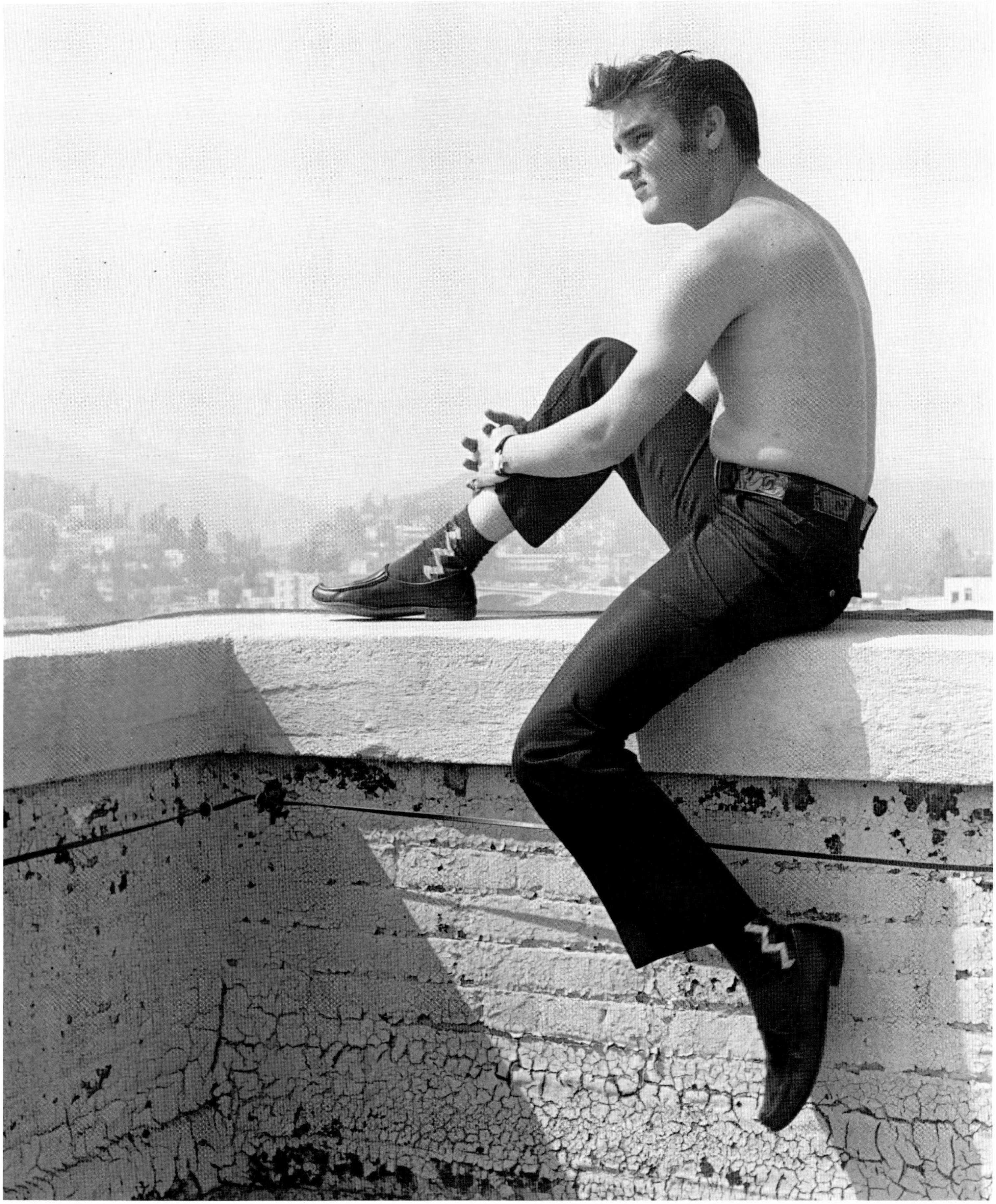

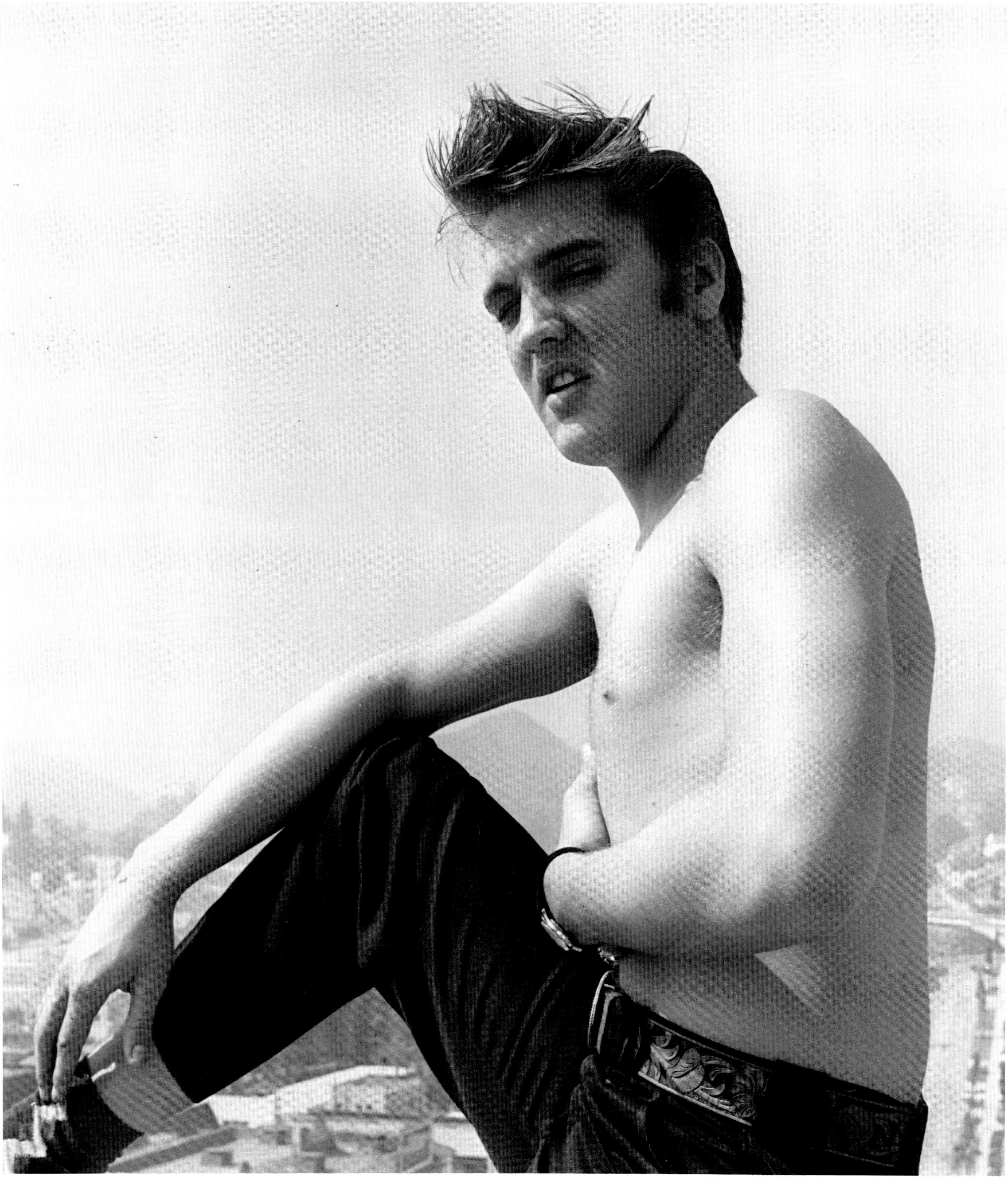

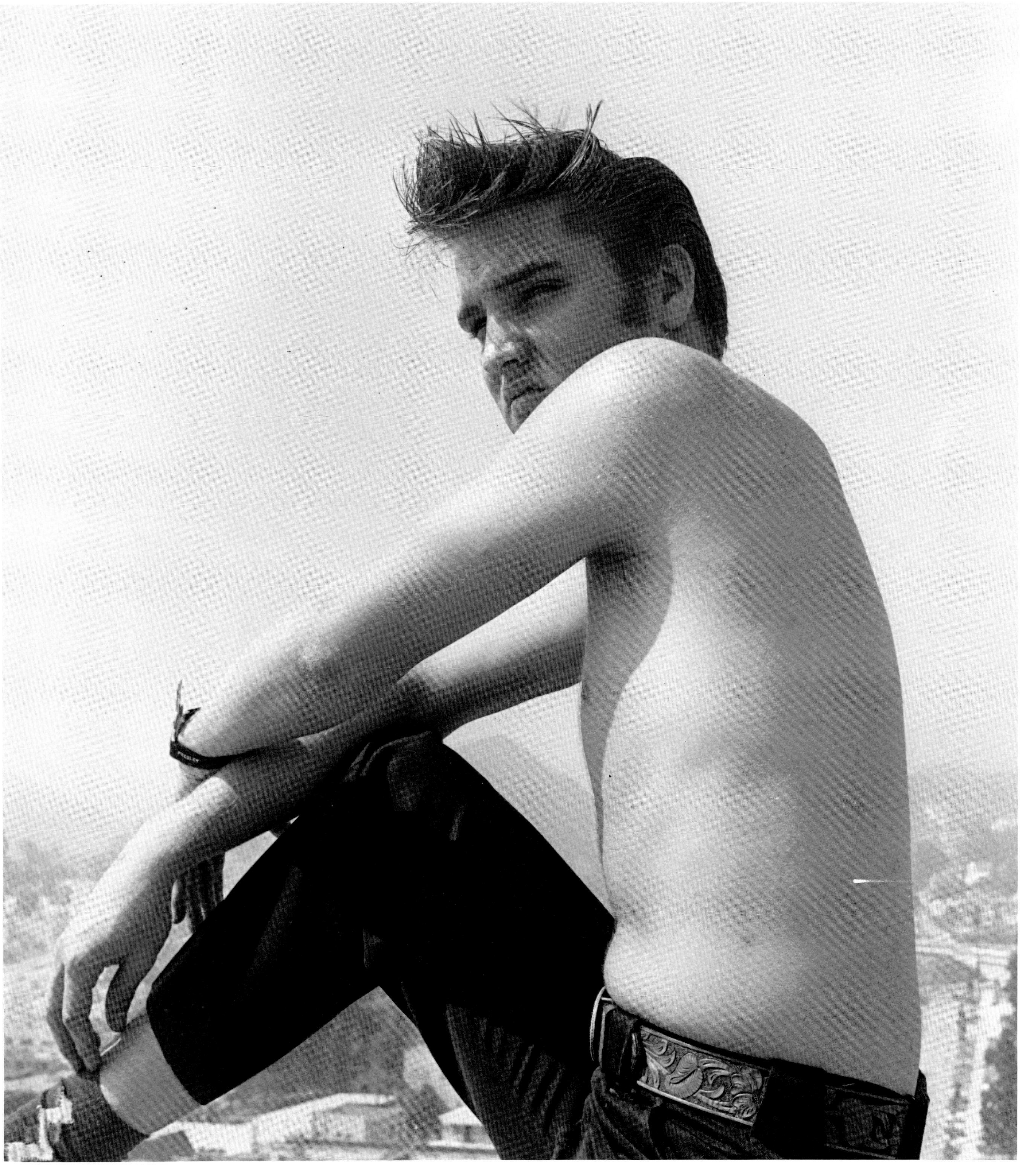

*All are architects of Fate,
Working in these walls of Time,
Some with massive deeds and great,
Some with ornaments of rhyme.*

Henry Wadsworth Longfellow

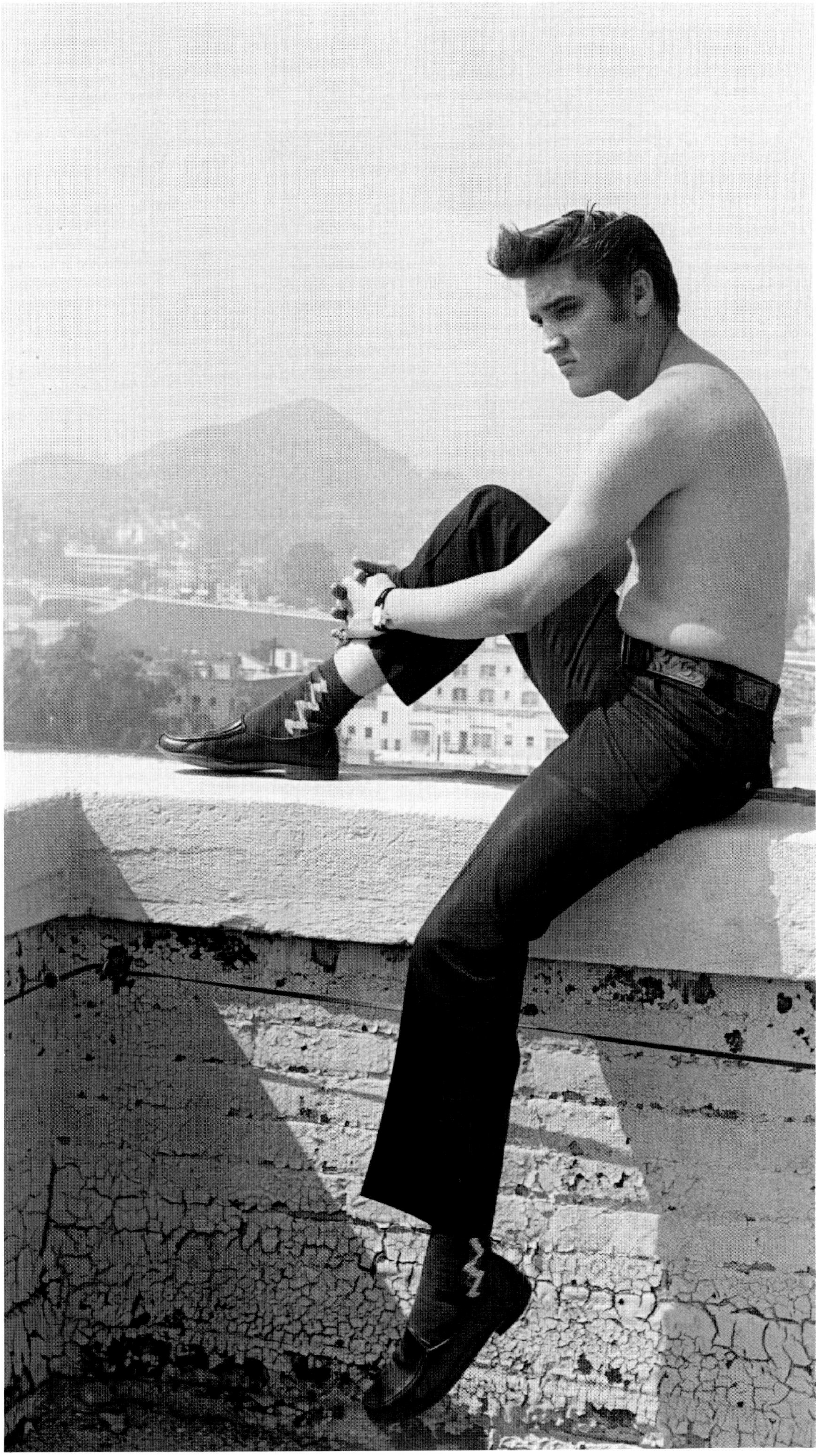

All thoughts, all passions, all delights,
Whatever stirs this mortal frame.
All are ministers of Love,
And feed his sacred flame.

Samuel Taylor Coleridge

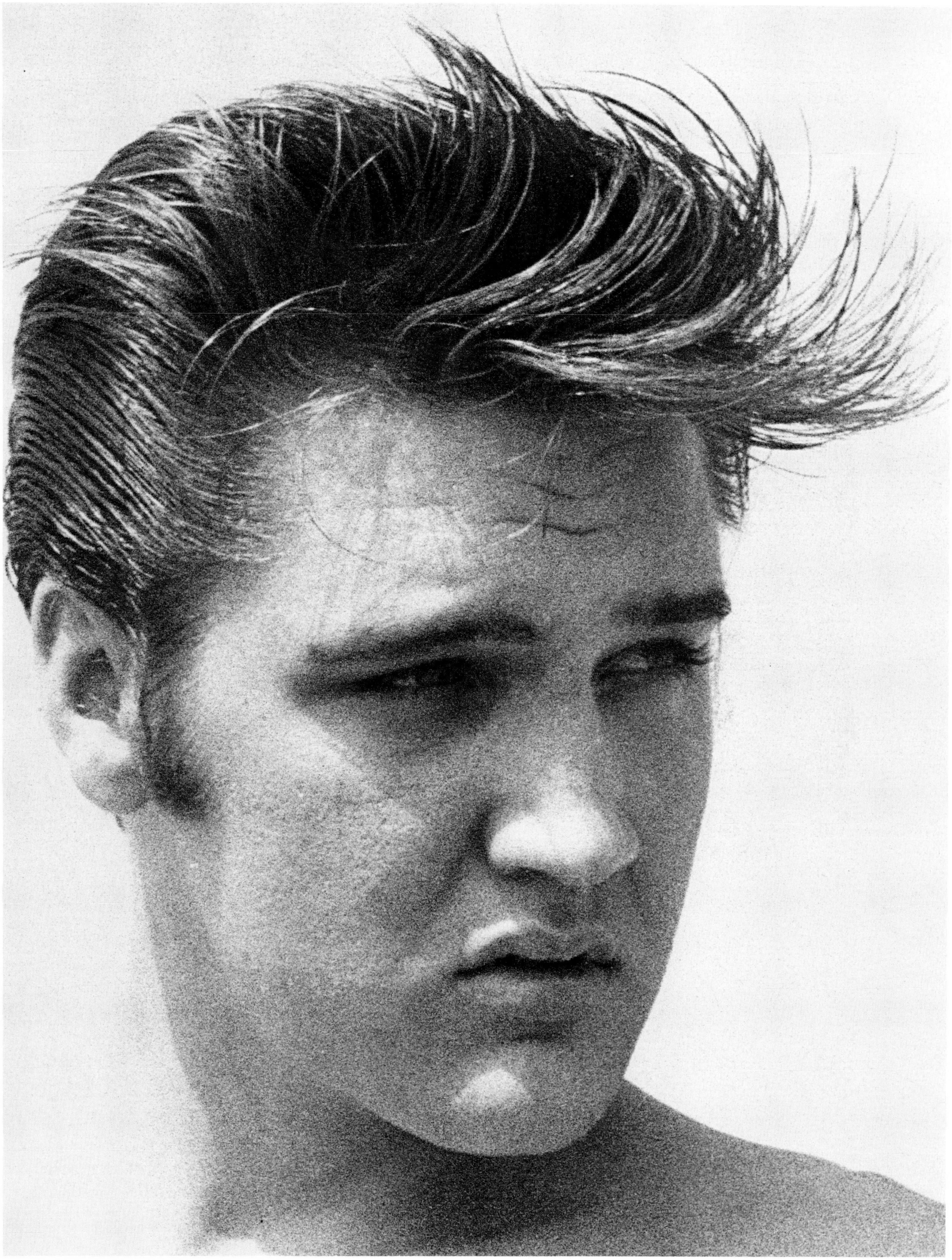

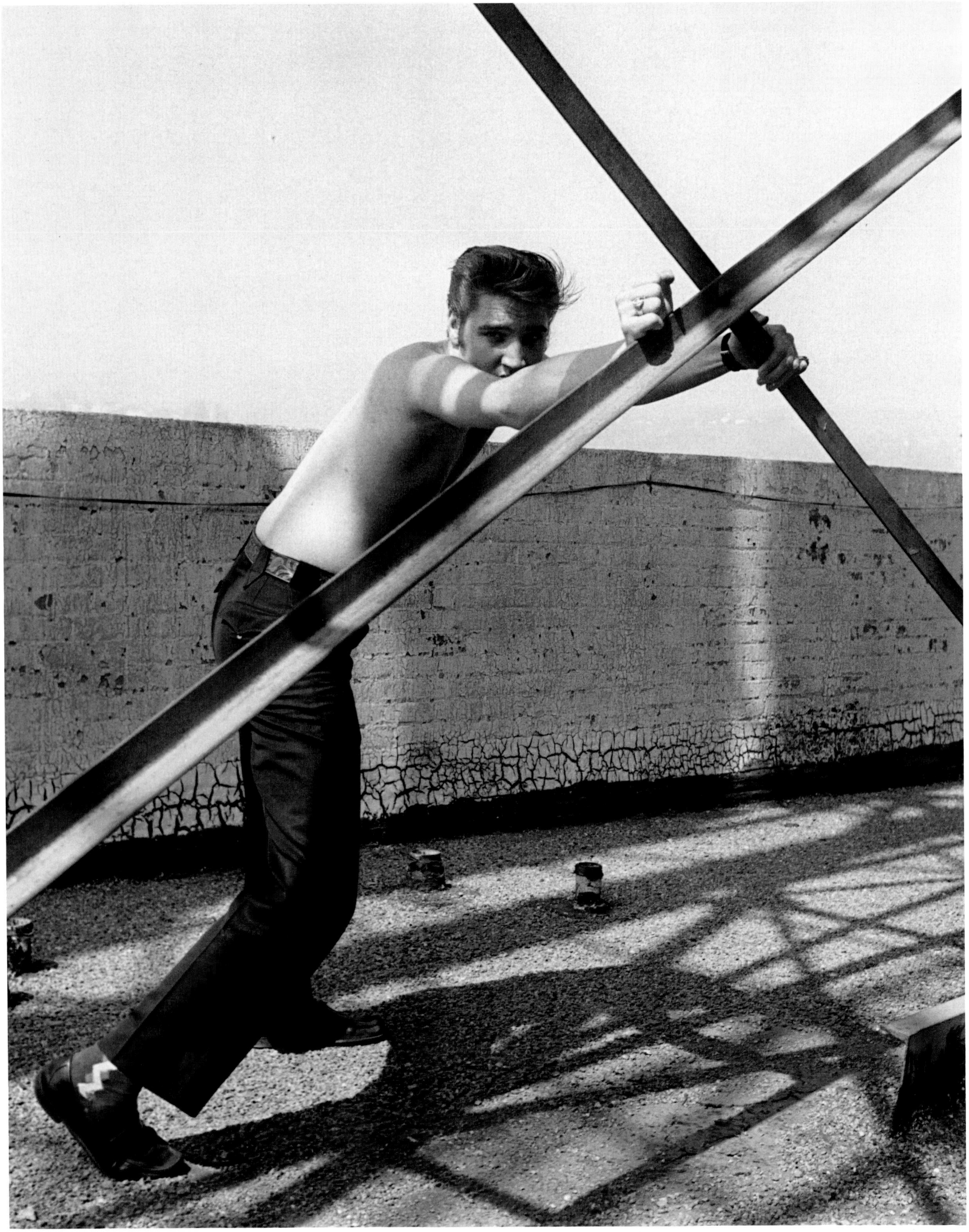

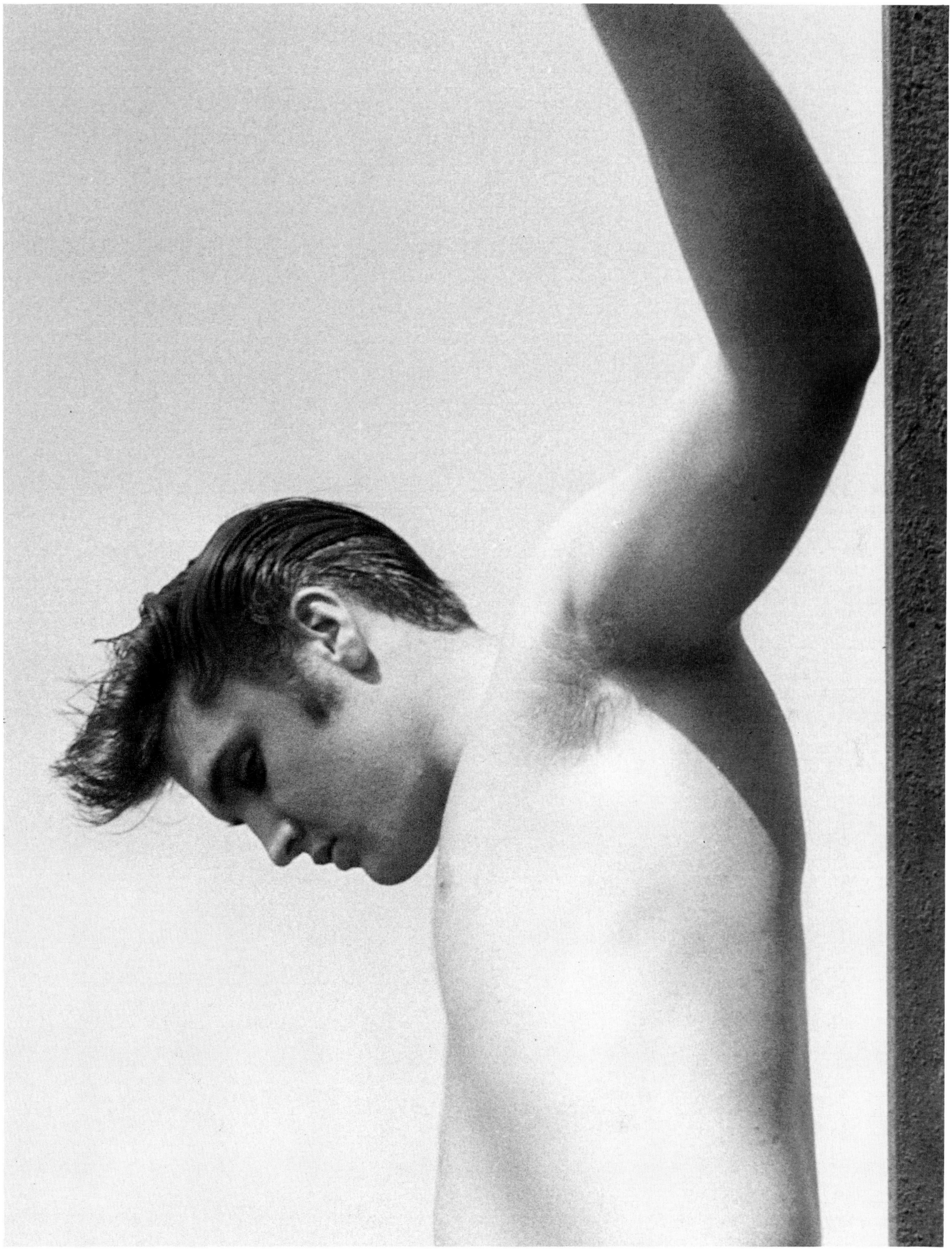

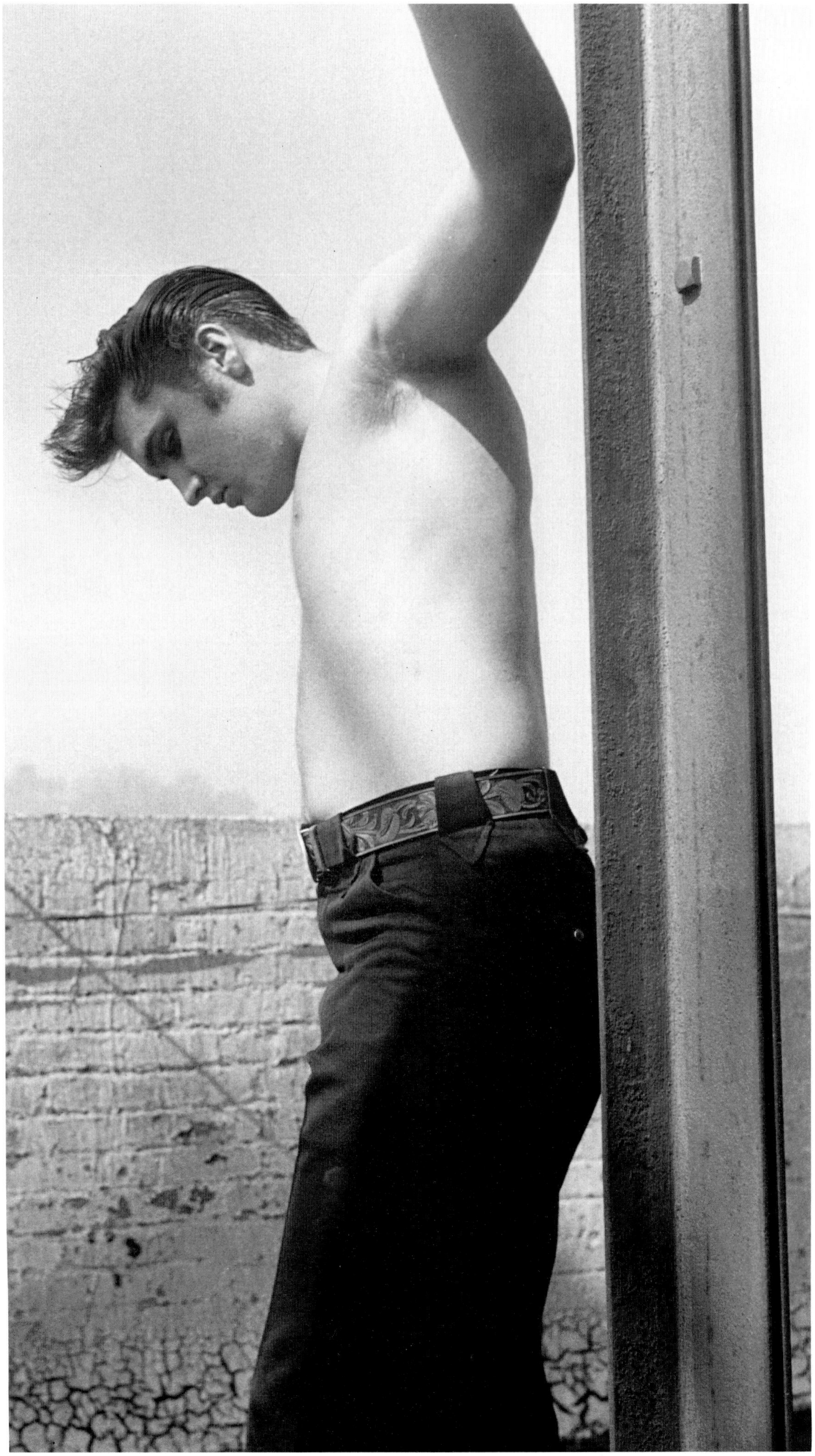

*Nothing is so strong as gentleness,
and nothing is so gentle as real strength.*

Ralph W. Sockman

*Memory is not so brilliant as hope,
but it is more beautiful, and a
thousand times as true.*

George Dennison Prentice

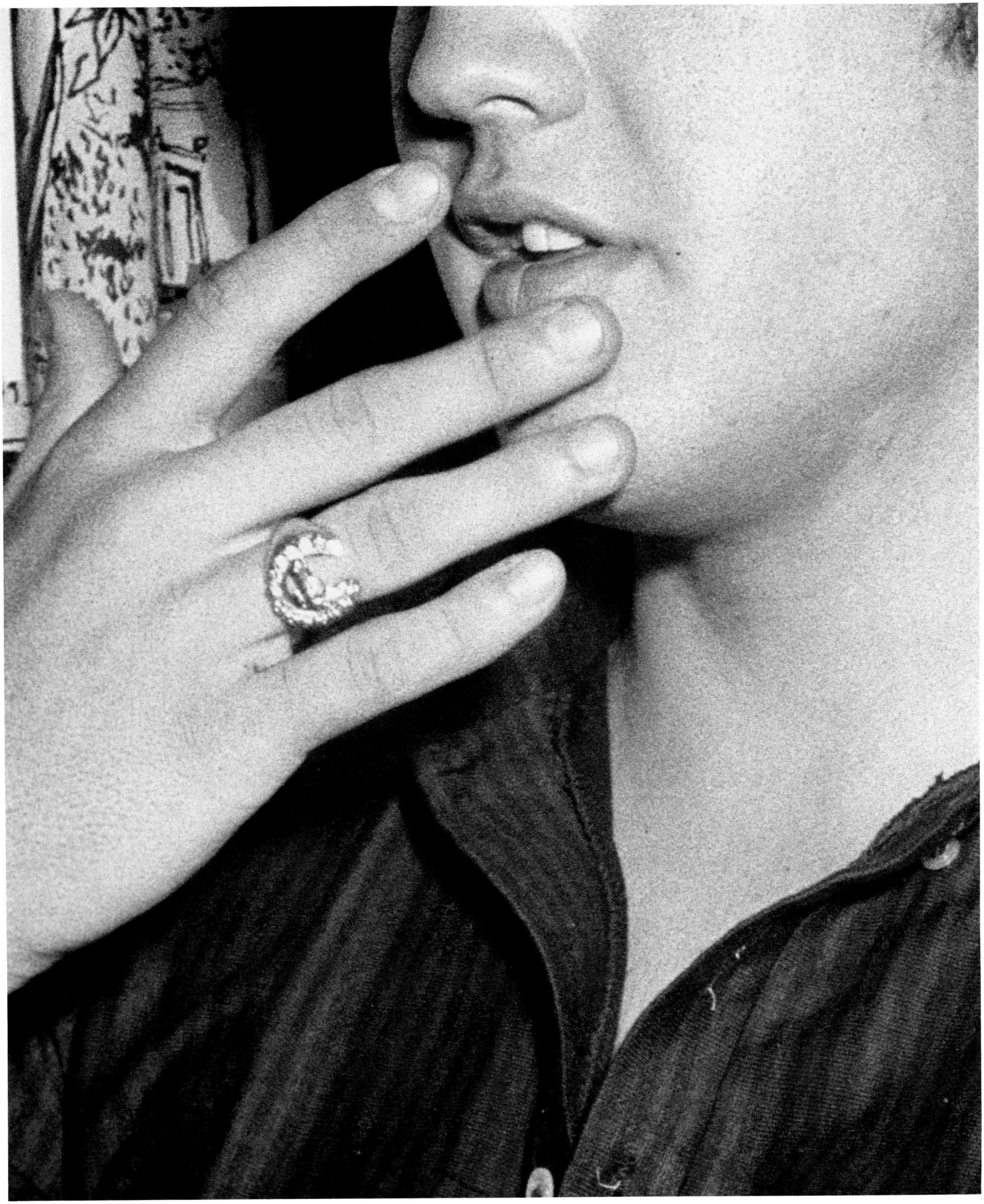

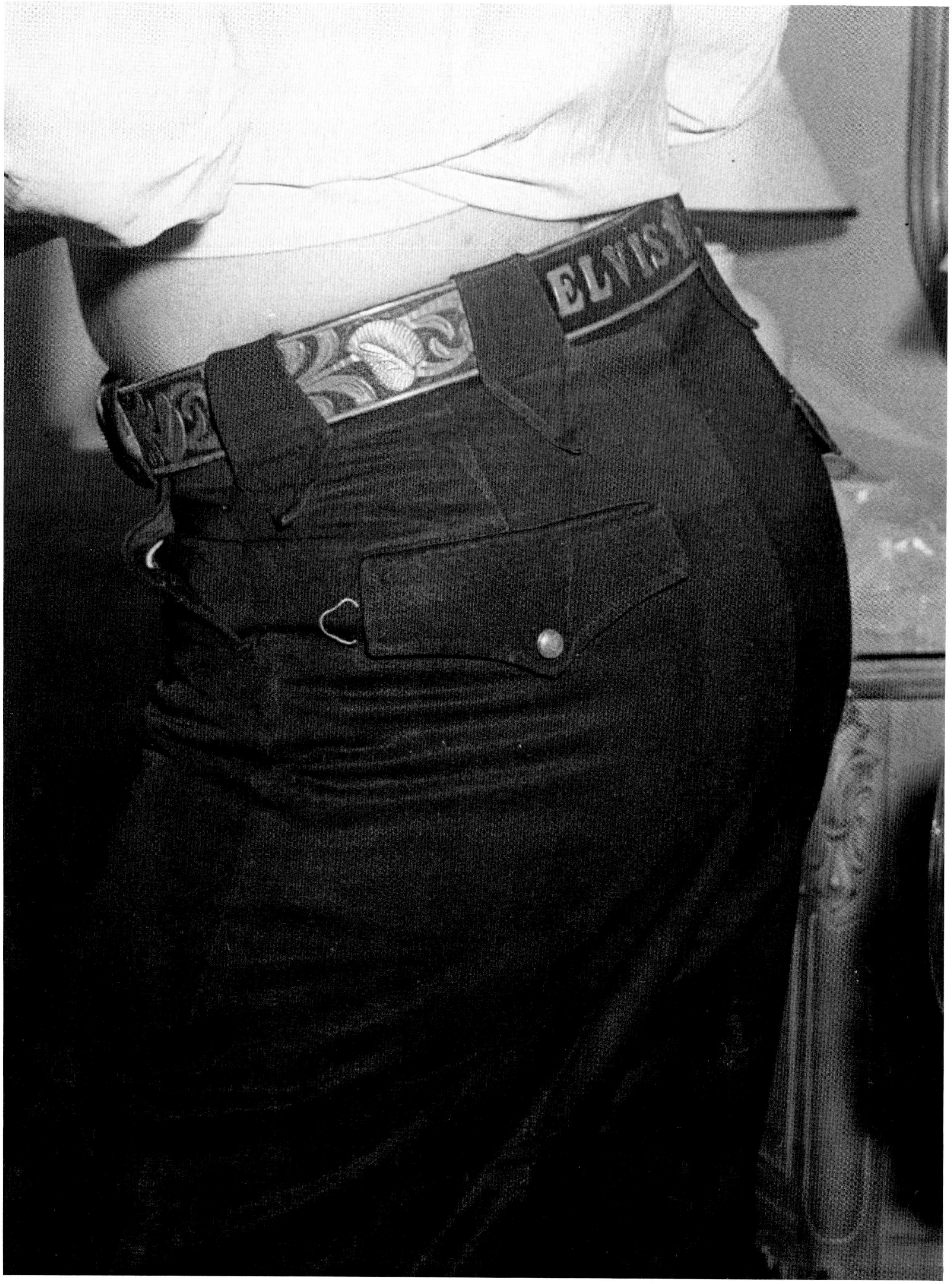
ELVIS

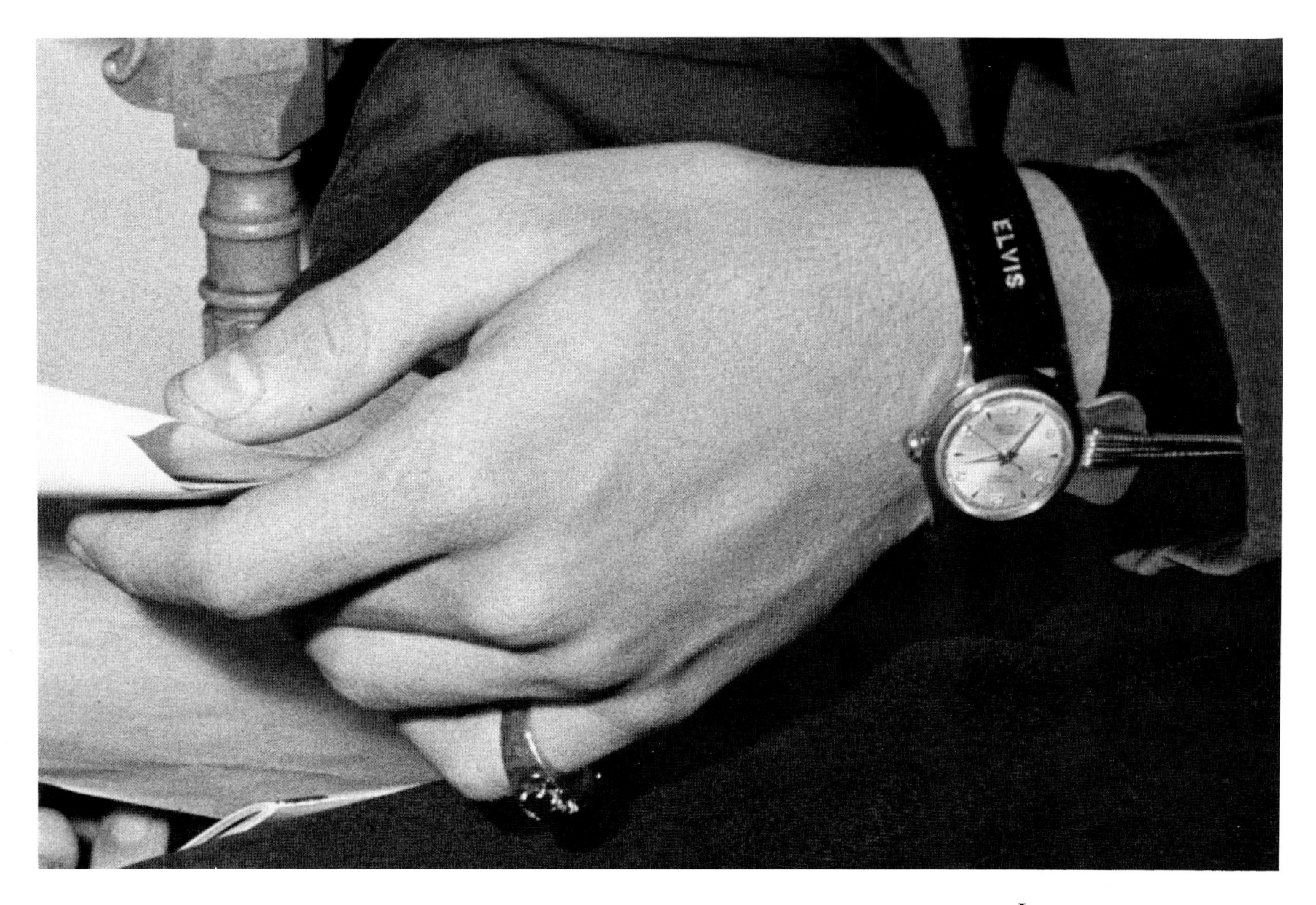

*In memory
everything seems to happen to music.*

Tennessee Williams

*Music is a means of giving form
to our inner feelings
without attaching them to events
or objects in the world*

George Santayana

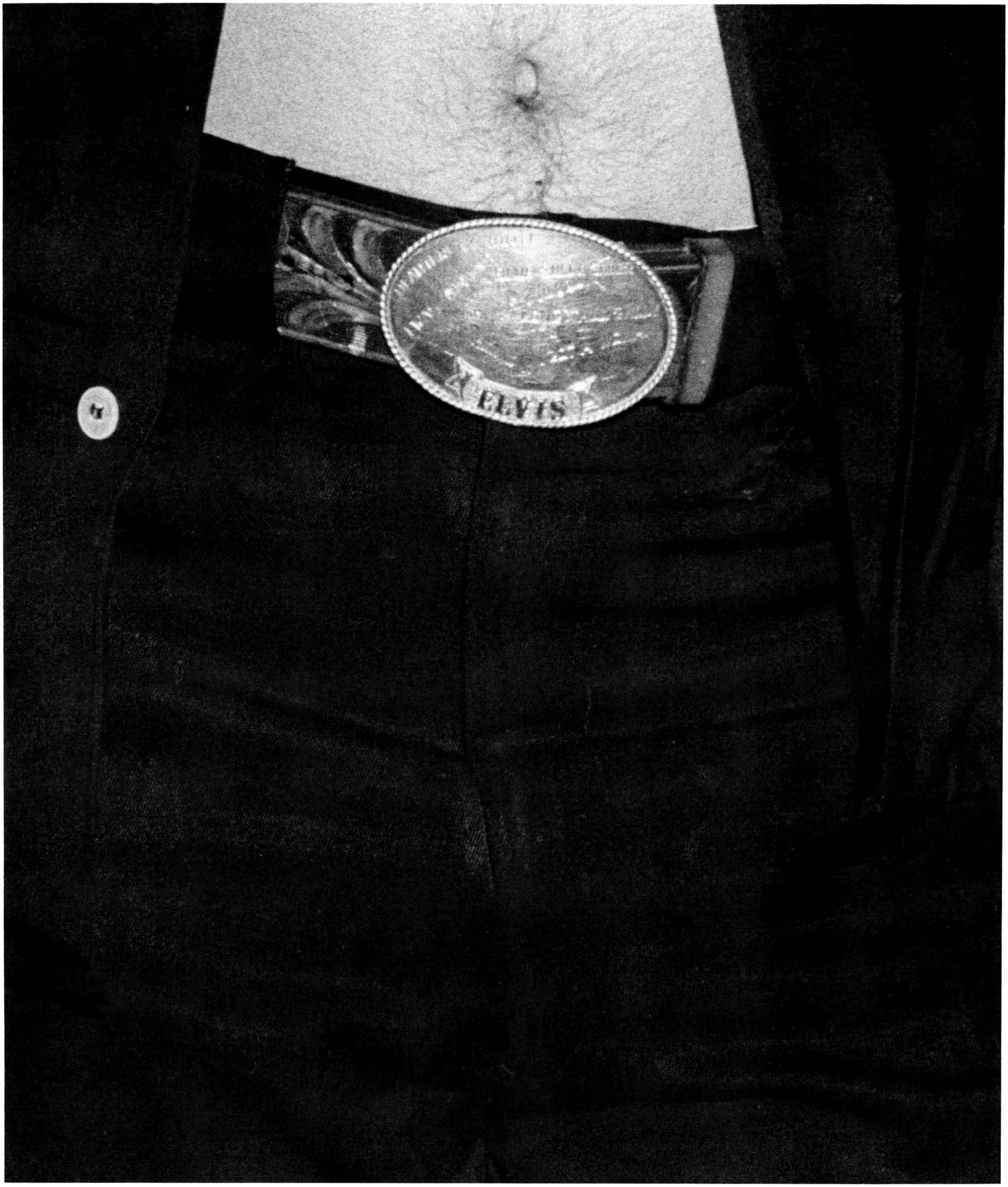
ELVIS

*Success is not the result
of spontaneous combustion.
You must set yourself on fire.*

Reggie Leach

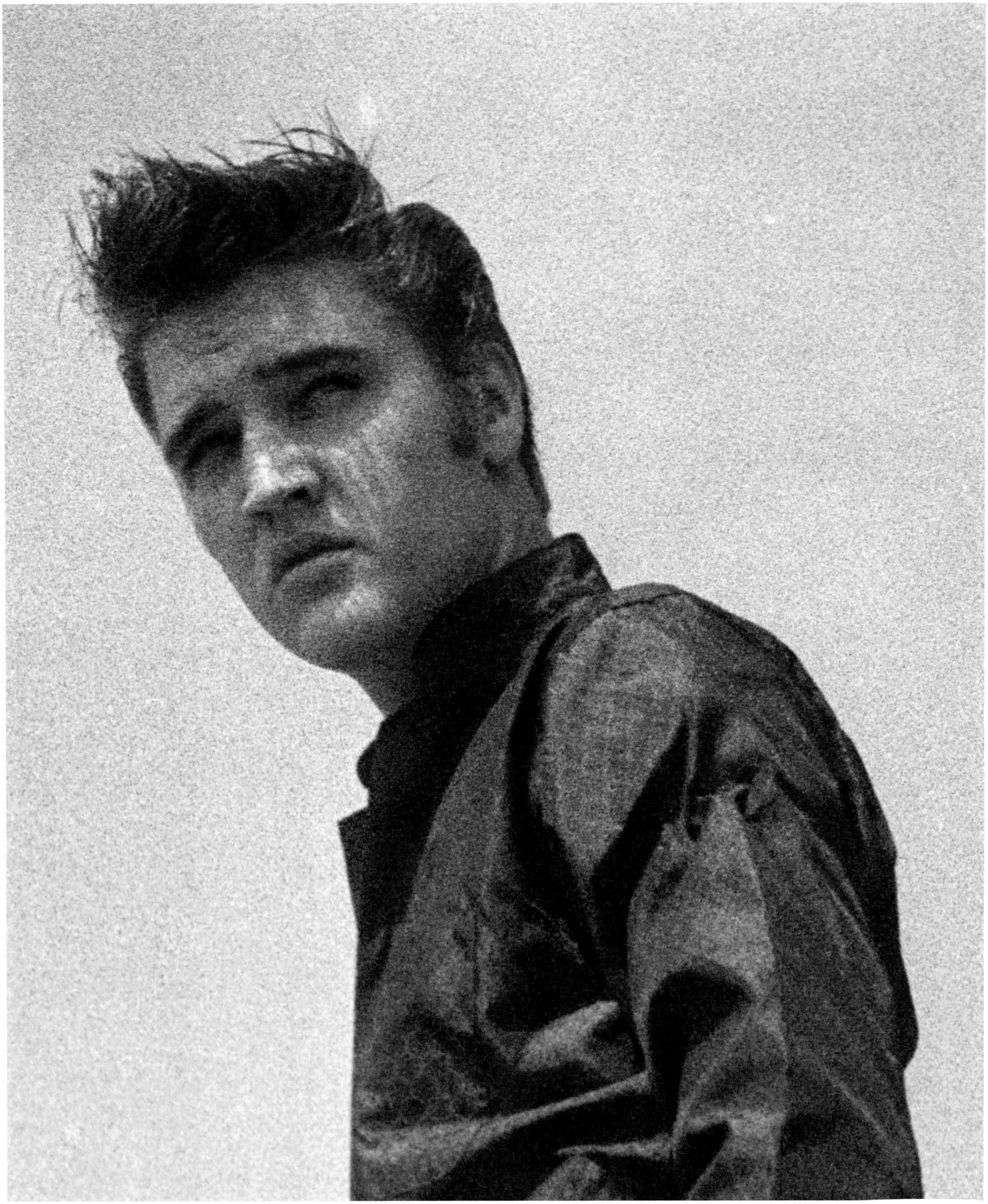

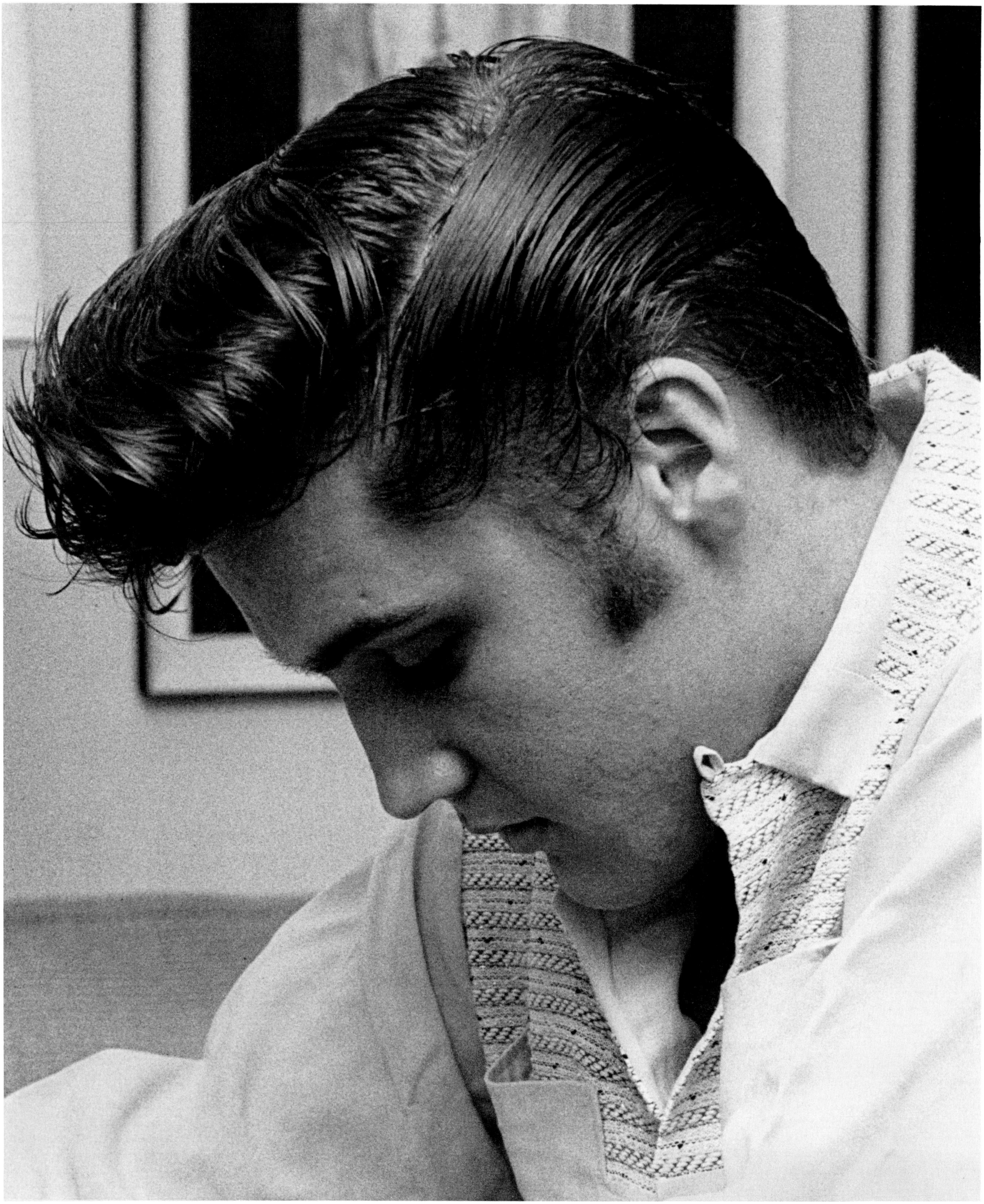

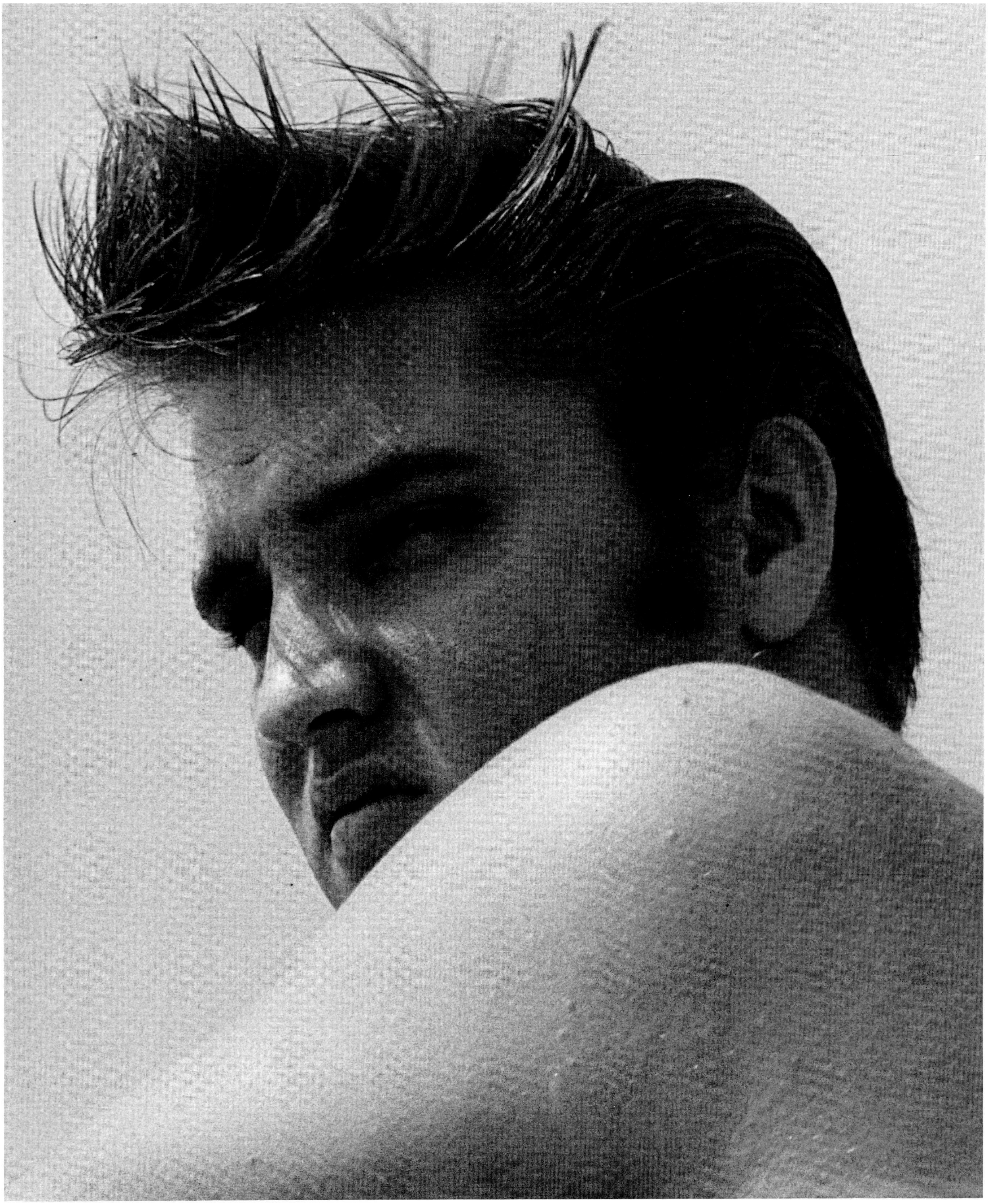

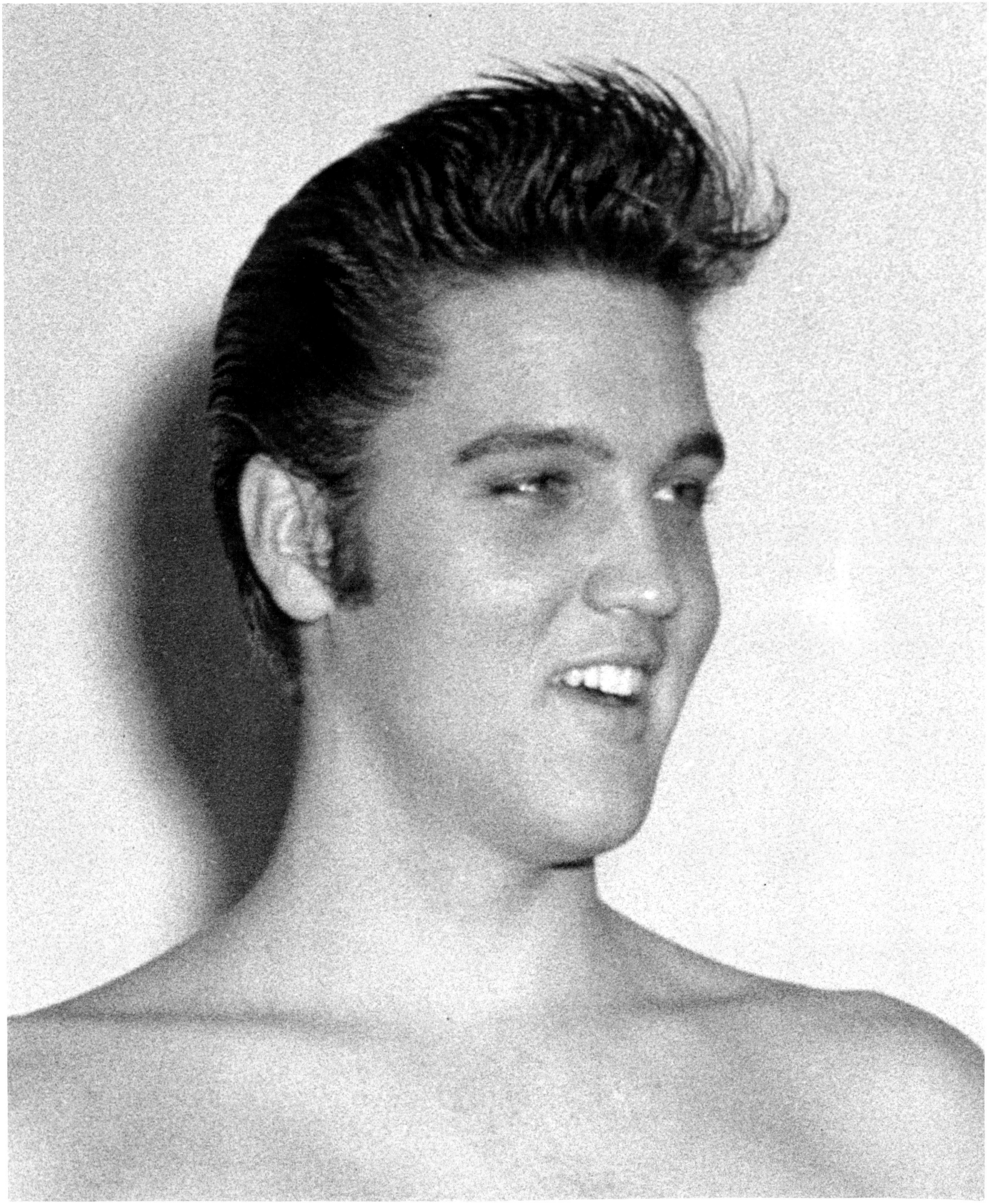

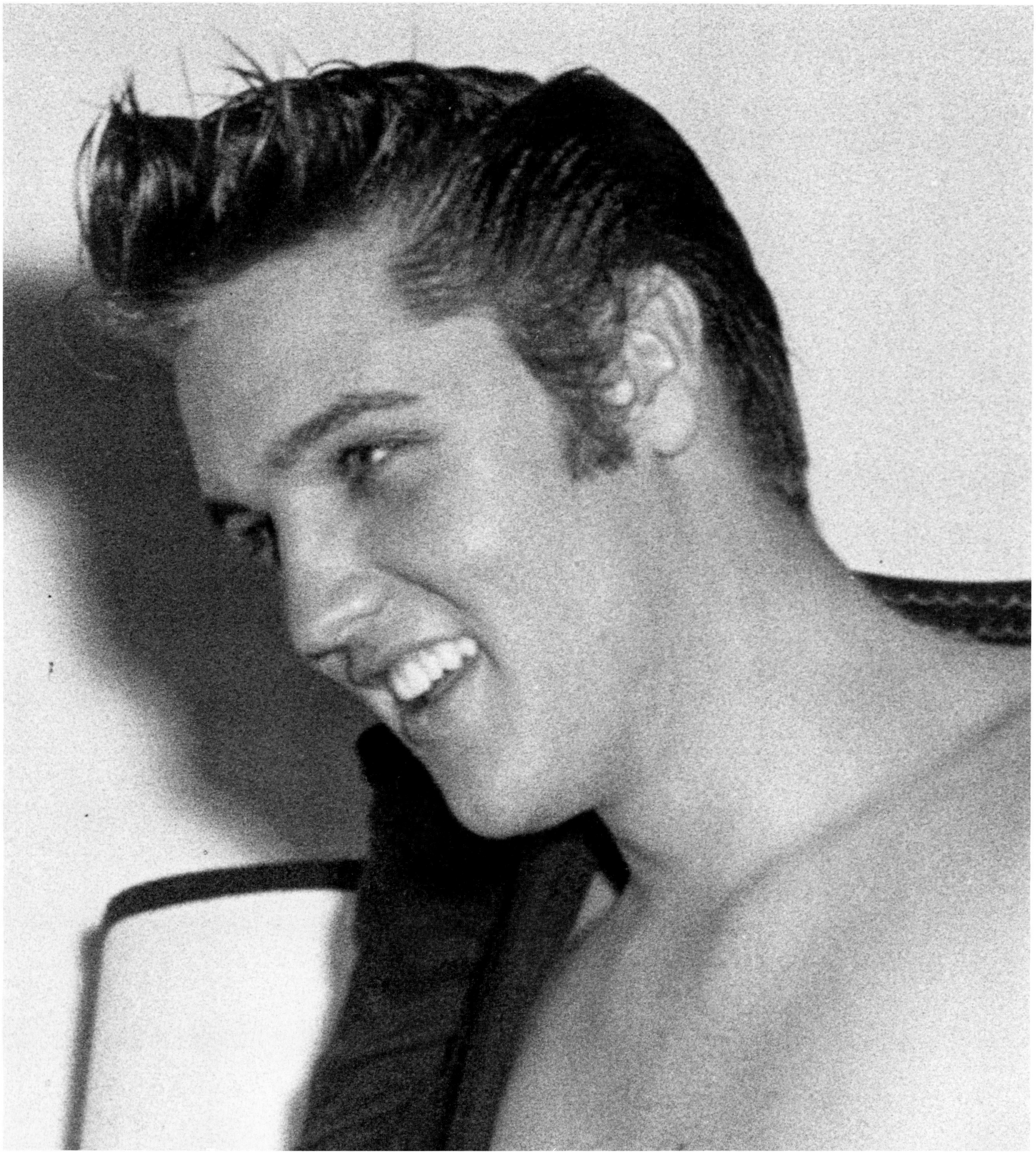

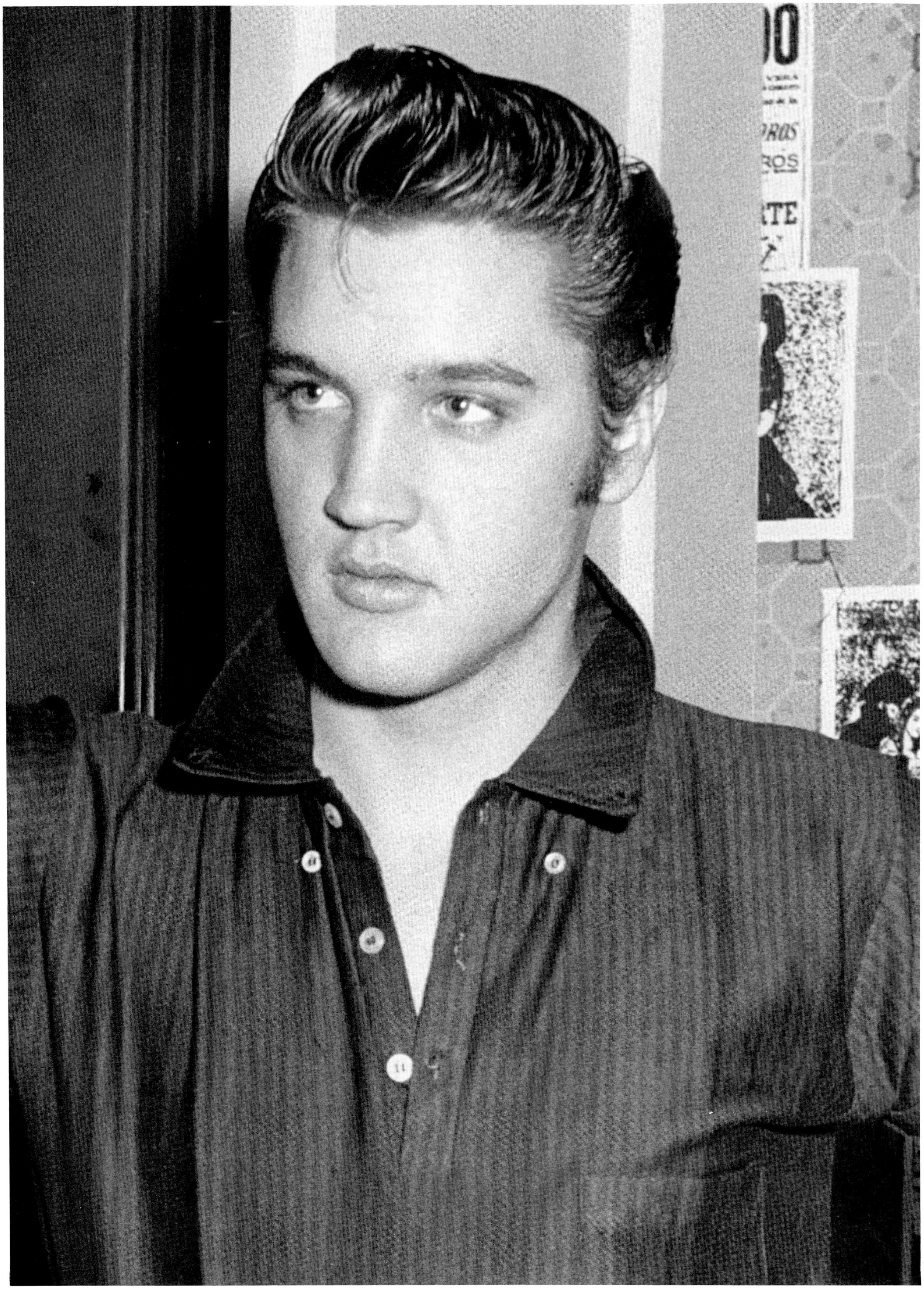

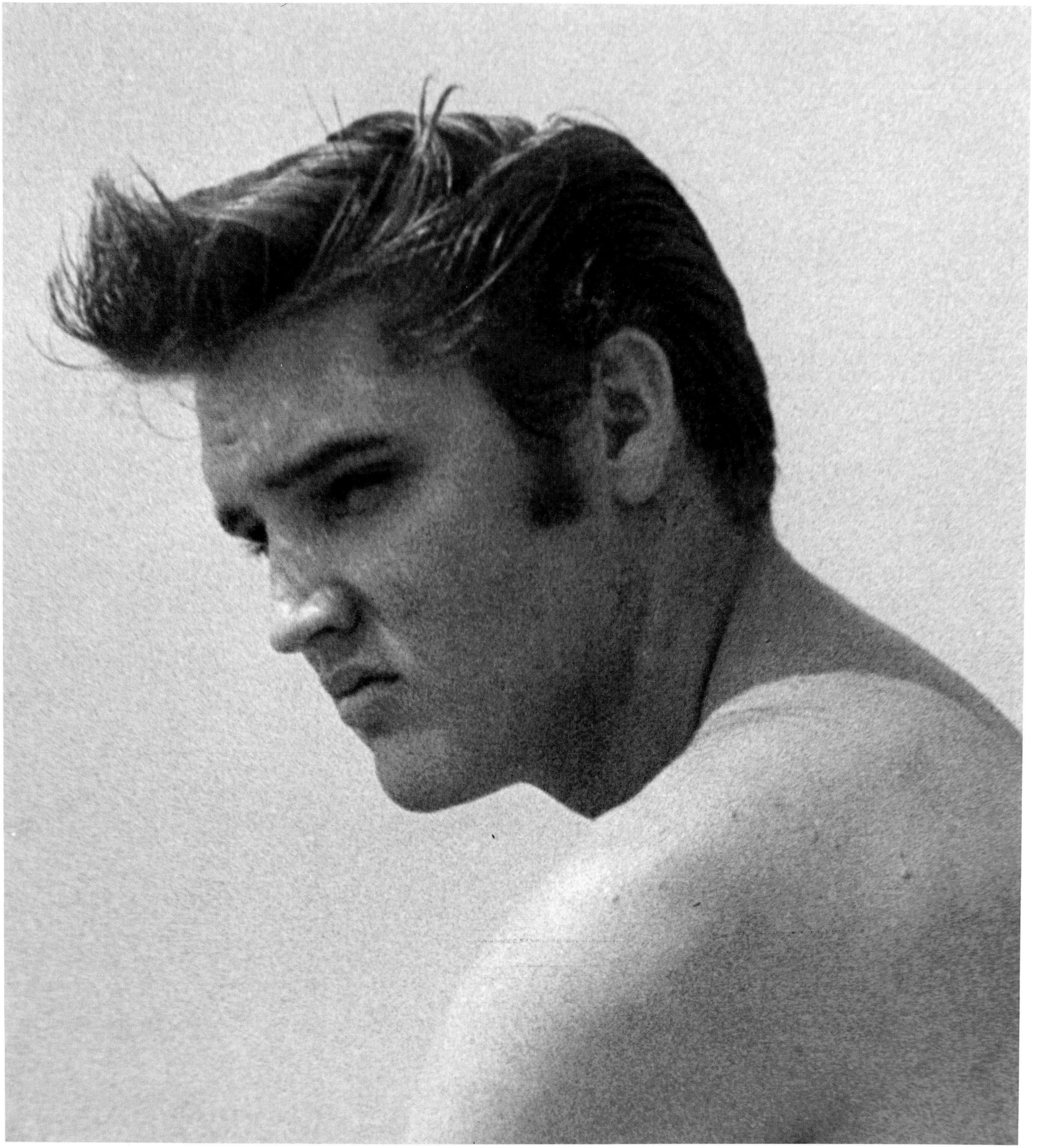

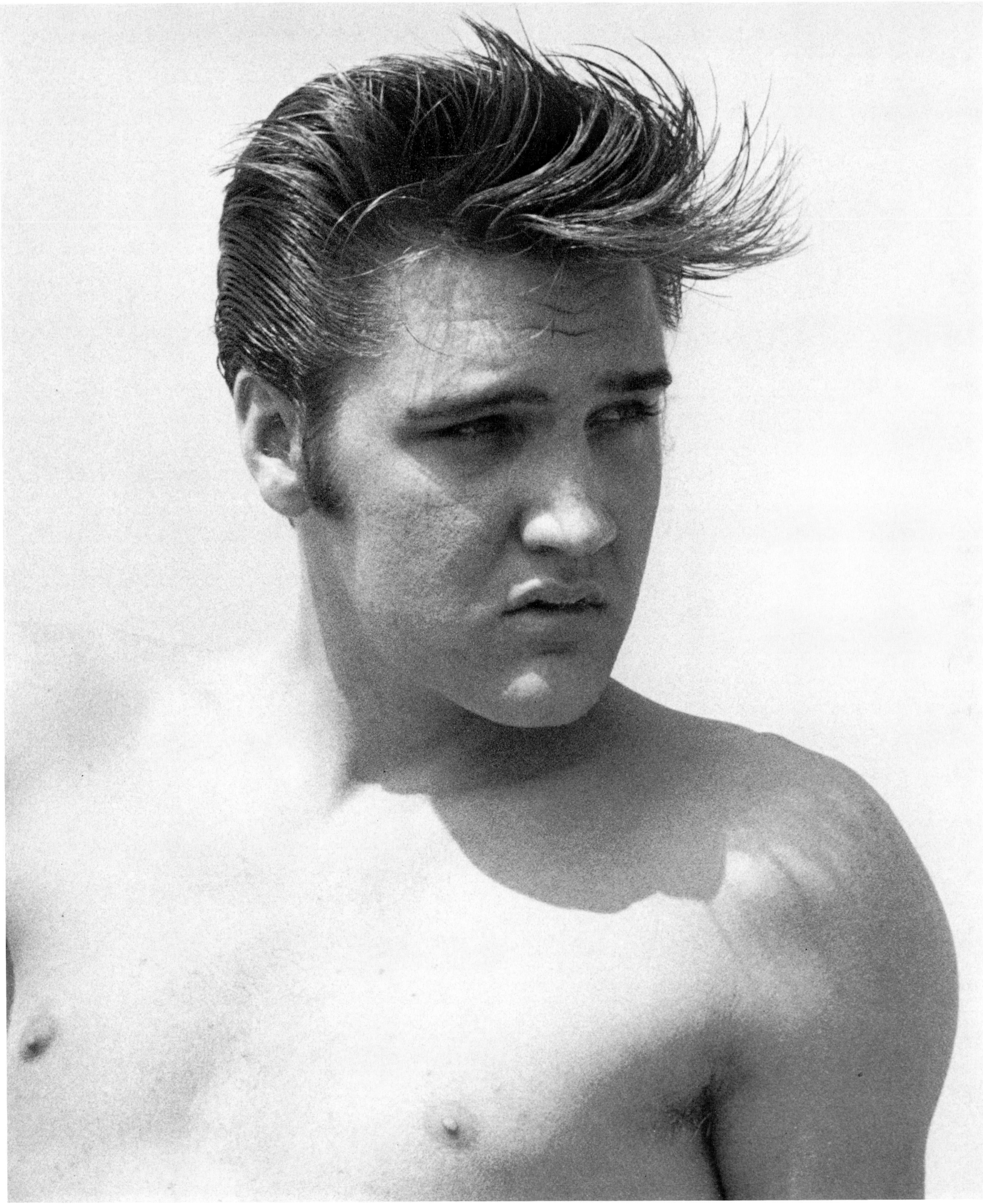

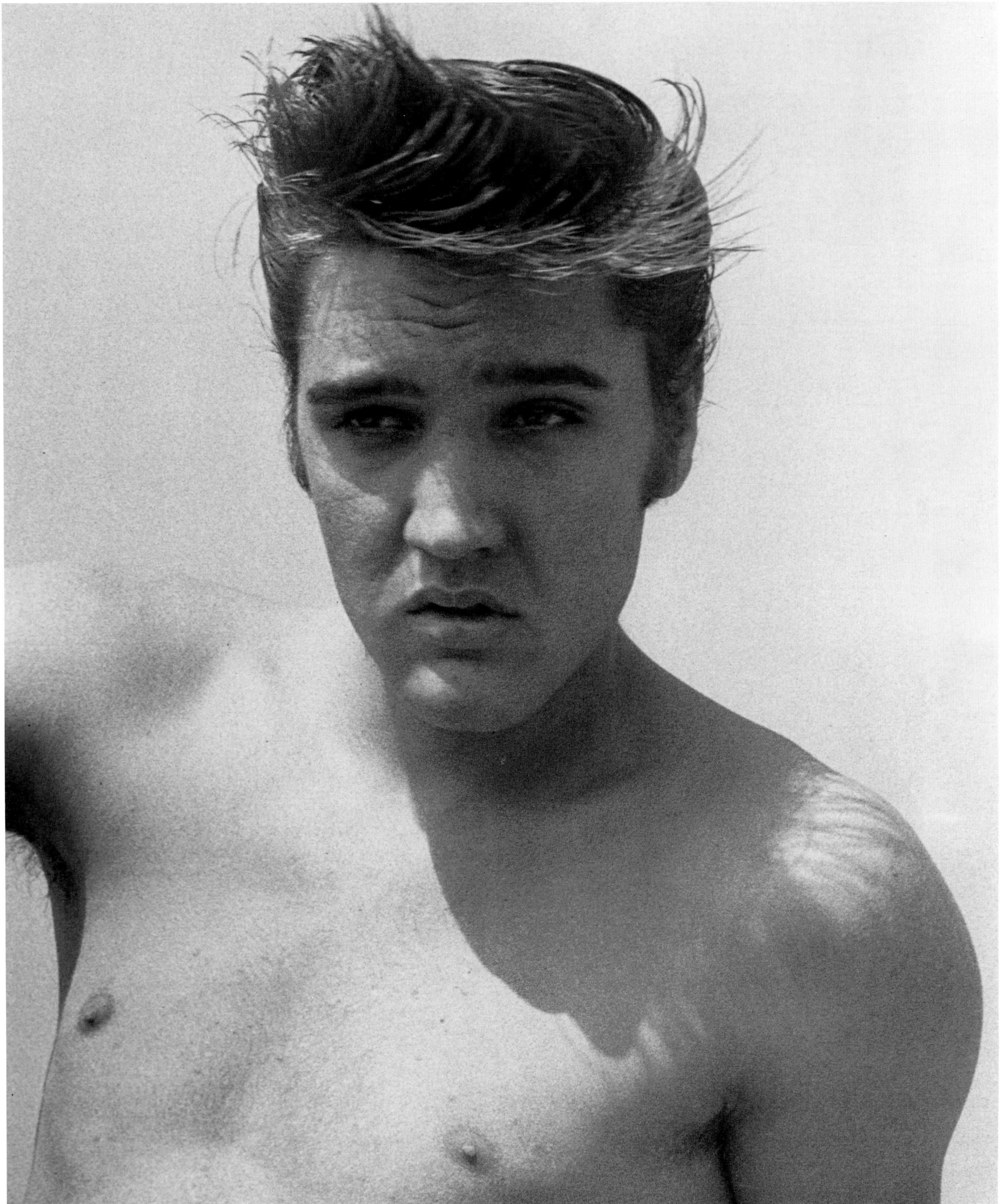

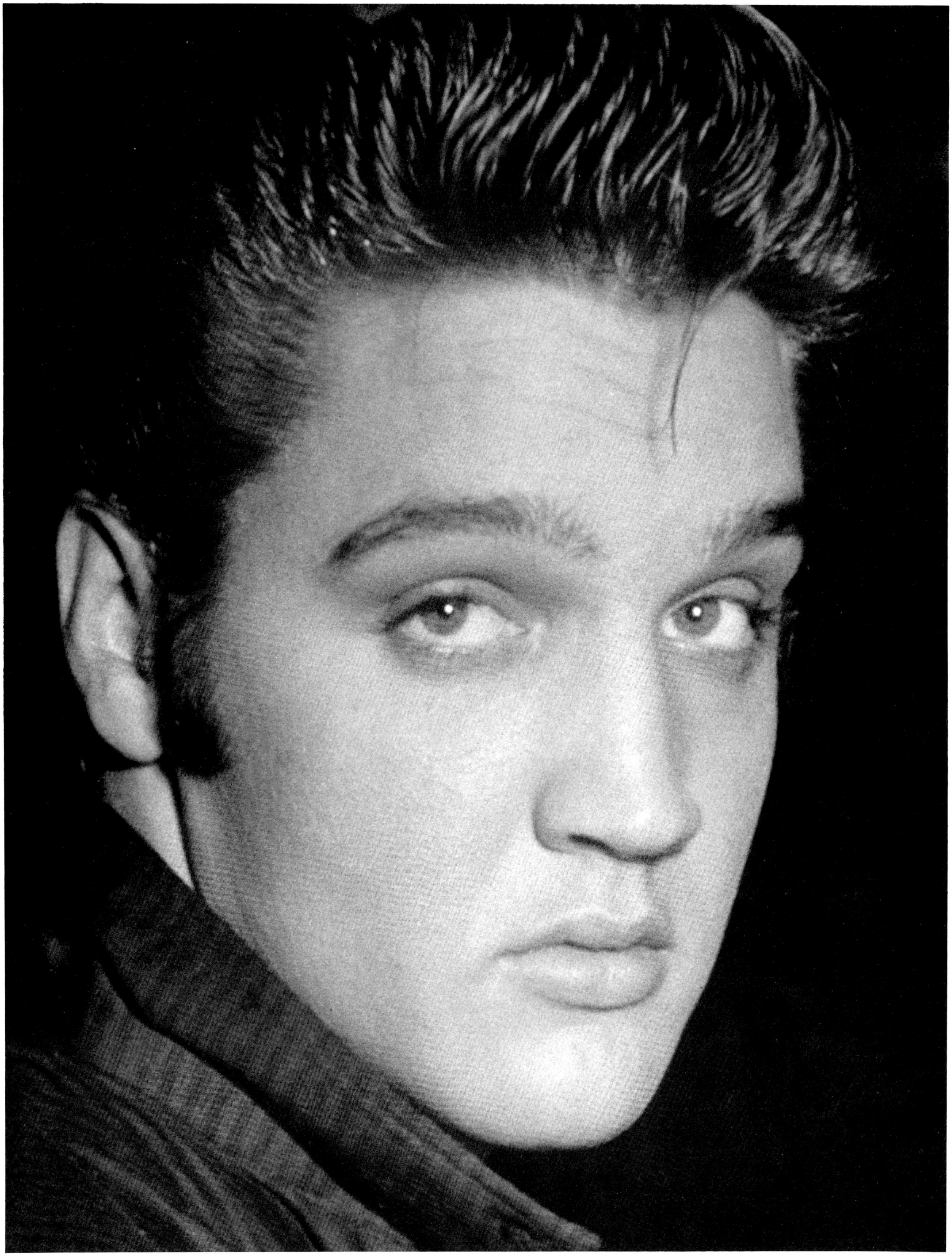

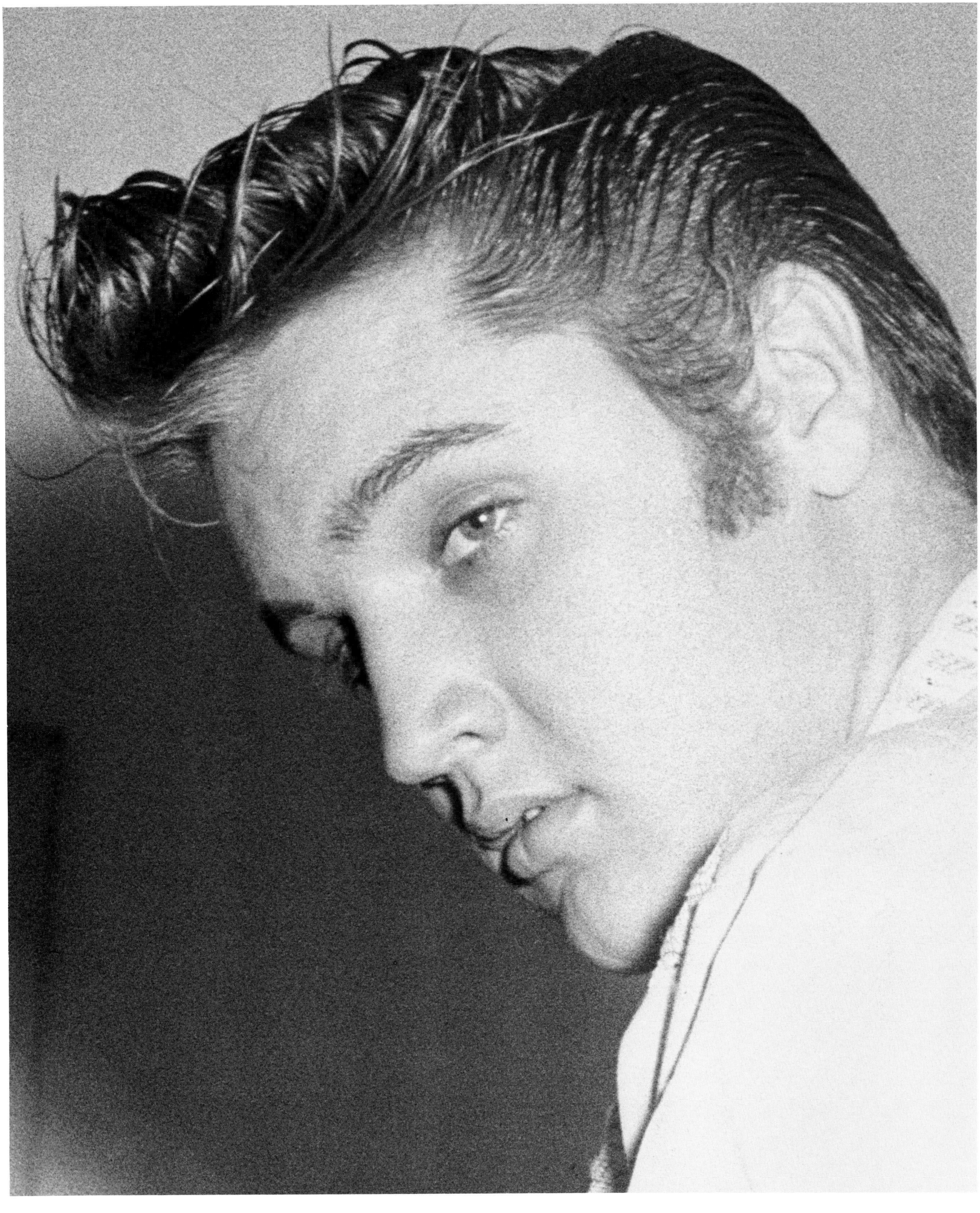

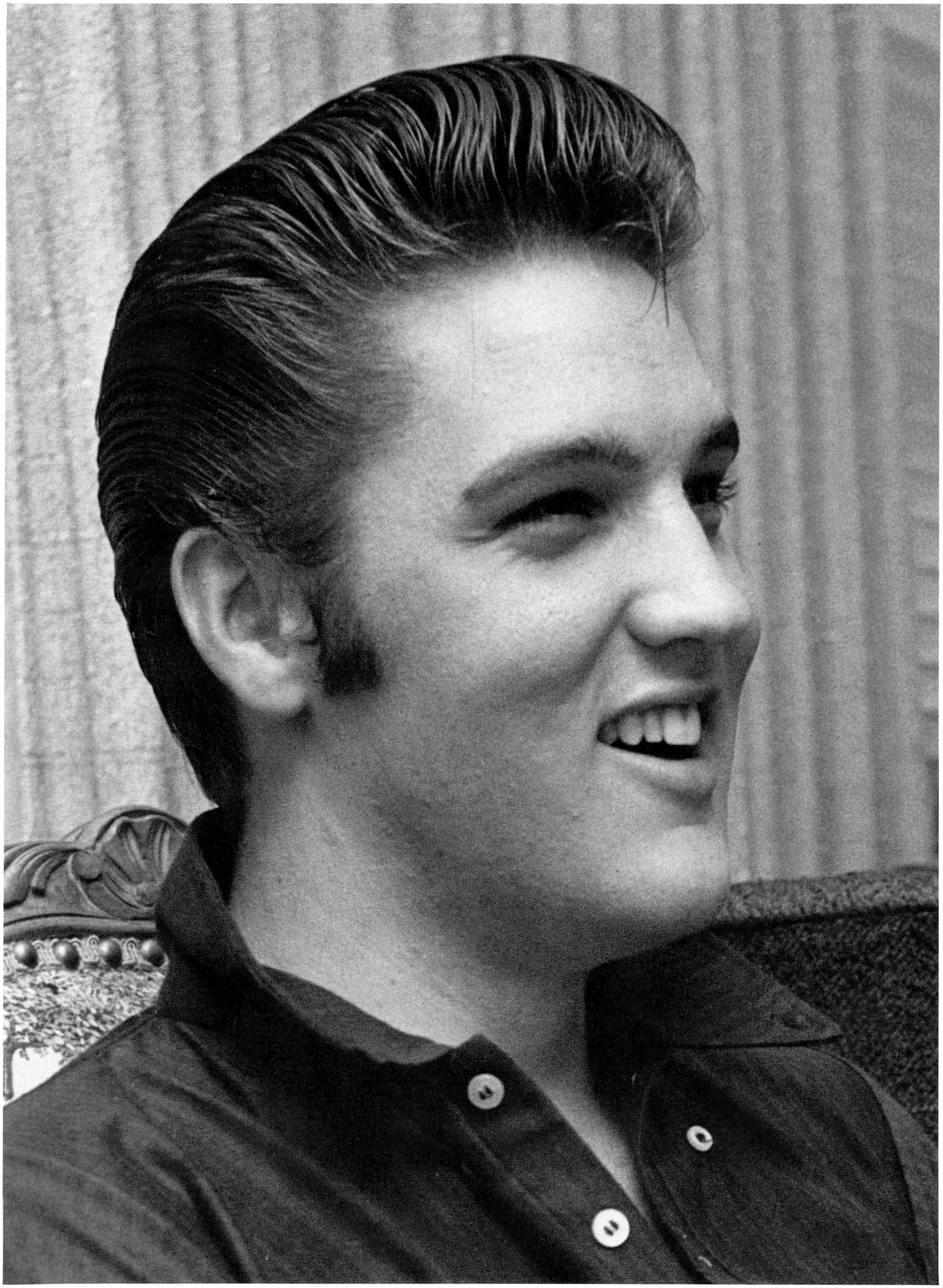

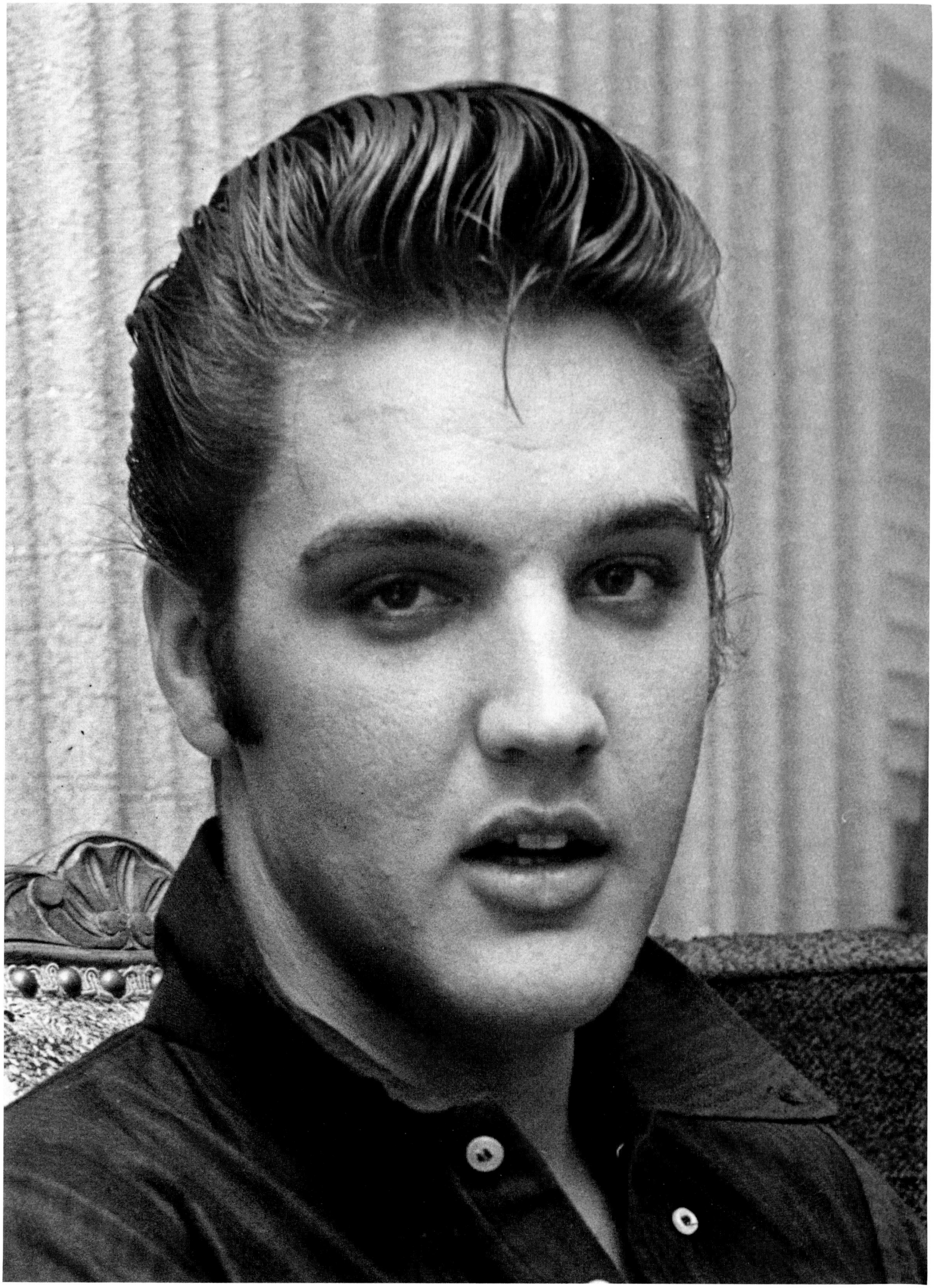

THE MEASURE OF A MAN

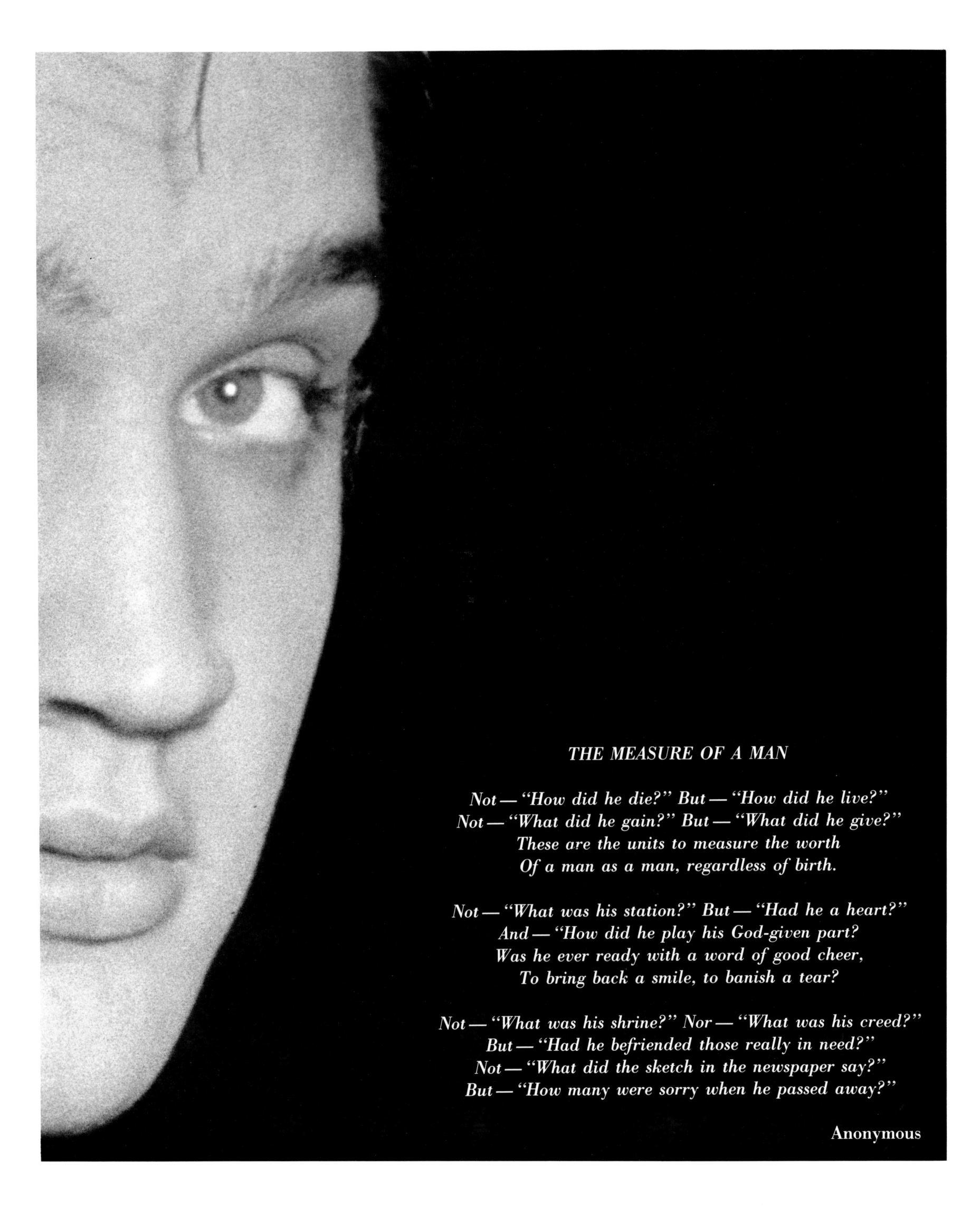

Not — "How did he die?" But — "How did he live?"
Not — "What did he gain?" But — "What did he give?"
These are the units to measure the worth
Of a man as a man, regardless of birth.

Not — "What was his station?" But — "Had he a heart?"
And — "How did he play his God-given part?
Was he ever ready with a word of good cheer,
To bring back a smile, to banish a tear?"

Not — "What was his shrine?" Nor — "What was his creed?"
But — "Had he befriended those really in need?"
Not — "What did the sketch in the newspaper say?"
But — "How many were sorry when he passed away?"

Anonymous

Reflections II

Chronology 1956

January

7	Saturday	C	Elvis appears on "Louisiana Hayride" in Shreveport, LA.
8	Sunday	G	Elvis celebrates his 21st birthday.
10	Tuesday	D	Elvis records "I Got a Woman," "Heartbreak Hotel," and "Money Honey" in that order during his first recording session with RCA Victor. The recordings take place in the RCA Studios in Nashville.
11	Wednesday	D	Continuing the recording session from last night, Elvis records "I'm Counting on You" and "I Was the One."
14	Saturday	C	Elvis appears on "Louisiana Hayride" in Shreveport, LA.
21	Saturday	C	Elvis reappears on "Louisiana Hayride."
27	Friday	D	"Heartbreak Hotel"/"I Was the One" is released by RCA Victor.
28	Saturday	T	Elvis appears on Tommy and Jimmy Dorsey's "Stage Show"—his first national television appearance. He sings "Shake, Rattle and Roll," "Flip, Flop and Fly," and "I Got a Woman." Elvis is paid $1,250 for this show.
29	Sunday	C	Elvis performs in Richmond, VA.
30	Monday	D	Elvis records "Blue Suede Shoes," "My Baby Left Me," "One-Sided Love Affair," "So Glad Your Mine," "I'm Gonna Sit Right Down and Cry (Over You)," and "Tutti Frutti."
31	Tuesday	D	The recording session from last night carries over until the morning hours.

February

		D	"Heartbreak Hotel" and "I Was The One" are released.
3	Friday	D	Elvis records "Lawdy Miss Clawdy," and "Shake, Rattle and Roll."
4	Saturday	T	Elvis appears on "Stage Show" and sings "Baby Let's Play House," and "Tutti Frutti." He is paid $1,250 for this show.
5	Sunday	C	Elvis performs in Norfolk, VA in the Monticello Auditorium.
6	Monday	C	Elvis performs in Greensboro, NC at the National Theater.
11	Saturday	T	Elvis appears on "Stage Show" and sings "Blue Suede Shoes" and "Heartbreak Hotel." He is paid $1,250 for this show.
15	Wednesday	D	"I Forgot To Remember To Forget" hits NO. 1 on *The Billboard's* Country & Western singles chart.
18	Saturday	T	Elvis appears on "Stage Show" and sings "Tutti Frutti" and "I Was The One." He is paid $1,250 for this show.
21	Tuesday	C	Elvis performs in Sarasota, FL in the Florida Theater.
22	Wednesday	D	"Heartbreak Hotel" enters *The Billboard's* "The Top 100" at position NO. 68 and enters the "Country's Best Sellers in Stores" list at the NO. 9 position.
25	Saturday	C	Elvis appears on "Louisiana Hayride" in Shreveport, LA.
29	Wednesday	D	"I Was The One" enters *The Billboard's* "The Top 100" at the NO. 84 position.

March

3	Saturday	N	*The Billboard*: PRESLEY HOT AS $1 PISTOL ON VICTOR
		C	Elvis appears on the "Louisiana Hayride" in Shreveport, LA.
7	Wednesday	D	"Heartbreak Hotel" hits NO. 1 on *The Billboard's* "Country Best Sellers in Stores" list.
10	Saturday	C	Elvis appears on "Louisiana Hayride" in Shreveport, LA.
14	Wednesday	C	Elvis appears in Atlanta, GA at the Fox Theater. The Jordanaires also perform on that show.
15	Thursday	G	Elvis signs a contract with Colonel Tom Parker to be Elvis' manager.
		C	Elvis performs for a second consecutive night at the Fox Theater in Atlanta, GA.

17	Saturday	T	Elvis appears on "Stage Show" and sings "Blue Suede Shoes" and "Heartbreak Hotel." He receives $1,250 for the show.
22	Thursday	C	Elvis appears in Richmond, VA at the Mosque Theater.
24	Saturday	T	Elvis appears on "Stage Show" and sings "Money Honey" and "Heartbreak Hotel." This is his final appearance on "Stage Show."
28	Wednesday	D	"Blue Suede Shoes" enters *The Billboard's* "The Top 100" at position NO. 88.
31	Saturday	D	The album *Elvis Presley*, enters *The Billboard's* "Best Selling Packaged Records—Popular Albums" at NO. 11 position.

April

		D	An extended play, double extended play, and long playing albums, all titled *Elvis Presley* are released by RCA Victor.
1	Sunday	F	Elvis has a screen test for Hal Wallis at Paramount Studios in Hollywood. He sings "Blue Suede Shoes" and performs a scene from *The Rainmaker*.
3	Tuesday	T	Elvis appears on "The Milton Berle Show" and sings "Blue Suede Shoes," and "Heartbreak Hotel." The show is broadcast from the USS Hancock, docked at the San Diego Naval Station.
4	Wednesday	C	Elvis performs in San Diego, CA at the San Diego Arena.
5	Thursday	C	Elvis performs for the second day at the San Diego Arena.
6	Friday	F	Elvis signs a 7-year contract with Hal Wallis and Paramount pictures. Elvis is to make 3 movies and to receive $100,000 for the first film, $150,000 for the second, and $200,000 for the third.
7	Saturday	C	Elvis appears on "Louisiana Hayride" in Shreveport, LA.
10	Tuesday	G	In an airplane flight to Memphis, Elvis' plane almost crashes.
11	Wednesday	N/D	"Heartbreak Hotel" sells over one million records, according to *Variety*.
		D	Elvis records "I Want You, I Need You, I Love You" at RCA Victor's Nashville studios. He is awarded a gold record for "Heartbreak Hotel," which had sold one million copies.
15	Sunday	C	Elvis performs in San Antonio, TX at the Municipal Auditorium.
16	Monday	C	Elvis performs in Corpus Christi, TX.

18	Wednesday	C	Elvis performs in Tulsa, OK. Eight thousand people were in the audience.
19	Thursday	C	Elvis performs in Amarillo, TX
20	Friday	C	Elvis performs in a concert in Fort Worth, TX at the Northside Convention Center. Seven thousand people were in the audience.
21	Saturday	C	Elvis performs in Dallas, TX.
22	Sunday	C	Elvis performs in San Antonio, TX at the Municipal Auditorium. Six thousand people attend two shows.
23	Monday	C	Elvis performs in the Venus room of the New Frontier Hotel in Las Vegas, NV. He is billed as "The Atomic Powered Singer." He is paid $12,500 for a two-week engagement.
25	Wednesday	D	"Heartbreak Hotel" hits NO. 1 in *The Billboard's*, "The Top 100." "Baby Let's Play House" enters "Country Best Sellers in Stores" at position NO. 13.
30	Monday	N	*Life* magazine: A HOWLING HILLBILLY SUCCESS. This is the first significant article about Elvis in a national news magazine.

May

		D	"I Want You, I Need You, I Love You"/"My Baby Left Me" is released by RCA Victor.
		D	"Heartbreak Hotel" (extended play album) is released by RCA Victor.
2	Wednesday	D	"Money, Honey" enters *The Billboard's* "The Top 100" at NO. 84 position.
5	Saturday	D	*Elvis Presley* (LP) reaches NO. 1 on *The Billboard's* "Best Selling Packaged Records — Popular Albums."
6	Sunday	C	Elvis ends his 2-week engagement at the New Frontier Hotel in Las Vegas, NV.
9	Wednesday	N	*Variety*: THE ELVIS PRESLEY STORY: HE'S MAKING MONKEYS OUT OF SINGERS
11	Friday	G	The Presleys buy a home at 1034 Audubon Drive in Memphis, TN.
12	Saturday	N	*The Billboard*: E.P. IS V.I.P. FOR VICTOR
13	Sunday	C	Elvis performs in St. Paul, MN.
14	Monday	N	*Newsweek*: HILLBILLY ON A PEDESTAL
		N	*Time*: TEENER'S HERO
		C	Elvis appears in La Crosse, WI.
15	Tuesday	C	Elvis performs in Memphis, TN.
16	Wednesday	C	Elvis performs in Little Rock, AR at the Little Rock Auditorium.
		D	"My Baby Left Me" and "I Want You, I Need You, I Love You" enter *The Billboard's* "The Top 100" at NO. 68 and NO. 90 positions respectively.

17	Thursday	C	Elvis appears in Springfield, MO at the Shrine Mosque.
18	Friday	C	Elvis performs in Des Moines, IA. Four thousand fans attend.
19	Saturday	C	Elvis performs in Lincoln, NE at the University of Nebraska Coliseum.
20	Sunday	C	Elvis appears in Omaha, NE.
23	Wednesday	D	"I Want You, I Need You, I Love You"/"My Baby Left Me" enters *The Billboard's* "Country Best Sellers in Stores" list at NO. 13 position.
24	Thursday	C	Elvis performs in Kansas City, MO. There are 2,500 fans in attendance.
25	Friday	C	Elvis performs in Detroit, MI in the Fox Theatre. There are 11,900 fans in attendance.
26	Saturday	C	Elvis performs in Columbus, OH at the Veteran's Memorial Auditorium.
27	Sunday	C	Elvis performs in Dayton, OH at the Field House of the University of Dayton. Each of the two shows are attended by 1,800 fans.

June

		D	*Elvis Presley* (extended play album) is released by RCA Victor.
3	Sunday	C	Elvis appears in Oakland, CA at the Oakland Auditorium Arena.
5	Tuesday	T	Elvis appears on "The Milton Berle Show" and sings "I Want You, I Need You, I Love You" and "Hound Dog." Elvis is paid $5,000 for the show.
6	Wednesday	C	Elvis performs in San Diego, CA at the San Diego Arena. 2,500 fans attend the show.
7	Thursday	C	Elvis performs in Long Beach, CA at the Long Beach Municipal Auditorium.
8	Friday	C	Elvis performs in Los Angeles, CA at the Shrine Auditorium.
11	Monday	N	*Newsweek*: HERO WORSHIP
16	Saturday	N	*The Billboard*: PRESLEY ON PAN BUT CASH KEEPS ROLLING
22	Friday	C	Elvis performs in Atlanta, GA at the Paramount Theatre.
23	Saturday	N	*America*: BEWARE ELVIS PRESLEY
		C	Elvis performs in Atlanta, GA at the Paramount Theatre.
24	Sunday	C	Elvis again appears in Atlanta, GA at the Paramount Theatre.
25	Monday	C	Elvis performs in Savannah, GA at the Auditorium. There are 3,500 fans in attendance at each of the two shows.

26	Tuesday	C	Elvis appears in Charlotte, NC at the Coliseum.
27	Wednesday	C	Elvis performs in Augusta, GA at the Bell Auditorium. Six thousand fans attend.
28	Thursday	C	Elvis performs in Charlotte, NC.
30	Saturday	C	Elvis performs in Richmond, VA at the Shrine Mosque Theatre.

July

		D	"Hound Dog" and "Don't Be Cruel" are released by RCA Victor.
1	Sunday	T	Elvis appears on "The Steve Allen Show" in New York and sings "I Want You, I Need You, I Love You" and "Hound Dog." Elvis receives $5,500 for the show. Later that evening, Elvis is interviewed from his hotel room by Hy Gardner on his local channel TV show "Hy Gardner Calling."
2	Monday	D	Elvis records "Hound Dog," "Don't Be Cruel," and "Anyway You Want Me."
4	Wednesday	C	Elvis performs in a benefit concert in Memphis, TN in Russwood Park. Over 14,000 fans attend.
		D	"I Want You, I Need You, I Love You," hits NO. 1 on *The Billboard's* "Country Best Sellers in Stores."
13	Friday	T	Elvis signs a contract for 3 appearances on "The Ed Sullivan Show" for $50,000.
14	Saturday	M	*The Billboard*: YOU CAN'T DO THAT TO ELVIS
16	Monday	N	*Newsweek*: DEVITALIZING ELVIS
21	Saturday	N	*Melody Maker*: ELVIS PRESLEY
23	Monday	N	*Newsweek*: QUESTION AND ANSWER
25	Wednesday	D	"Hound Dog" enters *The Billboard's* "The Top 100" at NO. 24 position.

August

		N	*Modern Screen* (August): ELVIS PRESLEY! WHO IS HE! WHY DOES HE DRIVE GIRLS CRAZY?
1	Wednesday	D	"Don't Be Cruel" enters *The Billboard's* "The Top 100" at NO. 28 position. "Hound Dog"/"Don't Be Cruel" enters *The Billboard's* "Country Best Sellers in Stores" at NO. 5 position.
3	Friday	C	Elvis performs in Miami, FL at the Olympic Theatre. Seven thousand fans attend the shows.
4	Saturday	N	*The Billboard*: PRESLEY GETS 3D GOLD DISK
		C	Elvis again appears in Miami, FL at the Olympic Theatre and again draws 7,000 fans for the shows.

5	Sunday	C	Elvis performs in Tampa, FL at the Fort Homer Hesterly Armory. Over 10,000 fans attend the shows.
6	Monday	C	Elvis performs in Lakeland, FL at the Polk Theatre. There are 5,500 fans in attendance at the three shows.
7	Tuesday	N	*Look*: ELVIS PRESLEY . . . HE CAN'T BE BUT HE IS
		C	Elvis performs in St. Petersburg, FL at the Florida Theatre. There are 6,500 fans in attendance.
8	Wednesday	C	Elvis performs in Orlando, FL. Seven thousand fans attend the two shows.
9	Thursday	C	Elvis appears in Daytona Beach, FL at the Peabody Auditorium. Over 5,000 fans attend the 2 shows.
10	Friday	C	Elvis performs in Jacksonville, FL at the Florida Theatre. There are 2,200 fans in attendance at each of the three shows.
11	Saturday	C	Elvis performs in Jacksonville, FL. A total of 15,000 fans attend the 3 shows.
12	Sunday	C	Elvis appears in New Orleans, LA at the Municipal Auditorium. About 13,000 fans attend.
18	Saturday	G	Photographic session at Hollywood Kickerbocker Hotel.
23	Thursday	F	Filming for The Reno Brothers that is later titled Love Me Tender begins at the 20th Century-Fox Movie Ranch near Hollywood, CA.
27	Monday	N	*Life*: ELVIS—A DIFFERENT KIND OF IDOL
		N	*Newsweek*: INEXTINGUISHABLE

September

		D	RCA Victor releases 6 singles simultaneously: "Blue Suede Shoes"/"Tutti Frutti;" "I Got a Woman"/"I'm Counting on You;" "I'll Never Let You Go (Little Darlin)"/"I'm Gonna Sit Right Down and Cry (Over You);" "Trying to Get to You"/"I Love You Because;" "Blue Moon"/"Just Because;" "Money Honey"/"One-Sided Love Affair;" "Shake, Rattle and Roll"/"Lawdy Miss Clawdy"
		N	*Coronet* (September): THE CRAZE CALLED ELVIS
		D	*The Real Elvis* (extended play album) is released by RCA Victor
1	Saturday	D	Elvis records "Playing for Keeps," "Love Me," "How Do You Think I Feel," and "How's the World Treating You." These recordings as well as those of the next two days are at Radio Recorders in Hollywood.

2	Sunday	D	Elvis records "Paralyzed," "When My Blue Moon Turns to Gold Again," "Long Tall Sally," "Old Shep," and "Too Much."
3	Monday	D	Elvis records "Ready Teddy," "Rip It Up," "First in Line," and "Any Place is Paradise."
		N	*Tupelo Daily Journal*: SEVEN PRESLEY RECORDS HIT NATION WITH BANG THIS WEEK
5	Wednesday	N/D	*Variety*: ELVIS IS EXPECTED TO SELL MORE THAN 10 MILLION RECORDS DURING HIS FIRST YEAR WITH RCA VICTOR. He has three gold records for "Blue Suede Shoes," "Heartbreak Hotel" and "Hound Dog."
		D	"Don't Be Cruel" hits NO. 1 on *The Billboard's*: THE TOP 100
		G	Elvis buys a pink cadillac.
8	Saturday	N	TV Guide. The first of a three-part series on Elvis.
9	Sunday	T	Elvis appears on "The Ed Sullivan Show" and sings "Don't Be Cruel," "Love Me Tender," "Ready Teddy," and "Hound Dog."
15	Saturday	N	*The Billboard*: VOX JOX
19	Wednesday	D	"Blue Moon" enters *The Billboard's* "THE TOP 100" at position NO. 87. "Don't Be Cruel"/"Hound Dog" hits NO. 1 on *The Billboard's* "Country Best Sellers in Stores."
		N	*Down Beat*: A PSYCHOLOGIST'S VIEWPOINT
		N	*Down Beat*: ELVIS PRESLEY. CAN 50 MILLION AMERICANS BE WRONG?
26	Wednesday	N	*Variety*: HALO, EVERYBODY, HALO: LATEST PRESLEY PITCH
		G	Tupelo, MI declares ELVIS PRESLEY DAY
		C	Elvis performs in Tupelo, MI at the Mississippi-Alabama Fair and Dairy Show. There are 7,500 fans in attendance at each of the 2 shows.
29	Saturday	N	*The Billboard*: PRESLEY JUGGERNAUT ROLLS. MERCHANDISING CAMPAIGN EXPECTED TO TOP $20 MIL SALES BY YEAR END

October

		D	"Love Me Tender"/"Anyway You Want Me" is released by RCA Victor.
		N	"House and Garden" (October): THE WAR OF THE GENERATIONS
3	Wednesday	N	*Tupelo Daily Journal*: ELVIS PRESLEY RECORD SALES TOP 10 MILLION
		D	"I Don't Care If The Sun Don't Shine" enters *The Billboard's* "THE TOP 100" at NO. 77 position.

8	Monday	N	*Time*: SWEET MUSIC
		N	*Newsweek*: MUD ON THE STARS
		F	Elvis completes filming of *Love Me Tender*.
10	Wednesday	D	"Love Me Tender"/"Any Way You Want Me" enters *The Billboard's* "Country Best Sellers in Stores" at NO. 9 position.
11	Thursday	C	Elvis performs in Dallas, TX at the 71st State Fair. There are 26,500 fans in attendance.
12	Friday	C	Elvis performs in Waco, TX at the Heart of Texas Coliseum.
13	Saturday	C	Elvis appears in San Antonio, TX.
14	Sunday	C	Elvis appears in Houston, TX.
15	Monday	C	Elvis performs in Corpis Christi, TX.
18	Thursday	G	Elvis is in a fight with Ed Hopper and Aubrey Brown at the service station in Memphis, TN.
20	Saturday	N	*The Billboard*: PRESLEY BUSTS ANOTHER MARK
		D	"Love Me Tender" enters *The Billboard's* "THE TOP 100" at NO. 12 position.
24	Wednesday	N	*Variety*: ELVIS A MILLIONAIRE IN 1 YEAR
26	Friday	N	*Colliers*: ROCK 'N' ROLL BATTLE. BOONE VS. PRESLEY
27	Saturday	N	*The Billboard*: ARMY TO GIVE ELVIS PRESLEY A G.I. HAIRCUT
28	Sunday	T	Elvis appears for the second time on "The Ed Sullivan Show" in New York and sings "Don't Be Cruel," "Love Me Tender," "Love Me," and "Hound Dog." Elvis receives his fifth gold record for "Love Me Tender" during the show.
29	Monday	N	*The New York Times*: PRESLEY RECEIVES A CITY POLIO SHOT
		N	*Time*: PEOPLE

November

		D	RCA Victor releases "I'm Counting on You;" "I'm Gonna Sit Right Down and Cry (Over You);" "Just Because;" "I'll Never Let You Go (Little Darlin');" "I Love You Because;" "I Got A Woman."
		D	*Elvis Volume I*, *Elvis Volume II* (extended play albums) and *Elvis* (long playing album) are released by RCA Victor.
		N	*The New Yorker* (November). "The Current Cinema" reviews *Love Me Tender*.
3	Saturday	N	*The Billboard*: VICTOR TO PLUG PRESLEY PORTABLE
5	Monday	N	*Newsweek*: GI JIVE
7	Wednesday	D	"Love Me" (from *Elvis — Volume I*) enters *The Billboard's* "THE TOP 100" at NO. 84 position.

		D	*Elvis* (album) enters *The Billboard's* "Best Selling Packaged Records—Popular Albums" at NO. 7 position.
		N	*Variety*: AS TO THAT PRESLEY LONGTERMER . . .
		D	"Love Me Tender" hits NO. 1 on *The Billboard's* "THE TOP 100"
13	Tuesday	N	*Look*: THE GREAT ELVIS PRESLEY INDUSTRY
15	Thursday	F	"Love Me Tender" premieres at the Paramount Theater in New York City.
21	Wednesday	F	"Love Me Tender" opens in 500 theatres across the country.
		D	"When My Blue Moon Turns to Gold Again" (from *Elvis—Volume I*) enters *The Billboard's* "THE TOP 100" at NO. 94 position.
23	Friday	C	Elvis performs in Toledo, OH at the Sports Arena. Thirteen thousand fans attend two shows.
25	Sunday	C	Elvis performs in Louisville, KY.
26	Monday	N	*Time*: Review of *Love Me Tender*.
28	Wednesday	N/F	*Love Me Tender* enters *Variety's* "National Box Office Survey" at position NO. 2.

December

		D	*Love Me Tender* (extended play album) is released by RCA Victor.
		N	*Cosmopolitan* (December): WHAT IS AN ELVIS PRESLEY?
		N	*TV WORLD* (December): SINGER OR SEXPOT?
		N	*TV and Radio Mirror* (December): Elvis and Ed Sullivan appear on the cover.
1	Saturday	N	*Melody Maker*: LET'S BE FAIR TO MR. PRESLEY
4	Tuesday	D	Elvis joins Carl Perkins, Jerry Lee Lewis, and Johnny Cash for "The Million Dollar Quartet."
8	Saturday	D	*Elvis* (Album) hits NO. 1 on *The Billboard's* "Best Selling Packaged Records—Popular Albums."
8	Saturday	N	*Saturday Review*: A review of *Love Me Tender*.
11	Tuesday	N	*Look*: THE FACE IS FAMILAR
16	Sunday	C	Elvis performs on "Louisiana Hayride" in Shreveport, LA. Nine thousand fans attend the show.
19	Wednesday	D	"Old Shep" (from *Elvis—Volume II*), "Poor Boy" (from *Love Me Tender*), and "Paralyzed" (from *Elvis—Volume I*), enter *The Billboard's* "THE TOP 100" at positions NO. 47, NO. 54, and NO. 78 respectively.
22	Saturday	N	*The Billboard*: PRESLEY TOP HOUND DOG
24	Monday	N	*The New Republic*: A STAR IS BORNE
31	Monday	N	*Wall Street Journal*: HEARTBREAK, HOUND DOGS PUT SALES ZIP INTO PRESLEY PRODUCTS

Concerts and Performances 1956

January

7 Shreveport, LA, "Louisiana Hayride"
14 Shreveport, LA, "Louisiana Hayride"
21 Shreveport, LA, "Louisiana Hayride"
28 New York, NY, The Dorsey Brothers "Stage Show"
29 Richmond, VA

February

4 New York, NY, The Dorsey Brothers "Stage Show"
5 Norfolk, VA
6 Greensboro, NC
11 New York, NY, The Dorsey Brothers "Stage Show"
18 New York, NY, The Dorsey Brothers "Stage Show"
21 Sarasota, FL
25 Shreveport, LA, "Louisiana Hayride"

March

3 Shreveport, LA, "Louisiana Hayride"
10 Shreveport, LA, "Louisiana Hayride"
14 Atlanta, GA
15 Atlanta, GA
17 New York, NY, The Dorsey Brothers "Stage Show"
22 Richmond, VA
24 New York, NY, The Dorsey Brothers "Stage Show"

April

3 San Diego, CA, "The Milton Berle Show"
4 San Diego, CA
5 San Diego, CA
7 Shreveport, LA, "Louisiana Hayride"
13 Wichita Falls, TX
15 San Antonio, TX
16 Corpus Christi, TX
17 Oklahoma City, OK
18 Tulsa, OK
19 Amarillo, TX
20 Ft. Worth, TX
21 Dallas, TX
22 San Antonio, TX
23 May 6 Las Vegas, NV, New Frontier Hotel

May

13 St. Paul, MN
14 LaCrosse, WI
15 Memphis, TN
16 Little Rock, AR
17 Springfield, MO
18 Des Moines, IA
19 Lincoln, NE
20 Omaha, NE
24 Kansas City, MO
25 Detroit, MI
26 Columbus, OH
27 Dayton, OH

June

3 Okland, CA
5 Los Angeles, CA, "The Milton Berle Show"
6 San Diego, CA
7 Long Beach, CA
8 Los Angeles, CA
22 Atlanta, GA
23 Atlanta, GA
24 Atlanta, GA
25 Savannah, GA
26 Charlotte, NC
27 Augusta, GA
28 Charlotte, NC
30 Richmond, VA

July

1   New York, NY, "The Steve Allen Show"

August

3   Miami, FL
4   Miami, FL
5   Tampa, FL
6   Lakeland, FL
7   St. Petersburg, FL
8   Orlando, FL
9   Daytona Beach, FL
10   Jacksonville, FL
11   Jacksonville, FL
12   New Orleans, LA

September

9   Los Angeles, CA, "The Ed Sullivan Show"
26   Tupelo, MS

October

11   Dallas, TX
12   Waco, TX
13   San Antonio, TX
14   Houston, TX
28   New York, NY, "The Ed Sullivan Show"

November

23   Toledo, OH
24   Cleveland, OH
25   Louisville, KY

December

16   Shreveport, LA, "Louisiana Hayride"

Television Performances 1956[1]

The Dorsey Brothers "Stage Show," New York, NY

January

28   "Shake, Rattle and Roll"/"Flip, Flop and Fly"
     "I Got a Woman"

February

4   "Baby, Let's Play House"
   "Tutti Frutti"
11   "Blue Suede Shoes"
    "Heartbreak Hotel"
18   "Tutti Frutti"
    "I Was the One"

March

17   "Blue Suede Shoes"
    "Heartbreak Hotel"
24   "Money Honey"
    "Heartbreak Hotel"

"The Milton Berle Show"

April — San Diego (U.S.S. Hancock)

3   "Heartbreak Hotel"
   "Blue Suede Shoes"

June — Hollywood

5   "Hound Dog"
   "I Want You, I Need You, I Love You"[2]

"The Steve Allen Show," New York, NY

July

1   "I Want You, I Need You, I Love You"
   "Hound Dog"

"The Ed Sullivan Show"

September — Hollywood[3]

9   "Don't Be Cruel"
   "Love Me Tender"
   "Ready Teddy"
   "Hound Dog"

October — New York

28   "Don't Be Cruel"
    "Love Me Tender"
    "Love Me"
    "Hound Dog"

[1] TV songs appeared on "Elvis Presley — A Golden Celebration" Album, 1984
[2] First time Jordanaires backed Elvis on TV
[3] Ed Sullivan had been in an auto accident on August 6 so actor Charles Laughton substituted as host for him in New York with Elvis performing in Hollywood.

Discography

The information in this section was obtained almost entirely from the archives of RCA. The RCA coding system enabled them to identify each record and side of the record or album. Each song has a master serial number that identifies the master disc (e.g., G2WB–0209 for "Heartbreak Hotel"). The first letter indicates the year (e.g., F for 1955; G for 1956). The W indicates the category of Country & Western. All of the songs Elvis recorded in 1956 were coded in this category. The last four numbers are the master number for each song. Each record has its own number for singles; a 20 prefix indicates a 78 RPM, and a 47 prefix a 45 RPM. Extended plays (EP) were 45 RPM records with four songs. The last letter A indicates a four song record, and only one has a B at the end, which indicates a double EP (eight songs). (EPB 1254 being the only double EP distributed to the public.) "LP" indicates long play albums (33⅓ RPM). The serial numbers for the EPs and LPs also show the side of the record; the lesser of the last numbers of the serial indicates the A side. For example, the serial number of the A side (side 1) for LPM 1382 is G2WP–7207 while the B side (side 2) is G2WP–7208. The EP and LP albums listed under each song are those albums in which the song appeared for the first time. Publishers listed in parentheses were the initial publishers. The "The Top 100" information refers to the chart date, not the issue date it appeared in *The Billboard*. Although *The Billboard* had other lists (Country & Western, Juke Box Plays, etc.) we have chosen to include only the data from the "The Top 100." Some of Elvis' songs reached NO. 1 on Country & Western charts before they reached NO. 1 on "The Top 100."

Recordings Released 1956

Singles

RELEASED	TITLE	RECORDED
February	"Heartbreak Hotel"/ "I Was The One"	January 1, 1956/January 11, 1956
May	"I Want You, I Need You, I Love You"/"My Baby Left Me"	April 11, 1956/January 30, 1956
July	"Don't Be Cruel"/"Hound Dog"	July 2, 1956/July 2, 1956
September	"Blue Suede Shoes"/"Tutti Frutti"	January 30, 1956/January 31, 1956
September	"I Got A Woman"/ "I'm Counting On You"	January 10, 1956/January 11, 1956
September	"I'll Never Let You Go (Little Darlin')"/"I'm Gonna Sit Right Down and Cry (Over You)"	September 10, 1954/ January 31, 1956
September	"I Love You Because"/ "Trying To Get To You"	January 20, 1956/July 11, 1955
September	"Just Because"/"Blue Moon"	September 10, 1954/July 6, 1954
September	"Money Honey"/ "One Sided Love Affair"	January 10, 1956/January 30, 1956
September	"Shake Rattle and Roll"/ "Lawdy Miss Clawdy"	February 3, 1956/February 3, 1956
October	"Love Me Tender"/ "Any Way You Want Me"	September 1, 1956/July 2, 1956

Extended Play Albums

RELEASED	ALBUM NOS.	TITLE
April	EPB 1254	*Elvis Presley*
April	EPA 747	*Elvis Presley*
May	EPA 821	*Heartbreak Hotel*
June	EPA 830	*Elvis Presley*
September	EPA 940	*The Real Elvis*
October	EPA 965	*Anyway You Want Me*
November	EPA 992	*Elvis Volume I*
November	EPA 993	*Elvis Volume II*
December	EPA 4006	*Love Me Tender*

Long Play Albums

RELEASED	ALBUM NOS.	TITLE
April	LPM 1254	*Elvis Presley*
November	LPM 1382	*Elvis*

Songs Recorded or Released in 1956

Anyway You Want Me (That's How I Will Be)

COMPOSER: Aaron Schroeder, Cliff Owens
PUBLISHER: (Ross Jungnickel, Inc.); Ann Rachel Music (ASCAP)
STUDIO: RCA Victor, New York
RECORDED: July 2, 1956
TAKE: 12
TIME: 2:12

SERIAL NO.	RECORD NO.	RELEASED
G2WB-5937	20-6643-A	October 1956
	47-6643-A	
G2WH-7105	EPA-965 side 1 band 1	October 1956
H2WP-8399	LPM-1707 side 2 band 6	March 1958

INSTRUMENTS
Leader & Guitar: Elvis Presley
Electric Guitar: Scotty Moore
Bass: William P. Black
Drums: D.J. Fontana
Piano: Shorty Long

VOCALISTS
"Jordanaires"
H. Gordon Stoker
Hugh T. Jarrett
Hoyt H. Hawkins
Neal Matthews, Jr.

Entered "The Top 100": 10-24-56
Position Entered: 56
Highest Position Reached: 27
Weeks at Top Position: 1
Total Weeks on List: 10

Anyplace Is Paradise

COMPOSER: Joe Thomas
PUBLISHER: Hill & Range, Inc.
STUDIO: Radio Recorders, Hollywood
RECORDED: September 3, 1956
TAKE: 22
TIME: 2:23

SERIAL NO.	RECORD NO.	RELEASED
G2WB-4929		
G2WH-7212	EPA-993 side 2 band 2	November 1956
G2WP-7208	LPM-1382 side 2 band 4	November 1956

INSTRUMENTS
Leader: Elvis Presley
Guitar: Scotty Moore
Bass: William P. Black
Drums: D.J. Fontana

VOCALISTS
"Jordanaires"
H. Gordon Stoker
Hoyt H. Hawkins
Neal Matthews, Jr.
Hugh T. Jarrett

Blue Moon

COMPOSER: Rodgers, Hart
PUBLISHER: Robbins Music Corp. ASCAP
STUDIO: Sun Studios, Memphis*
RECORDED: Date "Unknown" (Sun Record Co.)
TIME: 2:39

SERIAL NO.	RECORD NO.	RELEASED
F2WB-8117	20-6640-A	September 1956
	47-6640-A	September 1956
G2WH-3463	EPA-830 side 2 band 1	September 1956
G2PP-1283	LPM-1254 side 2 band 5	April 1956

INSTRUMENTS
Leader & Guitar: Elvis Presley
Guitar: Scotty Moore
Bass: William P. Black
Bongoes: Buddy Cunningham (possibly)

Entered "The Top 100": 9-16-56
Position Entered: 87
Highest Position Reached: 55
Weeks At Top Position: 1
Total Weeks on List: 17

*RCA purchased tapes from Sun Record Co.

Blue Suede Shoes

COMPOSER: Carl Perkins
PUBLISHER: Hi-Lo Music
STUDIO: RCA Victor, Studio 1, New York
RECORDED: January 30, 1956
TIME: 1:58

SERIAL NO.	RECORD NO.	RELEASED
G2WB-1230	20-6636-A	September 1956
	47-6636-A	September 1956
G2WH-1854	EPA-747 side 1 band 1	May 1956
G2WH-1850	EPB-1254 side 1 band 1	April 1956
G2PP-1282	LPM-1254	April 1956

INSTRUMENTS
Lead Guitar: Elvis Presley
Bass: William P. Black
Electric Guitar: Scotty Moore
Drums: D.J. Fontana

Entered "The Top 100": 3-28-56
Position Entered: 88
Highest Position Reached: 24
Weeks at Top Position: 1
Total Weeks on List: 12

Don't Be Cruel

COMPOSER: Otis Blackwell, Elvis Presley
PUBLISHER: Shalimar Music Corp. and Elvis Presley Music, Inc.
STUDIO: RCA Victor, New York
RECORDED: July 2, 1956
TAKE: 28
TIME: 2:03

SERIAL NO.	RECORD NO.	RELEASED
G2WB-5936	20-6604-B	July 1956
	47-6604-B	July 1956
G2WH-6136	EPA-940 side 1 band 1	August 1956

INSTRUMENTS
Leader & Guitar: Elvis Presley
Electric Guitar: Scotty Moore
Bass: William P. Black
Drums: D.J. Fontana
Piano: Shorty Long

VOCALISTS
"The Jordanaires"
H. Gordon Stoker
Hugh T. Jarrett
Hoyt H. Hawkins
Neal Matthews, Jr.

Entered "The Top 100": 8-1-56
Position Entered: 28
Highest Position Reached: 1
Weeks at Top Position: 7
Total Weeks on List: 27

First in Line

COMPOSER: Aaron Schroeder, Ben Weisman
PUBLISHER: Ross Jungnickel Inc.
STUDIO: Radio Recorders, Hollywood
RECORDED: September 3, 1956
TAKE: 27
TIME: 3:21

SERIAL NO.	RECORD NO.	RELEASED
G2WB-4931		
G2WH-7213	EPA-994 side 1 band 2	February 1957
G2WP-7207	LPM-1382 side 1 band 5	November 1956

INSTRUMENTS
Leader: Elvis Presley
Guitar: Scotty Moore
Bass: William P. Black
Drums: D.J. Fontana

VOCALISTS
"Jordanaires"
H. Gordon Stoker
Hoyt H. Hawkins
Neal Matthews, Jr.
Hugh T. Jarrett

Flip Flop and Fly

COMPOSER: Charles Calhoun, Lou Willie Turner
PUBLISHER:
RECORDED: January 28, 1956 from The Dorsey Brothers "Stage Show"

SERIAL NO.	RECORD NO.	RELEASED
OPA1-4199	CPL2-4031 side A band 4	March 1981

Heartbreak Hotel

COMPOSER: Mae Axton, Tommy Durden, Elvis Presley
PUBLISHER: Tree Music
STUDIO: RCA Victor, Nashville
RECORDED: January 10, 1956
TIME: 2:06

SERIAL NO.	RECORD NO.	RELEASED
G2WB-0209	20-6420-A	February 1956
	47-6420-A	February 1956
G2PH-2942	EPA-821 side 1 band 1	May 1956
H2WP-8398	LPM-1707 side 1 band 4	April 1958

INSTRUMENTS
Leader & Guitar: Elvis Presley
Piano: Floyd Cramer
Bass: William P. Black
Electric Guitar: Scotty Moore
Drums: D.J. Fontana
Guitar: Chet Atkins

Entered "The Top 100": 2-22-56
Position Entered: 68
Highest Position Reached: 1
Weeks at Top Position: 7
Total Weeks on List: 27

Hound Dog

COMPOSER: Jerry Leiber, Mike Stoller
PUBLISHER: (Elvis Presley Music and Lion Publishing); Jerry Lieber & Mike Stoller
STUDIO: RCA Victor, New York
RECORDED: July 2, 1956
TAKE: 31
TIME: 2:15

SERIAL NO.	RECORD NO.	RELEASED
G2WB-5935	20-6604-A	July 1956
	47-6604-A	
G2WH-6137	EPA-940 side 2 band 1	September 1956
H2WP-8398	LPM-1707 side 1 band 1	April 1958

INSTRUMENTS
Leader & Guitar: Elvis Presley
Electric Guitar: Scotty Moore
Bass: William P. Black
Drums: D.J. Fontana
Piano: Shorty Long

VOCALISTS
"Jordanaires"
H. Gordon Stoker
Hugh T. Jarrett
Hoyt H. Hawkins
Neal Matthews, Jr.

Entered "The Top 100": 7-25-56
Position Entered: 24
Highest Position Reached: 2
Weeks at Top Position: 3*
Total Weeks on List: 25

*Not consecutive

How Do You Think I Feel

COMPOSERS: Walker, Pierce
PUBLISHER: Cedarwood Music
STUDIO: Radio Recorders, Hollywood
RECORDED: September 1, 1956
TAKE: 7
TIME: 2:10

SERIAL NO.	RECORD NO.	RELEASED
G2WB-4923		
G2WH-7214	EPA-994 side 2 band 1	February 1957
G2WP-7268	LPM-1382 side 2 band 6	November 1956

INSTRUMENTS
Leader: Elvis Presley
Guitar: Scotty Moore
Bass: William P. Black
Drums: D.J. Fontana

VOCALISTS
"Jordanaires"
H. Gordon Stoker
Hoyt H. Hawkins
Neal Matthews, Jr.
Hugh T. Jarrett

How's The World Treating You

COMPOSER: Chet Atkins, Boudleaux Bryant
PUBLISHER: (Tanner Music); Acuff-Rose Publications
STUDIO: Radio Recorders, Hollywood
RECORDED: September 1, 1956
TAKE: 7
TIME: 2:20

SERIAL NO.	RECORD NO.	RELEASED
G2WB-4924		
G2WH-7214	EPA-994 side 2 band 2	February 1957
G2WP-7208	LPM-1382 side 2 band 4	November 1956

INSTRUMENTS
Leader: Elvis Presley
Guitar: Scotty Moore
Bass: William P. Black
Drums: D.J. Fontana

VOCALISTS
"Jordanaires"
H. Gordon Stoker
Hoyt H. Hawkins
Neal Matthews, Jr.
Hugh T. Jarrett

I Don't Care If The Sun Don't Shine

COMPOSER: Mack David; Marion Keisker (added verse to Elvis' version)
PUBLISHER: Famous Music
STUDIO: Sun Studios, Memphis*
RECORDED: September, 1954
TIME: 2:25

SERIAL NO.	RECORD NO.	RELEASED
F2WB-8042	20-6381A	September 1954
	49-6381A	September 1954
G2WH-7106	EPA-965 side 2 band 1	October 1956

INSTRUMENTS
Leader & Guitar: Elvis Presley
Guitar: Scotty Moore
Bass: William P. Black
Bongoes: Buddy Cunningham (possibly)

Entered "The Top 100": 10-3-56
Position Entered: 77
Highest Position Reached: 74
Weeks at Top Position: 1
Total Weeks on List: 6

*RCA purchased tapes from Sun Record Co.

I Forgot To Remember To Forget

COMPOSER: Kesler, Feathers
PUBLISHER: E.B. Marks Music Corp., BMI
STUDIO: Sun Studios, Memphis*
RECORDED: July, 1955
TIME: 2:28

SERIAL NO.	RECORD NO.	RELEASED
F2WB-8000	20-635-A	December 2, 1955
	47-635-A	December 2, 1955
G2PH-2943	EPA-821, side 2, band 2	May 1956
K2PP-1149	LPM-2011	August 1959

INSTRUMENTS
Leader & Guitar: Elvis Presley
Guitar: Scotty Moore
Bass: William P. Black
Drums: Johnny Bernero

*RCA purchased tapes from Sun Record Co.

I Love You Because

COMPOSER: Leon Payne
PUBLISHER: Fred Rose Music Inc., BMI
STUDIO: Sun Studios, Memphis*
RECORDED: July 6, 1954
TAKE: **
TIME: 2:39

SERIAL NO.	RECORD NO.	RELEASED
G2WB-1086	20-6639B	September 1956
	47-6639B	September 1956
G2WH-3462	EPA-830 side 1 band 2	September 1956
E2PP-1282	LPM-1254 side 1 band 5	April 1956

INSTRUMENTS
Leader & Guitar: Elvis Presley
Guitar: Scotty Moore
Bass: William P. Black

*RCA purchased tapes from Sun Record Co.
**Composite of takes 3 and 5

I Got A Woman

COMPOSER: Ray Charles
PUBLISHER: Progressive Music
STUDIO: RCA Victor, Nashville
RECORDED: January 10, 1956
TIME: 2:22

SERIAL NO.	RECORD NO.	RELEASED
G2WB-0208	20-6637-A	September 1956
	47-6637-A	September 1956
G2WH-1851	EPB-1254 side 2 band 1	April 1956
G2PP-1282	LPM-1254 side 1 band 3	April 1956

INSTRUMENTS
Leader & Guitar: Elvis Presley
Piano: Floyd Cramer
Bass: William P. Black
Electric Guitar: Scotty Moore
Drums: D.J. Fontana

I'll Never Let You Go (Little Darlin')

COMPOSER: Jimmy Wakely
PUBLISHER: (Sundance Music, BMI); Marlin Music Co.; ASCAP
STUDIO: Sun Studios, Memphis*
RECORDED: Date "Unknown" (Sun Record Co.)
TIME: 2:21

SERIAL NO.	RECORD NO.	RELEASED
F2WB-8116	20-6638-B	September 1956
	47-6638-B	September 1956
G2WH-1853	EPB-1254, side 4, band 2	April 1956
G2PP-1283	LPM-1254 side 2, band 4	April 1956

INSTRUMENTS
Leader & Guitar: Elvis Presley
Guitar: Scotty Moore
Bass: William P. Black

*RCA purchased tapes from Sun Record Co.

Paralyzed

COMPOSER: Otis Blackwell, Elvis Presley
PUBLISHER: (Shalimar Music Corp.); Travis Music Co.; Elvis Presley Music, Inc., BMI
STUDIO: Radio Recorders, Hollywood
RECORDED: September 2, 1956
TAKE: 12
TIME: 2:24

SERIAL NO.	RECORD NO.	RELEASED
G2WB-4922		
G2WH-7210	EPA-992 side 2 band 2	November 1956
G2WP-7207	LPM-1382 side 1 band 6	November 1956

INSTRUMENTS	VOCALISTS
Leader: Elvis Presley	"Jordanaires"
Guitar: Scotty Moore	H. Gordon Stoker
Bass: William P. Black	Hoyt H. Hawkins
Drums: D.J. Fontana	Neal Matthews, Jr.
	Hugh T. Jarrett

Entered "The Top 100": 12-19-56
Position Entered: 78
Highest Position Reached: 59
Weeks at Top Position: 1
Total Weeks on List: 7

Playing For Keeps

COMPOSER: Stanley A. Kesler
PUBLISHER: Hi-Lo Music Inc.; Hill & Range Songs, Inc.
STUDIO: Radio Recorders, Hollywood
RECORDED: September 1, 1956
TAKE: 7
TIME: 2:50

SERIAL NO.	RECORD NO.	RELEASED
G2WB-4920	20-6800-B	January 1957
	47-6800-B	January 1957
J2PP-8070	LPM 1990 side 1 band 4	February 1959

INSTRUMENTS	VOCALISTS
Leader: Elvis Presley	"Jordanaires"
Guitar: Scotty Moore	H. Gordon Stoker
Bass: William P. Black	Hoyt H. Hawkins
Drums: D.J. Fontana	Neal Matthews, Jr.
	Hugh T. Jarrett

Poor Boy

COMPOSER: Elvis Presley, Vera Matson
PUBLISHER: Elvis Presley Music Inc.
STUDIO: Tape acquired from 20th Century Fox Film soundtrack *Love Me Tender*
RECORDED: September 1, 1956
TIME: 2:13

SERIAL NO.	RECORD NO.	RELEASED
G2WB-7259		
G2WH-7524	EPA-4006 side 2 band 1	December 1956
J2P-8070	LPM-1990 side 1 band 5	February, 1959

Entered "The Top 100": 12-19-56
Position Entered: 54
Highest Position Reached: 35
Weeks at Top Position: 2
Total Weeks on List: 11

Ready Teddy

COMPOSER: Blackwell, John Marascaleo
PUBLISHER: Elvis Presley Music, Inc.; Venice Music, Inc., BMI
STUDIO: Radio Recorders, Hollywood
RECORDED: September 3, 1956
TAKE: 12
TIME: 1:55

SERIAL NO.	RECORD NO.	RELEASED
G2WB-4930		
G2WH-7212	EPA-993 side 2 band 1	November 1956
G2WP-7208	LPM-1382 side 2 band 3	November 1956

INSTRUMENTS	VOCALISTS
Leader: Elvis Presley	"Jordanaires"
Guitar: Scotty Moore	H. Gordon Stoker
Bass: William P. Black	Hoyt H. Hawkins
Drums: D.J. Fontana	Neal Matthews, Jr.
	Hugh T. Jarrett

Rip It Up

COMPOSER: Robert Blackwell, John Marascaleo
PUBLISHER: Venice Music, Inc. and Elvis Presley Music, Inc.
STUDIO: Radio Recorders, Hollywood
RECORDED: September 3, 1956
TAKE: 19
TIME: 1:52

SERIAL NO.	RECORD NO.	RELEASED
G2WB-4932		
G2WH-7209	EPA-992 side 1 band 1	November 1956
G2WP-7207	LPM-1382 side 1 band 1	November 1956

INSTRUMENTS
Leader: Elvis Presley
Guitar: Scotty Moore
Bass: William P. Black
Drums: D.J. Fontana

VOCALISTS
"Jordanaires"
H. Gordon Stoker
Hoyt H. Hawkins
Neal Matthews, Jr.
Hugh T. Jarrett

Shake, Rattle, and Roll

COMPOSER: Charles Calhoun
PUBLISHER: Progressive Music
STUDIO: RCA Victor, Studio 1, New York
RECORDED: February 3, 1956
TIME: 2:27

SERIAL NO.	RECORD NO.	RELEASED
G2WB-1294	20-6642-A	September 1956
	47-6642-A	September 1956
G2WH-3462	EPA-830 side 1 band 1	September 1956
	LPM-1990 side 2 band 3	February 1959

INSTRUMENTS
Leader & Guitar: Elvis Presley
Bass: William P. Black
Electric Guitar: Scotty Moore
Drums: D.J. Fontana
Piano: Shorty Long

So Glad You're Mine

COMPOSER: Arthur Crudup
PUBLISHER: Elvis Presley Music
STUDIO: RCA Victor, Studio 1, New York
RECORDED: January 30, 1956
TIME: 2:18

SERIAL NO.	RECORD NO.	RELEASED
G2WB-1233		
G2WH-7211	EPA-993 side 1 band 1	November 1956
G2WP-7208	LPM-1382 side 2 band 1	November 1956

INSTRUMENTS
Leader & Guitar: Elvis Presley
Bass: William P. Black
Electric Guitar: Scotty Moore
Drums: D.J. Fontana
Piano: Shorty Long

Too Much

COMPOSER: Lee Rosenberg, Bernard Weinman
PUBLISHER: Southern Belle; Elvis Presley Music, BMI
STUDIO: Radio Recorders, Memphis
RECORDED: September 2, 1956
TAKE: 12
TIME: 2:30

SERIAL NO.	RECORD NO.	RELEASED
G2WB-4928	20-6800-A	January 1957
	47-6800-A	
H2WP-8398	LPM-1707 side 1 band 7	March 1958
K2PH-6306	EPA-5141 side 2 band 1	March 1960

INSTRUMENTS
Leader: Elvis Presley
Guitar: Scotty Moore
Bass: William P. Black
Drums: D.J. Fontana

VOCALISTS
"Jordanaires"
H. Gordon Stoker
Hoyt H. Hawkins
Neal Matthews, Jr.
Hugh T. Jarrett

Trying To Get To You

COMPOSER: Singleton, McCoy
PUBLISHER: (Hill & Range, BMI); Motion Music Co.
STUDIO: Sun Studios, Memphis*
RECORDED: Date "Unknown" (Sun Record Co.)
TIME: 2:31

SERIAL NO.	RECORD NO.	RELEASED
F2WB-8039	20-6639-A	September 1956
	47-6639-A	September 1956
G2WH-1852	EPB-1254 side 3 band 2	April 1956
G2PP-1283	LPM-1254 side 2, band 2	April 1956

INSTRUMENTS
Leader & Guitar: Elvis Presley
Guitar: Scotty Moore
Bass: William P. Black
Drums: Johnny Bernero
Piano: Elvis Presley

*RCA purchased tapes from Sun Record Co.

Tutti Frutti

COMPOSER: Dorothy La Bostrie, Richard Penniman ("Little Richard")
PUBLISHER: Venice Music
STUDIO: RCA Victor, Studio 1, New York
RECORDED: January 31, 1956
TIME: 1:57

SERIAL NO.	RECORD NO.	RELEASED
G2WB-1255	20-6636-B	September 1956
	47-6636-B	September 1956
G2WH-1852	EPB-1254 side 3 band 1	March 1956
G2WH-1854	EPA-747 side 1 band 2	April 1956
G2PP-1283	LPM-1254 side 2 band 1	April 1956

INSTRUMENTS
Leader & Guitar: Elvis Presley
Bass: William P. Black
Electric Guitar: Scotty Moore
Drums: D.J. Fontana
Piano: Shorty Long

We're Gonna Move

COMPOSER: Elvis Presley, Vera Matson
PUBLISHER: Elvis Presley Music, Inc.
STUDIO: Tape acquired from 20th Century Fox Film soundtrack *Love Me Tender*
RECORDED: September 1, 1956
TIME: 2:28

SERIAL NO.	RECORD NO.	RELEASED
G2WB-7260		
G2WH-7524	EPA-4006, side 2 band 2	December 1956
K2PP-1149	LPM-2011 side 2 band 3	September 1959

When My Blue Moon Turns To Gold Again

COMPOSER: Wiley Walker, Gene Sullivan
PUBLISHER: Peer Intl. Group. 1941
STUDIO: Radio Recorders, Hollywood
RECORDED: September 2, 1956
TAKE: 10
TIME: 2:20

SERIAL NO.	RECORD NO.	RELEASED
G2WB-4925		
G2WH-7210	EPA-992 side 2 band 1	November 1956
G2WP-7207	LPM-1382 side 1 band 2	November 1956

INSTRUMENTS
Leader: Elvis Presley
Guitar: Scotty Moore
Bass: William P. Black
Drums: D.J. Fontana

VOCALISTS
"Jordanaires"
H. Gordon Stoker
Hoyt H. Hawkins
Neal Matthews, Jr.
Hugh T. Jarrett

Entered "The Top 100": 11-21-56
Position Entered: 94
Highest Position Reached: 27
Weeks at Top Position: 1
Total Weeks on List: 15

Extended Play Albums (EP-45 RPM)

Elvis Presley

RECORD NO. EPB-1254

SIDE ONE
"Blue Suede Shoes"
"I'm Counting On You"

SIDE TWO
"I Got A Woman"
"One-Sided Love Affair"

SIDE THREE
"Tutti Frutti"
"Trying To Get To You"

SIDE FOUR
"I'm Gonna Sit Right Down And Cry (Over You)"
"I'll Never Let You Go"

RELEASED: April 1956

NOTE: The only double extended play for public release

Elvis Presley

RECORD NO. EPA-747

SIDE ONE
"Blue Suede Shoes"
"Tutti Frutti"

SIDE TWO
"I Got A Woman"
"Just Because"

RELEASED: April 1956

Heartbreak Hotel

RECORD NO. EPA-821

SIDE ONE
"Heartbreak Hotel"
"I Was The One"

SIDE TWO
"Money Honey"
"I Forgot To Remember To Forget"

RELEASED: May 1956

Elvis Presley

RECORD NO. EPA-830

SIDE ONE
"Shake, Rattle, And Roll"
"I Love You Because"

SIDE TWO
"Blue Moon"
"Lawdy Miss Clawdy"

RELEASED: June 1956

The Real Elvis

RECORD NO: EPA-940

SIDE ONE
"Don't Be Cruel"
"I Want You, I Need You, I Love You"

SIDE TWO
"Hound Dog"
"My Baby Left Me"

RELEASED: September 1956

Anyway You Want Me

RECORD NO: EPA-965

SIDE ONE
"Anyway You Want Me"
"I'm Left, Your Right, She's Gone"

SIDE TWO
"I Don't Care If The Sun Don't Shine"
"Mystery Train"

RELEASED: October 1956

Elvis Volume 1

RECORD NO: EPA-992

SIDE ONE
"Rip It Up"
"Love Me"

SIDE TWO
"When My Blue Moon Turns To Gold Again"
"Paralyzed"

RELEASED: November 1956

Elvis – Volume II

RECORD NO: EPA-993

SIDE ONE
"So Glad You're Mine"
"Old Shep"

SIDE TWO
"Ready Teddy"
"Anyplace Is Paradise"

RELEASED: November 1956

Love Me Tender

RECORD NO: EPA-4006

SIDE ONE
"Love Me Tender"
"Let Me"

SIDE TWO
"Poor Boy"
"We're Gonna Move"

RELEASED: December 1956

Strictly Elvis*

*Includes songs recorded in 1956

RECORD NO: EPA-994

SIDE ONE
"Long Tall Sally"
"First In Line"

SIDE TWO
"How Do You Think I Feel"
"How's The World Treating You"

RELEASED: February 1957

Long Play Albums (LP-33⅓ RPM)

Elvis Presley

RECORD NO: LPM–1254

SIDE ONE
"Blue Suede Shoes"
"I'm Counting On You"
"I Got A Woman"
"One Sided Love Affair"
"I Love You Because"
"Just Because"

SIDE TWO
"Tutti Frutti"
"Tryin' To Get To You"
"I'm Gonna Sit Right Down And Cry (Over You)"
"I'll Never Let You Go (Little Darlin')"
"Blue Moon"
"Money Honey"

RELEASED: April 1956

Elvis

RECORD NO: LPM 1382

SIDE ONE
"Rip It Up"
"Love Me"
"When My Blue Moon Turns To Gold Again"
"Long Tall Sally"
"First In Line"
"Paralyzed"

SIDE TWO
"So Glad You're Mine"
"Old Shep"
"Ready Teddy"
"Anyplace Is Paradise"
"How's The World Treating You"
"How Do You Think I Feel"

RELEASED: November 1956

Filmography 1956

Elvis wanted very much to be an actor and in 1956 had the opportunity to make his first film. While under contract with Paramount he was lent to 20th Century Fox to make *Love Me Tender*. We can imagine the excitement and anticipation Elvis and his fans felt when the film premiered in New York City on November 15, 1956. People started lining up for tickets at 8 AM and were greeted by a 40-foot high likeness of Elvis.

Love Me Tender
Studio: 20th Century Fox   Producer: David Weisbart   Director: Robert D. Webb

CAST

Vance Reno	Richard Egan
Cathy Reno	Debra Paget
Clint Reno	Elvis Presley
Mr. Siringo	Robert Middleton
Brett Reno	William Campbell
Mike Garvin	Neville Brand
Martha Reno	Mildred Dunnock
Major Kincaid	Bruce Bennett
Ray Reno	James Drury
Ed Galt	Russ Conway
Mr. Kelso	Ken Clark
Mr. Davis	Barry Coe
Pardee Fleming	L. Q. Jones
Jethro	Paul Burns
First Train Conductor	Jerry Sheldon
Storekeeper	James Stone
Auctioneer	Ed Mundy
First Soldier	Joe DiReda
Station Agent	Bobby Rose
Paymaster	Tom Greenway
Major Harris	Jay Jostyn
Second Train Conductor	Steve Darrell

PRODUCTION CREW

Screenplay	Robert Buckner
Based on a Story by	Maurice Geraghty
Director of Photography	Leo Tover
Art Directors	Lyle R. Wheeler, Maurice Ransford
Set Decoration	Walter M. Scott, Fay Babcock
Special Photographic Effects	Ray Kellogg
Editor	Hugh S. Fowler
Makeup	Ben Nye
Hairstyles	Helen Turpin
Costumes	Mary Wills
Executive Wardrobe Designer	Charles Lemaire
Assistant Director	Stanley Hough
Technical Advisor	Col. Tom Parker
Sound Recording	Alfred Bruzlin, Harry M. Leonard
Cinemascope Lenses by	Bausch & Lomb
Music	Lionel Newman
Vocal Supervision	Ken Darby
Orchestration	Edward B. Powell

SONGS FROM FILM

"We're Gonna Move"
"Love Me Tender"
"Let Me"
"Poor Boy"
    Leader: Elvis Presley
    Guitar: Via Mumolo
    Vocals: Chuck Prescott
              John Dodson
              Red Robinson
              others

Newspapers and Periodicals

January

25   *Downbeat*, p. 14: RCA EXCITED. Elvis Presley, a Country & Western singer, has been signed by RCA Victor and is described as a combination between Frankie Laine, Billy Daniels, and Johnnie Ray. RCA paid him $40,000 in cash and gave him a new convertible because they felt he was so hot a prospect.

February

3   *The Charlotte News*, p. 9A: SINGING STAR TO APPEAR HERE. Elvis, who has skyrocketed to fame will appear at the Carolina Theater on Friday with shows beginning at 2:30, 4:15, 7:20, and 9:30 PM. Elvis sings both hillbilly and popular music, mixing country music with bop.

11   *The Charlotte News*, Section 2, p. 1: OUR GIRLS GO GA-GA OVER ELVIS. Over 6,000 teenagers came to 4 Elvis shows in the Carolina Theater yesterday. About 1,000 were turned away. When told that some people call him a hillbilly, Elvis stated, "No, don't call me that . . . I don't know what style I have. I never could answer that question." Nevertheless, Charlotte teenagers jumped out of their seats, waved their arms; and one even did a flip on the floor in front of the stage. Denied permission to go backstage after the show, one teenager stated, "I'll just die if I don't shake his hand."

15   *Tupelo Daily Journal*, p. 8: ELVIS PRESLEY: THE TWO-CADILLAC MAN WITH A STYLE LIKE A STEAM-ENGINE. A columnist spoke of Elvis' electrifying effect on his audience. How a crowd of 5,000 in Jacksonville mobbed Elvis after a performance and his pink shirt and white jacket were

shredded souvenirs. He put Elvis in the Sinatra/Johnny Ray category. He then reviewed Elvis' recent history beginning as a truck driver and emerging as a star. He quotes Elvis as saying, "It's all happening so fast, there's so much happening to me . . . that some nights I just can't fall asleep. It scares me, you know . . . it just scares me."

24   *Jacksonville Journal*, p. 7: ELVIS PRESLEY COLLAPSES. Elvis collapsed after a show last night and was taken to the hospital where doctors said he suffered from exhaustion brought on by his strenuous, 4-week, nationwide tour. He was kept overnight in the hospital and released the next day.

March

3   *The Billboard*, p. 54: A WINNAH, PRESLEY HOT AS A $1 PISTOL ON VICTOR. Elvis Presley who has been on the RCA Victor label for only about 2 months, is the hottest artist for RCA this week. Six of his records are in RCA's list of top 25 best sellers. Five of these have been previously issued on the Sun label where they had done well on their own.

April

11   *Variety*, p. 43, ELVIS PRESLEY HITS GOLD PLATTER CIRCLE. Elvis Presley, RCA Victor's hottest entertainer, has hit the 1 million mark in sales for "Heartbreak Hotel." Currently, Elvis has 6 out of 15 of RCA Victor's best sellers.

21   *The Billboard*, p. 27: 75G DAILY AIN'T HAY. SHOLES HAY. SHOLES HAS LAST LAUGH AS PRESLEY RINGS UP SALES. "They laughed when Steve Sholes sat down to write out that $40,000 check for Elvis Presley's recording contract." However, this week Elvis is selling around $75,000 daily in retail record stores. His records are selling at a rate of 50,000 a day (pop singles) accounting for about 50 percent of RCA's total pop business.

23   *The Houston Press*, p. 1: ELVIS SANG—AND THE GIRLS SQUEALED. SQUADS OF POLICE KEPT SINGER'S BLUE SUEDE SHOES FROM BEING TRAMPLED. The columnist interviewed Elvis backstage between shows. When questioned about the hysteria he causes, Elvis remarked, "That makes me work harder—I know they like me." When asked about his dance on stage, Elvis remarked, "It's just the way I feel." Someone remarked that "Elvis just can't stand to hurt anybody's feelings." One of the police remarked how the teenagers affected one another. When a few were allowed to get autographs a while ago, a huge crowd descended on Elvis

when the policemen's backs were turned, and the police got him out just in time.

30 *Life*, Vol. 40, p. 64: A HOWLING HILLBILLY SUCCESS. Elvis Presley's latest record "Heartbreak Hotel" is the best selling record in the country this week. Elvis, who "howls, mumbles, coos and cries his way through it" is "the biggest singing attraction for teenagers in the USA." Elvis will earn $12,500 for a week's entertainment in Las Vegas.

May

9 *Variety*, pp. 1, 63: THE ELVIS PRESLEY STORY: HE'S MAKING MONKEYS OUT OF SINGERS. A large group of Elvis imitators are trying to cash in on his style and success. Other labels are hiring singers who perform in Elvis' style. Currently, there are more than a dozen singers who have recorded and who have definitely been inspired by Elvis. RCA Victor's plants are working overtime and "Heartbreak Hotel" has sold over 1 million records. There has been an advance sale of 400,000 records for "I Want You, I Need You, I Love You" and "My Baby Left Me." Although Elvis has been "very hot with the bobby soxers," he has failed to impress the clientele at the New Frontier Hotel in Las Vegas where he was replaced two days ago (May 7) by Roberta Sherwood.

9 *Variety*, p. 63: 10 COPS FOR ELVIS PART OF THE 15G OVERHEAD. Ten policemen have been hired as bodyguards to protect Elvis from his admirers for an upcoming matinee and evening appearance at St. Paul and Minneapolis on October 13.

9 *Variety*, p. 63: WITH BRITISH TEENAGE SET. British teenagers are beginning to regard Elvis as the "new singing sensation." Elvis' British representatives are trying to arrange for performances in Britian next year.

14 *Newsweek*, p. 82: HILLBILLY ON A PEDESTAL. Elvis is described as a combination of Marlon Brando and James Dean. A fan stated, "I like him because he looks so mean." The article stated that last week Presley ended his 2-week performance at the New Frontier Hotel in Las Vegas where the older crowd did not appreciate his performances. "I don't want no more night clubs," Elvis remarked. In discussing his 7-year contract with Hal Wallis and Paramount Theaters, Elvis stated, "I wouldn't want no regular spot on no TV program . . . Movies are the thing. I love to act. I don't care nothing whatsoever about singing in no movie."

14 *Time*, pp. 53–54: TEENERS' HERO. "In the spotlight, the lanky singer flails furious rhythms on his guitar every now and then breaking a string. In a pivoting stance, his hips swing sensuously from side to side and his entire body takes on a

frantic quiver, as if he had swallowed a jackhammer. Full-cut hair tausles over his forehead, and sideburns frame his petulant, full-lipped face. His style is partly hillbilly, partly socking Rock 'n' Roll. His loud baritone goes raw and whining in the high notes, but down low it is rich and round." This is Elvis Presley, "a drape-suited, tight-trousered young man . . . who drives teenagers wild."

As a child Elvis received a guitar before he was twelve. "I beat on it for a year or two, . . . Never did learn much about it." He sang church hymns with a heavy beat but had no interest in a musical career. But last week, "Heartbreak Hotel" reached NO. 1 on the Best Selling record list.

30   *Variety*, pp. 41, 46: ELVIS PRESLEY — DIGITATION CHURNS UP TEEN TANTRUMS, SCRIBE RAPS, SO-SO B.O. Elvis Presley is whipping up considerable noise through his personal appearance swing through the Midwest. This comes from hysterical teenagers and "irate editorialists, who've been blasting Presley for his torso-twisting singing style." On October 24, 2,500 teenagers "literally tore up the show" in Municipal Auditorium in Kansas City. Elvis only sang six songs before the teenagers broke through the police blockade and jumped on stage. Elvis had to leave when they began tearing his costume. The relatively small turnout for the performance was felt to be due to the $2.50 admission. The editorial rap came from a columnist in St. Paul in an "open letter to Elvis." The columnist called Elvis "nothing more than a male burlesque dancer." The columnist felt that these small attendances were due to "Moms and Dads [who] had seen you on TV and didn't like your unnecessary bump and grind routine. . . . You disillusioned many of your fans needlessly. Why, Elvis, do you resort to your 'Pelvis Presley' routine? You'd better drop it before more and more people drop you."

30   *Downbeat*, p. 39: PRESLEY INVADES H'WOOD WITH IMPACT OF A BRANDO. Elvis Presley signed a long-term contract with Hal Wallis, the moviemaker, solely based on his screen test. He is being hailed as one of the most promising new dramatic actors since Marlon Brando. "I just can't thank Mr. Wallis enough for givin' me this big break. Never thought I'd turn out to be a movie actor. Never did nothin' but jump around and sing 'cause that's the way I feel all the time."

June

4   *Oakland Tribune*, pp. 1, 13: ELVIS SENDS 6,400 HERE INTO FRENZY. Elvis gave two performances at the Oakland Auditorium Arena in front of 6,400 screaming fans and sang, among other songs, "Blue Suede Shoes" and "Heartbreak

Hotel." The screams of the crowd made it impossible for him to be heard. Elvis wore a Kelly green tweed jacket and was backed up by the Jordanaires, a combo of drums, bass, and guitar. He had to be escorted through a secret entrance to prevent being mobbed. Offstage, he appeared quite natural, intelligent, and with a disarming frankness. He remarked, "I don't like to stand still; I get nervous. . . . As long as I keep on doing okay, I'll keep doing what I'm doing. I really want to be an actor. A good actor . . ." "I date quite a few girls but nothing real serious. I don't play the guitar as much as I used to, because I break too many strings." After one of the performances, exhausted as he was, he was very willing to sign autographs for the few people who eluded the police. One of the Jordanaires said, "I've never seen anything to compare with this guy. The reaction he gets is the wildest I've ever seen."

4 *San Francisco Chronicle*, p. 20: ELVIS HITS AND TEENAGERS TURN OUT. Elvis Presley sang for 20 minutes at the Oakland Auditorium Arena yesterday. Elvis stalked onto the stage and sang for 20 minutes. The roar of the crowd that greeted him subsided only when he sang "Heartbreak Hotel." Dressed in black denim pants, Elvis was greeted with screams whenever one of his knees shot out while he sang. Elvis, his hair in a duck tail and hanging in his eyes, grabbed the microphone and dragged it around the stage, sometimes petting it, sometimes turning upon it with his "manly wrath." "If he did that same stuff on the streets, we'd lock him up," said a disgusted Oakland police officer. The admission to the performance was $2.50, and "programs" were 50 cents, each containing 10 pages of pictures and space for autographs. Song books sold for $1 a copy. Autographed pictures sold for 50 cents. One of the fans wore a quilted skirt with Elvis' name on the skirt in red.

4 *The San Francisco News*, p. 11: ELVIS SHMELVIS: IT'S ELVIS. Three thousand five hundred teenage girls went into ecstasy over Elvis' 20-minute performance in Oakland's Auditorium. "The gyrations are generally indescribable. They must be seen to be believed." He wore a bottle-green sportcoat, black loafers, and black denim trousers. As he sang, the girls swayed, screamed, clapped, swooned, and sobbed. To the worrying mothers, "a word of advice: Take it easy."

4 *San Francisco Examiner*, p. 1: PRESLEY 'SENDS' THRONGS WITH BUMPS, GRINDS. Three thousand five hundred teenage girls created deafening screams for Elvis' concert at the Oakland Auditorium. The Oakland police kept Elvis from being smothered by the teenagers. The audience delighted and swayed to the rhythm of Elvis' gyrating performance, pulling their hair, weeping, shrieking, and tapping their feet. He never stopped singing for 20 minutes and the performance was

indescribable. The fans screamed so loud that it shook the auditorium everytime he started a new number. At the end of his last song, he edged slowly into the wings with his sulking staggering walk that has been a trademark. He stopped just out of view, and with one hand, waved goodbye; the crowd stampeded towards the stage but were detoured by the police.

5   *San Francisco Chronicle*, p. 19: PRESLEY LEAVES YOU IN A BLUE SUEDE FUNK. The reaction of the audience, mainly teenage girls, at Sunday night's concert in Oakland was "frightening." At the evening show, two young ladies collapsed from hysteria, and another fainted at the opportunity of acquiring an autograph from Elvis. The performance that he gives in concert is not what you will see on "The Milton Berle Show" tonight, when he makes his appearance. "It's a bit rugged for TV." Following the show, a few fans were able to get by the police. For those few, Elvis was very friendly and casual and gave each a peck on the cheek. "His emotional power is frightening."

6   *The New York Times*, p. 67: ELVIS PRESLEY RISES TO FAME AS VOCALIST WHO IS VIRTUOSO OF HOOTCHY-KOOTCHY. The columnist had negative comments regarding Elvis' performance on "The Milton Berle Show" last night. He did not care for his singing ability and called his performance a variation on the "Hootchy-Kootchy," comparing Elvis' body movements with burlesque performers.

6   *The Philadelphia Inquirer*, p. 36: ROCK 'N' ROLL EARFUL SHATTERS CRITIC. "Offhand, we'd say this tall, dark, and heavy-lidded 21-year-old from Mississippi is like Johnny Ray, only more so with the torso. To the basic Ray, Presley has added an emphatic Hip, Hip. It's easy to understand why critics have nicknamed him "Pelvis Presley." Man, you never did see such writhing, wriggling, prancing, shivering and shaking! . . . This fellow is perpetual motion and emotion. . . . He's handsome in a dark, brooding way. He looks a little like the late James Dean—hair unkempt, long in the nape, long in the sideburn." "It's exciting in a primitive, sexual way, and the excitement seems to be contagious, judging from the glee in the faces of several young girls in last night's studio audience."

8   *The San Francisco News*, p. 9: IS PELVIS ELVIS ANOTHER FRANKIE? In this article, the writer compared Elvis to a "male strip-teaser." He gave negative comments regarding "Stage Show" and about Elvis in particular. ". . . it struck me that here was the most decadent-looking, unhealthy, inherently unpleasant face I had ever seen on TV." In his final comment, he was hopeful that the teenagers who have fallen for Elvis were going through a phase similar to what their mothers went through with Frank Sinatra.

11	*Newsweek*, pp. 66–67: HERO WORSHIP. An ex-wife of a sugar heir flew from Los Angeles to Atlanta, bought a blue cadillac convertible, and drove to Memphis just to buy three copies of a newspaper in which there was a picture of her taken with Elvis Presley.
13	*Variety*, pp. 51, 58: ROCK 'N' ROLL: PROS 'N' CONS. A review of several recently published articles critical of Elvis and a disc jockey's comments imploring Elvis to "drop the hoochy-cootchy gyrations or end up as "Pelvis' Presley."
15	*The San Francisco News*, p. 9: GYRATE SOME MORE, ELVIS, THEY LOVE IT. The columnist received angry mail for his comments made about Elvis on June 8. He presented some of the positive letters from Elvis' fans. One of the fans responded, "Since when does someone with an insipid mug like yours call a good-looking guy like Elvis Presley 'decadent-looking,' . . ."
16	*The Billboard*, p. 18: $ GYRATIONS. PRESLEY ON PAN BUT CASH KEEPS ROLLING. Elvis' appearance on "The Milton Berle Show" last week drew explosive comments from the local press the next day. The New York Times' Jack Gould described him as "a Rock 'n' Roll variation on one of the most standard acts in show business, the virtuoso of the hootchy-kootchy." Another columnist commented, "Elvis Presley wiggled and wiggled with such abdominal gyrations that burlesque bombshell Georgia Southern really deserves equal time to reply in gyrating kind."
	A disc jockey in New York told his audience that he thought Elvis and the people handling him should be concerned with his future and build him more lasting popularity than just a craze. However, NBC noted that Elvis' controversial appearance on "The Milton Berle Show" resulted in topping Phil Silver's ratings at the competitive time for the first time in several months.
18	*Newsweek*, p. 14: SHOWS OF THE WEEK. Milton Berle with the help of Elvis Presley ended his 8th complete TV season with a "frenzied close."
22	*The San Francisco News*, p. 9: ELVIS-PELVIS DEBATE ROCKS 'N' ROLLS ON. The columnist received and presented more pro-Elvis mail, as well as anti-Elvis mail stemming from his article on June 8. "Your cutting remarks with regards to Mr. Presley only lead me to believe that you are extremely jealous of this tall, talented, handsome, American youth."
22	*Atlanta Journal*, p. 34: ELVIS TO ROCK 'N' ROLL HERE. "Elvis Presley Rock 'n' Roll, Country & Western, and popular singing artist came to Atlanta Friday for a 3-day engagement at the Paramount Theater."
23	*America*, Vol. 95, pp. 294–295: BEWARE ELVIS PRESLEY. The columnist wrote a negative article regarding Elvis'

	personal appearances and quoted other columnists. He attacked NBC for allowing Presley to be on television. He felt that Elvis' performance, although not as distasteful as that in La Crosse, WI, was nevertheless "in appalling taste" (according to the San Francisco Chronicle). He implored television to stop allowing such performances like Elvis'.
23	*Atlanta Journal*, p. 6: TEEN-AGE SQUEALS. PRESLEY ROCKS FANS, $15 SHIRT RIPPED OFF. "Elvis rolled into Atlanta Friday, rocked through three performances at the Paramount Theater and had one of his $15 white jersey shirts ripped off by enthusiastic female fans."
26	*Look*, Vol. 20, p. 40: THE GREAT ROCK 'N' ROLL CONTROVERSY. The article reviews previous musical "fads," and the current maligning of Rock 'n' Roll music.
27	*The Charlotte News*, p. 7A: IN ELVIS' DEFENSE. 'NEW SIDE OF THE BOY': STEVE ALLEN. Steve Allen, in an open letter to Charles Mercer, answering Mr. Mercer's recent column regarding Elvis, defended his booking of Elvis after "The Milton Berle Show." He mentioned that he had booked Elvis before "The Milton Berle Show" and that Elvis had appeared on many TV shows without causing any significant controversy. He felt that it was illogical for anyone to insist that he, Steve Allen, ban Elvis from the show. Mr. Allen felt that Elvis can appear on television anytime but that he wanted to make certain that "he conducts himself in a gentlemanly manner." We are going to present the "'new' Elvis Presley."
27	*The Charlotte News*, p. 7A: RIGHT FOR YOUNG FOLK: BERLE IVES. Berle Ives, commented favorably on Elvis, "A lot of people are knocking this Elvis Presley. Why, I think he's alright." He stated that it's the same kind of music that he danced to in 1927 when he [Ives] was in college.

July

2	*The Philadelphia Inquirer*, p. 22: ELVIS GETS TO ALLEN—SO? 'NOTHING MUCH.' "Depending on whether you are a teenager or an old fogey of 25 or more, Elvis Presley distinguished or disgraced himself on a Milton Berle show a few weeks back when his hips went rushing off every which way. Steven Allen, grabbing at every likely weapon to cut into Ed Sullivan's rating, promptly announced he was going to bring Presley back alive. . . . Allen observed that he believed in doing a show for all the family. And lo! There was Elvis all duded up in white tie, tails, white gloves, and collapsible top hat—'The new Elvis Presley,' Allen declared, 'making his first comeback.' 'I think I have something on not quite correct,' Elvis said diffidently. "Blue suede shoes," . . . Without the

shim–sham–shim distractions, Presley sounds okay. . . ." Afterwards, displaying a slow, rather attractive grin, Presley sang "You Ain't Nothin' But a Hound Dog" to a bored top-hatted basset.

14 *The New York Times*, p. 33: PRESLEY SIGNED BY ED SULLIVAN. Ed Sullivan signed Elvis to a $50,000 contract for 3 performances. Elvis had been paid $5,000 and $5,500 for the Steve Allen show performances. Elvis has become the center of controversy after appearing on Milton Berle's show. His body motions were considered in poor taste by some critics and viewers. On "The Steve Allen Show" he was "relatively placid" much to the satisfaction of his critics.

16 *Newsweek*, p. 59: DEVITALIZING ELVIS. The article reviewed Steve Allen's curtailing Elvis' performance on his show. "When Allen made his move last week to mute and frustrate Presley for the good of mankind, the proceedings were instructive, but somewhat saddening . . . Presley was distraught . . . Allen's ethics were questionable from the start. He fouled Presley" . . . Having him dress in a tuxedo with tie and tails and trying to make a comic out of Elvis. However, Elvis recovered. Leaving the hall after the show, Elvis came upon some teenagers. "And he bloomed like a rose, they tell me, and writhed again as of old."

21 *Melody Maker*, p. 3: ELVIS PRESLEY. "Elvis Presley has it. His soap-box is the Rock 'n' Roll beat; his oratory is bluesy; his emotional attack is Johnny Ray with a dash of Laine . . . Though I shall never buy a Presley disc, I don't hate him; and I can listen to his records without either foaming with ecstasy or fuming. Vaguely, they depress me. Without any doubt, he's a dynamic performer and I don't regard his rise as a strange or shameful accident."

23 *Newsweek*, p. 69: QUESTION AND ANSWER. "The Steve Allen Show" with Elvis' help and publicized appearance upset "The Ed Sullivan Show" in the ratings. Sullivan then immediately signed Elvis to $50,000 for 3 appearances.

23 *Time*, p. 67: SUNDAY AT 8 (CONT.). In the battle between Steve Allen and Ed Sullivan, Allen with Elvis on his show, beat Sullivan decisively. Sullivan remarked that he would not have Elvis on his show for any amount and that Elvis was not his "cup of tea" for his family type program. Without Elvis, Sullivan again beat Allen, and realizing Elvis' impact on Allen's previous victory, Sullivan then signed Elvis to a 3-show $50,000 contract.

28/29 *Tupelo Daily Journal*, p. 5: TEACHER RECALLS ELVIS' FAVORITE TUNE WHILE AT LAWHON WAS OLD SHEP. Mrs. J.C. Grimes, Elvis' fifth-grade teacher had glowing remarks regarding Elvis. She noted that he spent every free moment learning how to play the guitar and sing. He never took a lesson but had a talent with which he was blessed. She noted that "Old Shep" was a song he often sang and sang it with much feeling and emotion. She said, "Often Elvis would sing in chapel, . . ." She remembered him as well-mannered and obedient. She remarked that he got good grades and was interested in his studies. She commented that "I couldn't have asked for a better pupil." His aunt commented that success has never changed Elvis' attitudes or has gone to his head and that he visited her recently. "Just a good little boy . . . He used to play with my kids and I never had any trouble at all with him fighting and squabbling like the other children. He always liked music."

August

4   *The Billboard*, p. 18: PRESLEY GETS 3D GOLD DISK. Elvis is to receive his third straight gold disc from RCA this week. "Hound Dog," which had been on the market for only two weeks, was expected to hit the 1 million mark on July 31, which would have been record time. "Heartbreak Hotel" and "I Want You, I Need You, I Love You" are two of Elvis' previous hits that sold over 1 million records.

6   *Modern Screen* (August) pp. 41, 90–91: ELVIS PRESLEY! WHO IS HE? WHY DOES HE DRIVE GIRLS CRAZY? A review of the last few years regarding Elvis' life, and performances. They remarked how fans "formed a human pyramid trying to reach the high window of his dressing room backstage." "His singing style is unlike that of the great crooners or sobbers who have come before him. Elvis just lets go — but with tempo." Elvis, commenting on his over-protected childhood, remarked, "I couldn't go out with the other boys, go swimming, or even play away from the house until I was fifteen." "First thing you know, when I was 15 and a sophomore, I fell in love with a girl who is 19 and a senior." When he arrived for a screen test with Hal Wallis and was asked how much acting experience he had, Elvis remarked, "Never read a line in my life." Commenting on Elvis' charitable performances — that he once sang without charging a fee with proceeds going toward a night baseball park for youngsters. "For recreation he likes to hunt up an amusement park and play the games of chance along the midway . . . One day he came home with 24 kewpie dolls he had won at a carnival."

7   *Look*, Vol. 20, pp. 82–85: ELVIS PRESLEY . . . HE CAN'T BE . . . BUT HE IS. The article states that Elvis' fame is a legend of the "American Dream." It discusses his rise, the fact that he never took a music lesson on his guitar, could not read music, paid $4 to make his first record, then became a star in

the hillbilly circuit in 1955 without any significant promotion, and his rise to success in 1956. But the article then states that his success "is overshadowed by a nightmare of bad taste," which include his gyrations on stage and his leers at the audience. When he asked Elvis about the sexual aspect of his performance, Elvis replied, "Ah don't see anything wrong with it. Ah just act the way Ah feel."

10   *Jacksonville Journal*, pp. 1–2: TROUBLES MOUNT FOR ELVIS IN JAX. Local Juvenile Court Judge, Marion W. Gooding, warned Elvis to "keep it clean" while he performed in Jacksonville or face Court charges. The Judge invited Elvis to his chambers for a pre-show session to "put him straight," but Elvis ignored the invitation. Judge Gooding claimed that he didn't "want to make a martyr" of Elvis, but also didn't want to "see obscenity and vulgarity in front of our children." In addition, the American Guild of Variety Artists again asked Elvis to join their union, since his controversial body motions and dance routine put him under the jurisdiction of the Variety Artists.

10   *The Florida Times-Union*, p. 6, Editorial: THE PRESLEY PRESSURE CAN FRACTURE ANYBODY. Elvis Presley, who is the biggest national craze since Davey Crockett, comes to Nashville today and will appear in three shows. Elvis has been the center of mob scenes wherever he appeared during his recent Florida tour, scenes reminiscent of Frank Sinatra during wartime and Rudolf Valentino in the 1920s. "What's important right now is to avoid being trampled in the rush as Presley gets around town."

11   *Jacksonville Journal*, pp. 1, 3: ELVIS' PERFORMANCE SATISFIES GOODING. Judge Gooding, along with 2,200 screaming youngsters, watched Elvis' first performance and felt that Elvis complied with his order. Elvis was confused at Gooding's request yesterday; "I can't figure out what I'm doing wrong . . . I know my mother approves of what I'm doing. . . ."

    In addition, the matter of the American Guild of Variety Artists was cleared up before the show when Elvis accepted membership in the organization. Between performances, Elvis answered reporters and posed for pictures for magazines, television, and newspaper photographers.

19   *The Dallas Times Herald*, p. 1: HE'S REAL COOL' MUSICRATS PUSH WARBLER ELVIS FOR PRESIDENT. The first "Presley for President Club" in Texas, most likely in the nation, was organized this week. With loud shouts and placards waving, the Musicratic National Conventional got under way to choose a candidate for the Presidential Election. Undoubtedly, Elvis would most likely be the only candidate chosen. Their campaign yell is: "Extra, Extra, Read All About

It! We've Got a Cat and We're Gonna Shout It! He's the Best in the Land to Strike Up the Band. Sing, Presley, Sing 'cause You Can, Can, Can!"

22 *Downbeat*, p. 8: ELVIS IS AWFUL, BUT I LOVE HIM. In a hotel lobby, there was a teen-age girl sitting with a frown on her face. "He's ghastly . . . just ghastly," she said. . . ."The doll!" Elvis had commented that he had had five watches and four rings ripped from him by fans.

27 *Newsweek*, p. 68: INEXTINGUISHABLE. The article remarked that interest in Elvis is still high and mentioned some stories. One woman won First Prize which was a bear hug from Elvis in a national essay contest "Why I Like Elvis." Her reason: "He is the brightest star in the eternal heavens." A Boston disc jockey had a contest offering 7 strands of Elvis' hair for the 7 most ridiculous reasons for wanting his hair. He received 18,400 replies in 1 week. One winning answer from a mother stated that if she had Elvis' hair, she "would cut it in three pieces, braid it, and hang myself to the tune of Hound Dog." Elvis was also surprised to find that he had won the "Apollo Award" given by newspapermen and disc jockies claiming Elvis as the latest reincarnation of the god of art, music, and poetry.

27 *Life*, Vol. 41, pp. 101–110: ELVIS—A DIFFERENT KIND OF IDOL. "Up to a point, the country can withstand the impact of Elvis Presley as a familiar and acceptable phenomenon." Whenever Elvis howls his combination of hillbilly and Rock 'n Roll, "he is beset by teen-age girls yelling for him. They dote on his side-burns and pegged pants, cherish cups of water dipped from his swimming pool, covet strands of his hair, boycott disc jockeys who dislike his records . . ." "But with Elvis Presley, the daffiness has been deeply disturbing to civic leaders, clergymen, and some parents. He does not just bounce to accent his heavy beat. He uses a bump and grind routine usually seen only in burlesque. His young audiences, unexposed to such goings-on, do not just shout their approval. They get set off by shock waves of hysteria, going into frenzies of screeching and wailing, winding up in tears. . . . When he starts a show, Elvis takes a few swipes at his guitar, then lurches into one of his scorchers. . . . The girls in the front of the audience go into screams and seizures. From that point, most of them do not hear what Elvis is singing as he brings his "subsceptible audience to the breaking point." Said one fan, "When he does that on TV, I got down on the floor and scream."

There were interesting items shown in pictures. Hairs from Elvis' sideburns and two letters from a contest in which a Boston disc jockey offered a prize for the best letters expressing why they wanted Elvis' hair. One of them stated "Dear Sir, I would like some Elvis Presley hair because I'm bald"; another stated "Dear Norm, If I had a hair from Elvis Presley's sideburns, I would tack it over the front door of my house and over it I would have a big sign reading—Elvis Presley Was 'Hair'." Another picture showed a skirt with Elvis Presley written on it. Another showed teenagers with water-warped records. Another picture showed teenagers praying for Elvis' salvation after the minister stated that Elvis had "achieved a new low in spirtual degeneracy."

31 *Tupelo Daily Journal*, p. 1: GOV. COLEMAN TO VISIT HERE 'PRESLEY DAY'. General Manager of the Mississippi-Alabama Fair said that the governor agreed to present Elvis Presley with a recognition scroll at the opening of his performance at the Fair. He will also be presented with a key to the city. Elvis is to give two performances—2:30 and 7:30 PM with 10,000 seats available for each show.

September

Coronet, Vol. 40, pp. 153–157: A CRAZE CALLED ELVIS. The article reviews Elvis' background and rise to fame. His rise from driving a delivery truck 2 years ago after graduating high school; to his singing career, which earned him $55,000 last year; to his $1 million expected earnings from record sales, personal appearances, and record TV performances this year. It states that Elvis accounted for more than one half of RCA Victor's pop-records just 3 months after he was signed by RCA. His popularity in the South and Southwest were at record-breaking pace. Although some critics have accused Elvis of performing deliberately in an erotic manner, "Elvis himself doesn't deny the accusation. . . . 'Ah cain't he'p it. It's the way ah fee'-ul!.'" Elvis stated that during his childhood, "The only time I ever sang in public was maybe in a little variety show at school." Currently, Elvis earned 4.5 cents in royalties for every 89 cent record and a proportionate percentage for his $3.98 LPs, which will amount to $400,000 for 1956. Elvis earns $25,000 a week and is on great demand for performances. Elvis' wardrobe consists of more than 20 each of sport jackets, pants, suits, and pairs of shoes, and it is constantly changing. Although he has a reputation as a flashy dresser, he states that he favors "conservative clothes" for every day dress. His weight has risen from 153 to 184 lbs. this past year, owing mainly to his diet. Elvis has very intense work ethics and stamina, often performing 2 or 3 and even up to 5 shows a day, then hitting the road for the next show. Most of his travel at this time is by limousine for the short trips and trainer planes for the long trips. During this past year, Elvis rarely has more than 3 or 4 hours sleep each night, and stated,

"I lie there thinkin' will this last? My heart gets to beatin' and I can't sleep." Elvis is devoted to his parents and bought them a ranch house in Memphis. However, he rarely has more than a day or two at home each time he visits. Regarding his choice in girls, he stated "I haven't got a dream girl of any kind in mind. But I know one thing for sure. I don't want anybody who is more or less of a snob or a put-on. I like girls to be themselves." He was recently given a 7-year contract with Paramount Theaters. Regarding acting, Elvis stated "I'd like to learn to act in the movies, and I think I can do it." The article closed with a complimentary comment stating that no matter how popular Elvis appears to be, the degree of success has not gotten to him. They stated that recently following a show in Denver, when the group went to the airport the next morning and the flight was called, Elvis could not be found. Frantically looking for Elvis, Colonel Parker finally found him pitching pennies with a taxidriver out in the back.

Modern Screen (September) p. 16: LOUELLA PARSONS IN HOLLYWOOD. OPEN LETTER TO ELVIS PRESLEY

"I believe that you are very serious about becoming a good actor as well as a sensational singer. . . . You can bet on one thing—there won't be any bad taste slipping by in your screen performances. So why not drop it now? . . . I want to congratulate you on the many appearances you make for worthwhile charities. . . . You have talent and looks. Just drop the 'freak' stuff, Elvis."

3   *Tupelo Daily Journal*, p. 1: SEVEN PRESLEY RECORDS HIT NATION WITH BANG THIS WEEK: RCA Victor released 7 Elvis records at one time, all taken from his album even though "Hound Dog" and "Don't Be Cruel" are high on the nation's record list.

5   *Variety*, p. 1: YOU CAN'T LAUGH OFF PRESLEY'S PHENOMENAL 10,000,000 RECORDS. Elvis has 1 million record sales already with "Blue Suede Shoes," "Heartbreak Hotel," and "Hound Dog." RCA has just released 7 single records from Elvis' albums and the singles are selling at the rate of 12,000 a day. Elvis has become quite a bargain for RCA Victor as his contract with Sun Record Company was purchased for $30,000 last year plus an additional $5,000 bonus. Already, Elvis has sold 10 million records with $5 million for RCA. In the past few weeks, RCA has been so busy pressing Elvis' records that it had to use facilities of both Decca and MGM to keep up with the demand. This is the first time that RCA Victor has used outside presses. Presently, Elvis' recordings account for two thirds of RCA's daily singles output.

8   *TV Guide* (September 8–14) pp. 4–7: ELVIS PRESLEY. PART 1. THE PEOPLE WHO KNOW SAY HE DOES HAVE

	TALENT. Part one of a three part series commenting on Elvis' talents.
8/9	*Tupelo Daily Journal*, p. 1: 'PRESLEY HOMECOMING' THEME OF PARADE ON CHILDREN'S DAY. "Elvis Homecoming" will be the theme of the Annual Children's Day parade to be held on September 26th at the Mississippi–Alabama Fair. Titles of Elvis' songs will be the themes of the floats entered in the parade. Elvis' manager stated that it would be too dangerous for Elvis to ride in the parade.
9	*The Dallas Times Herald*: ELVIS PRESLEY: WHAT MAKES HIM TICK? "Elvis Presley—a figure who is both hated and loved, scorned and worshiped, condemned and exhaulted; a youth of humble beginnings who has inspired a cult of fanatic followers through his voice, appearance, and gyrations—is returning to television tonight" on "The Ed Sullivan Show." "One thing is certain—almost everyone will react one way or another. There seems to be no middle ground." However you feel about him, knowing him may help understand him. "One minute he is frantically singing and leaping about. The following moment he may slip into a mood of deep despondency." "He is an amazing worker, apparently driven by some force inside himself. He has tremendous respect for his fans and often signs autographs for hours. He neither smokes nor drinks. He's unruly and wild and is a constant source of trouble for those booking his act. He is the physical epitome of a trouble-making teenager, with long sideburns, slicked back hair, and drooping eyelids." Although he cannot read music, he has a feel for the beat that is essential in Rock 'n' Roll rhythms. Many experts feel he is an example of defiance that any teenagers seek to express. They find an outlet for pent-up energies in him that they cannot release in society. Elvis Presley cannot continue to be the "perpetual teenager" and remain the sensation he is now. His voice is not really bad. "Presley, then, is a phenomenon of our age. He's a young, bewildered by success, singer. He is the elected ruler of a cult of defiant fans, not king by talent or choice, but simply because he was born at the right moment. There is one thing left to say—there are more cultural, social, and economic advances being nutured today than ever before. Perhaps our civilization needs a Presley to hold up, inspect and study. It makes our advances more than satisfying."
10	*Tupelo Daily Journal*, p. 4: MOVIE RENAMED TO FIT NEW PRESLEY RECORD. Twentieth Century-Fox renamed the *Reno Brothers*, Elvis' first movie *Love Me Tender*.
10	*The New York Times*, p. 55: A paragraph commenting on Elvis' appearance on "The Ed Sullivan Show" against which NBC did not try to compete, giving Steve Allen the night off and running an English film instead.

10   *The Philadelphia Inquirer*, p. 26: "SULLIVAN'S $50,000 BOY CUT OFF AMIDSHIPS." "The Ed Sullivan Show" displayed one third of its $50,000 worth of Elvis Presley and what the absent Ed got for his money, mostly, was half a man. Elvis sang four songs . . . he strode out in horse—blanket jacket and open collar shirt and went into his legs-apart, toss-turned-in singing stance. But then the cameras soared to his waist and resolutely aimed there or higher so that "Elvis the Pelvis" could just have well have been "Elvis the Epiglottis." Judging from the girlish shrieks and shouts, a lot was going on out of camera range while Presley was singing "Don't Be Cruel." Certainly it couldn't have been his voice, or even his shoulder-twitching, forehead wiping, lip-smacking or lip-licking that inspired all the commotion. Or could it? Immediately after this strenuous workout, all Elvis could manage was a weary 'whew.' The camera man gradually gained a little confidence, so that by the time Presley went into his finale, "Hound Dog," he was on display from tip to toe, every wildly squirming inch of him. No sexy 'bumps,' though." Charles Laughton, who introduced Presley, commented "Music hath charms to sooth the savage beast."

13   *Tupelo Daily Journal*, p. 11: ELVIS, ACTRESS NATALIE WOOD ARE TWOSOME. Natalie Wood confessed today that she and Elvis have been keeping steady company since he arrived for his movie debut. "He's really great and the most totally real boy I've ever met. He's a real pixie and has a wonderful little boy quality." She commented how he was very courteous and polite and sweet. "He is the nicest boy I know. A wonderful dancer—and he sings all the time to me." She commented that he was not "big headed" and completely unaware of how popular he really was. "I can't believe anyone with all this success can be as terrific as he is."

16   *The New York Times*, Section 2, p. 13: ELVIS PRESLEY. LACK OF RESPONSIBILITY IS SHOWN BY TV IN EXPLOITING TEENAGERS. TV broadcasters should be expected to display "adult leadership and responsibility in areas where they do have some significant influence." They have not done this in the case of Elvis Presley. Mr. Presley made another appearance on "The Ed Sullivan Show," attracting record audiences, but in some ways, it was the most unpleasant of his recent performances. "Mr. Presley initially disturbed adult viewers—and instantly became a martyr in the eyes of his teenage following—for his striptease behavior" on last spring's Milton Berle program." However, he was more sedate when he performed on "The Steve Allen Show." When he appeared on "The Ed Sullivan Show," he "injected movements of the tongue and indulged in wordless singing that were singularly distasteful. At least some parents are puzzled

or confused by Presley's almost hypnotic power; others are concerned; perhaps most are a shade disgusted and content to permit the Presley fad to play itself out." Teenagers with their numbers growing, have found a rallying point in Presley "who seems to be on their side." In addition to television, expose magazines and the music-publishing industry are the culprits. "Selfish exploitation and commercialized overstimulation of youth's physical impulses is certainly a gross national disservice."

18 *Atlanta Journal*, p. 25: FIREMEN SUPERIOR TO ELVIS AS DATE, SECRETARY SAYS. "A gal who knows them both says she would rather date a city fireman than Elvis Presley. This despite the fact she once broke a date with her fireman friend to meet Elvis after midnight. . . ." 'I first got interested in Elvis,' she said, 'when I saw they were having a magazine contest on the subject, "Why I would like to meet Elvis." She "was somewhat taken aback when her letter was judged the best of 95,000 submitted. A national picture magazine ran her photo and she received a considerable amount of mail herself." "We met after the show. . . . and I drove him in my car. . . . We sat there in the car with about a thousand little girls milling around us for a lot of the time, although we did get to talk some." . . . "On the stage, he is dynamic and off the stage . . . he is the same Elvis, the same Mississippi boy he has been for 21 years. He likes to tease but he doesn't tell any jokes. We just talked about his career, movies, and his songs, and what other people were saying about him. He asked about my job and what I wanted to do, and I told him I wanted to be a writer."

19 *Downbeat*, pp. 42–43, 46: A PSYCHOLOGIST'S VIEWPOINT. A New York disc jockey and a psychologist were analyzing the appeal of Rock 'n' Roll on his radio program. In a question put to the psychologist regarding Elvis Presley's performances, the psychologist said, "I guess it would be important to watch him in action. I see before me one of the record covers. I think that the way he grimaces . . . (I understand he really rocks his body in the course of performing a song) . . . I think there, too, the suggestiveness comes across . . . the sexual suggestiveness comes across." When asked if this is a necessary evil or a normal outlet for youngsters' urges, the psychologist replied, "In my opinion, the adolescent in every generation has the same kind of problem. There is an emergence of new urges that he probably doesn't understand. There are many cultural pressures that make it difficult for him to experience these urges freely, and in view of this kind of thing, I don't think that this is anything that is particularly evil. I think that if anyone . . . any of the adults in our generation . . . look back at their own adolescence, they would be able to pick out a particular style of music that

gave them an outlet for expressing what couldn't be expressed through channels that nature provided."

Later in the discussion the psychologist added, "There is certainly an antiformalism in Presley's style, and I think that this is in part . . . I think it's due to the fact this is in part what all adolescents do. It's a kind of rebellious mood . . . some may idolize their parents, others may feel that their parents failed and they would like to strike out anew, for this is an antiformalism I think is one of the characteristics. . . . One of the things that is necessary for this kind of rebellion. But I think that the emphasis is on the moment of experience . . . the immediate experience as you call it . . . the return of naturalism, to get away. Well, this is something that all adolescents go for, to get away from the phoniness that the adults are emmersed in."

19 *Downbeat*, p. 41: ELVIS PRESLEY. CAN FIFTY MILLION AMERICANS BE WRONG? "Do what you will to Elvis Presely—slander him, mock him, step on his blue suede shoes—he'll still be king to his insuppressible army of fans." This raises an interesting question, "Can fifty million Americans possibly be wrong?" As soon as Elvis became popular, the intimate aspect of his life was revealed to the public whether it was accurate or not. "From correspondence and personal conversations I have had with Presley's staunchest teenage supporters, it has become clear that they favor him as much for his looks, his reputed kindnesses, his concern for his parents, and for the Horatio Alger character of his climb as they do for his vocal and physical gyrations."

19 *Atlanta Journal*, p. 22: 'ROSE REAL COOL' TO PRESLEY. Billy Rose described Rock 'n' Roll music . . ." as musical monstrosities." "Maybe it's the age difference between today's youth and an older generation that lived on memories, but a great many people will agree with Billy Rose that the untalented twitchers and twisters seemed to have pushed real musicians into the background."

21 *Tupelo Daily Journal*: PRESLEY DAY WILL EMPHASIZE THAT TUPELO IS PROUD OF HIM. It was announced that in addition to a theme for the annual parade around Presley's hit recording, there will be a giant banner welcoming Elvis and strung across Main Street; "Merchants will be asked to decorate their windows with an Elvis Presley theme for the day."

22 *TV Guide* (September 22–28) pp. 17–19, ELVIS PRESLEY. PART 2. THE FOLKS HE LEFT BEHIND HIM. Part two of the series discussing Elvis' relatives and friends. As one of his friends remarked, "He's too restless and he drives himself too hard. For his own good, he should learn to slow down."

24 *Newsweek*, p. 68: THE ED SULLIVAN SHOW. Elvis' appearance boosted Ed Sullivan's top rated show to 82.6

percent of the viewing public—an all time high even though Elvis refrained from his controversial routine.

25 *Tupelo Daily Journal*, p. 11: ELVIS AT MILAM JUNIOR HIGH LOVED MUSIC, WAS QUIET LAD. Mrs. Quay Webb Camp, Elvis' sixth grade teacher stated that Elvis "is an example of a good American citizen." "He was a good little boy who never did anything that needed to be corrected." She stated that he made "good grades in school and was a good average student." She recalled that Elvis had brought his guitar to play and sing in schoolroom programs and that he had "made straight A's in Music."

25 *Tupelo Daily Journal*, p. 1: ELVIS TRAFFIC BRINGS BAN ON MAIN PARKING. Parking is prohibited along the downtown areas of Main Street from 6 PM to midnight on Wednesday as an aid to control the expected heaviest flow of traffic in Tupelo's history, owing to Elvis' performance and the parade scheduled for the Mississippi–Alabama Fair.

25 *Tupelo Daily Journal*, p. 1: THE WELCOME MAT IS OUT FOR PRESLEY HOMECOMING. Magazine and news reporters will occupy a special press section in front of the grandstand for the Mississippi–Alabama Fair. Cameramen will be on hand from TV news and Fox Movietone to record Elvis' homecoming for nationwide distribution. Some newsmen, realizing that their seating in front row seats put them in the path of danger from screaming fans, erected signs that read "Don't Be Cruel."

26 *Tupelo Daily Journal*, p. 1: CEDAR HILL WINS $150 COMMUNITY AWARDS; SPOTLIGHT TODAY ON PRESLEY. Elvis will be in the spotlight at the Mississippi–Alabama Fair and Dairy Show. The homecoming will start officially at 2:30 PM when Governor J.P. Coleman will present Elvis with a scroll and a key to the city. Elvis will then perform in the afternoon and then again at 7:30 PM. About 30,000 to 40,000 people are expected at the fairgrounds.

26 *Variety*, pp. 1, 16: HALO, EVERYBODY, HALO: LATEST PRESLEY PITCH. 20th Century Fox wants to recreate Elvis into "an influence for the good," particularly with emphasis on "the kids" and the juvenile delinquency problem.

27 *Tupelo Daily Journal*, p. 1: 20,000 PERSONS, MOSTLY SCREAMING TEENAGERS, WELCOME PRESLEY HOME. National guardsmen called out for the night performance were occupied by hysterical teenage girls who fought blockades placed around the stage. They shoved and scratched, trying to get a chance to touch Elvis Presley, who was able to stay out of their reach. Elvis received awards from the Governor after which he began his matinee performance before a screaming crowd of about 5,000. At one point, Elvis got too close to his hysterical fans, who tore silver buttons from his blue velvet

shirt sleeve. Photographers and reporters scrambled onto the stage for safety when Elvis started singing, and the teenagers rushed forward toward Elvis. One of the teenagers actually got onto the platform, threw her arms about Elvis, and was dragged screaming from the stage. Several of the fans fainted and were nearly trampled. Footlights were torn from their sockets as the teenagers tried desperately to touch Elvis. Elvis received $5,000 plus a 60 percent of the gate for the two performances. Elvis' parents were present for the homecoming events.

27 *Tupelo Daily Journal*, p. 1: ELVIS PRESLEY MERCHANDISE SALES ALREADY TOPPING DAVY CROCKETT; MAY CONTINUE YEARS. The young people of American are now being deluged with Elvis Presley items, many in his favorite colors of black and emerald green. Skirts, separates, scarves, bracelets, necklaces, lipsticks, cologne, purses, and kerchiefs are just some of the items. They feature Elvis' picture, the names of his hit records, and a picture of a guitar or a hound dog.

27 *The New York Times*, p. 42: HOMETOWN HONORS PRESLEY. A paragraph remarking how Elvis received a scroll from the Governor of Mississippi and a citation from the Mayor of Tupelo and a comment about his 45-minute concert at the Mississippi–Alabama Fair.

29 *The Billboard*, pp. 31, 34: PRESLEY JUGGERNAUT ROLLS. MERCHANDISING CAMPAIGN EXPECTED TO TOP $20 MIL SALES BY YEAR END. A merchandising campaign for Elvis products is expected to sell more than $20 million worth of items before the end of the year. This will overcome such competition as Mickey Mouse, Hopalong Cassidy, and Davy Crockett. Such Elvis merchandise includes T-shirts, blue jeans, bobby-socks, hats, kerchiefs, sneakers, other items of clothing, purses, billfolds, charm bracelets, necklaces, magazines, gloves, guitar, lipstick, cologne, stuffed 'Hound-Dogs', stationery, and recently, a soft drink. Also expected is a glow-in-the-dark picture of Elvis—the image lasting about 2 hours after the lights have been turned off. Major department stores will be handling the merchandise. There are approximately 200,000 fan club members. A magazine titled "Elvis Presley Answers Back" will be sold for about 50 cents.

29 *The Billboard*, p. 31: LIP ROUGE TO ROCK 'N' ROLL. There is to be a new lipstick called "Teenagers Lipstick" that will soon be marketed as Presley merchandise. It will be available in three shades: "Heartbreak Pink," "Hound Dog Orange," and "Tutti Frutti Red."

29 *TV Guide* (September 29–October 5) pp. 20–23: ELVIS PRESLEY. PART 3. HE TELLS HOW THE LITTLE WIGGLE GREW. Comments of Elvis' and others' regarding his gyrations during his performances.

29/30	*Tupelo Daily Journal*, p. 1: GIRL DOESN'T LIKE PICTURE, ELVIS SETTLES FOR $5,500. Elvis, in an out-of-court settlement, gave a young lady $5,500 as she threatened to sue him for having a picture of Elvis' head on her shoulder that was published in "Elvis Presley Speaks."

October

House and Garden (October), pp. 40–41: THE WAR OF THE GENERATIONS. In this article, the columnist stated that he didn't think that television should be censored for allowing Elvis to perform. "There is nothing inherently harmful in any sort of music itself or in the performance of it before audiences of any age. The rhymthic monotity of Rock 'n' Roll, the crudeness of its melodic and harmonic structure, the primitive and often suggestive nature of its lyrics—none of these things in itself incites youngsters to violence, sexual laxness, or any of the other ills that have been blamed on the music. . . . What is really bothering us *adults*, I suspect, is not that television has chosen to satisfy this teenage audience, but that such a distinctive audience exists at all—that within our own society there is a large, well-defined group whose standards of taste and conduct we find baffling, and even terrifying. These are our children, and we want badly for them to identify themselves with us. But somehow we have failed to inspire in them a respect for our own standards. . . . Like it or not, a little hostility between generations is a fact of life, and the kids will have their special idols. . . ."

Modern Screen (October) pp. 37, 90–92, I FLIPPED WHEN ELVIS HELD ME IN HIS ARMS. A young Elvis fan relates how she started "the first" fan club in America. Of her fan club members she said, "Ninety-five percent of my 3,000 club members are from nice, stable families, and attend church regularly." She wrote many letters to radio stations to have Elvis' records played. She received permission from Colonel Parker to visit Elvis backstage prior to a concert and to be backstage during his performance. She felt like Elvis Presley resembled Apollo, the symbol of youth and beauty. "Close up, he is fantastically good-looking." "His clothes are of unusual color combinations, such as green, purple, and blue; or pink, green, and black." They had conversation, and she mentioned to him that "all the girls in Dallas were wearing the Elvis bob now, with the sideburns and everything." At the end of their conversation, Elvis suddenly kissed her and then went on stage to perform.

3   *Tupelo Daily Journal*, p. 1: ELVIS PRESLEY RECORD SALES TOP 10 MILLION. Elvis has sold 10 million records

thus far. There is a backlog of more than 856,000 orders for "Love Me Tender" and "Any Way You Want Me," soon to be released. It has also been reported in a weekly magazine, *Parade*, that Elvis hired a bodyguard, stemming from an attempt of sailors to beat him up recently.

8   *Newsweek*, p. 58: MUD ON THE STARS. After Ed Sullivan paid a record $50,000 for three Elvis Presley appearances, his advertising agency thought that other networks would follow. The new asking price of $300,000 offered to NBC and CBS was rejected.

8   *Time*, pp. 96, 98, 100: SWEET MUSIC. The record industry is having its best year since the record player was invented. The reason is that "records are cheaper ($1.98–$3.98 for a long-player versus $5.95 in 1954) and technically better than ever," . . . and they are "being played on phonographs that are cheaper (less than $100 for a hi-fi) and better than ever." RCA Victor has an all time high advance sale of 1 million records for Elvis' "Love Me Tender."

9   *San Francisco Chronicle*, p. 25: ELVIS TO STAR IN FILM WITH JAYNE MANSFIELD. Twentieth Century Fox announced that Elvis Presley and Jayne Mansfield are to star in a movie entitled *The Love Maniac*.

11 *The Dallas Times Herald*: PLANS KEPT SECRET. ELVIS HUSH—HUSH IRKS EAGER FANS. Thousands of young Dallas fans were upset that they were not able to find out Elvis' whereabouts in Dallas. Some threatened to boycott his show at the Cotton Bowl. Obviously the plan was to prevent Elvis from getting mobbed as he had been in other cities. There were rumors that a wire fence would be placed around the stage, on the football field, to which fans remarked, "He can't do that to us. We'll show him. We'll get wire clippers."

12 *The Dallas Morning News*, pp. 106–109: ELVIS PRESLEY DISTURBANCE SURELY HIT SEISMIC SCALE. Twenty-six thousand five hundred frenzied fans gathered on the eastern slope of the Cotton Bowl for an Elvis Presley performance. Prior to the concert, a Dallas County deputy sheriff served Elvis with papers on a $38,000 suit alleging that Elvis' management broke a contract. For the show, Elvis entered in an open car as a spotlight followed him around the field and up to the platform, which was positioned at the 50-yard line. "High-pitched, ear-splitting screams began and never let up "when Elvis was first sighted until when the show was over. Elvis had sung a half dozen songs. Ninety-five police officers and an 8-ft. high fence kept the fans from Elvis. Elvis wore a green tweed jacket, white buckskin, high-top shoes with red heels, a white raw silk shirt with pleats, a blue tie, and charcoal trousers. Elvis began the concert with "Heartbreak Hotel" as he shuffled and staggered with the microphone. Sometimes it

appeared that he was doing a "classical Indian war dance." Other times, he threw his famous pelvis from the 50-yard line to the 35. Some of the fans screamed so hard that they became hoarse and could only sit, weep, and moan. Prior to the concert, Elvis had a press conference and claimed that he had only slept about 4 hours in the last 48, showing the strains of the rigorous touring. When questioned by one of the reporters, "Why are you so humble?" Elvis replied "I know that the Lord can give and that the Lord can take away. I might be herding sheep next year."

12 *The Dallas Morning News*: CHEERS CONSTANT. PRESLEY THRILLS CROWD OF 26,500. Twenty-six thousand five hundred fans cheered almost continuously during a 35-minute performance in the Cotton Bowl football arena. It was the largest crowd ever to pay to see an entertainer perform in Dallas. A spotlight centered over Elvis in the backseat of a convertible as the car approached the field. The roar of the crowd grew louder as his car circled the football field and then became "an ear-splitting crescendo," becoming even greater when Elvis waved his hand. The crowd quieted momentarily, but then as Elvis tossed his head back, "pandemonium broke loose" and the noise did not subside. He started his performance with "Have Some Fun Tonight," and the performance was complete with the "gyrating pelvic motions."

15 *The San Francisco News*, p. 1: WHAT MAKES ELVIS ROLL ON. STORY OF A JELLY-KNEED KID. The columnist in the first of a three-part series, reviews Elvis' life up to the present, including his childhood, his early recordings, and his recent successes. Quoting an RCA Victor official "Presley's the biggest thing since Gene Austin. We're the biggest record company in the country, and we've got Decca and MGM pressing records for us right now because we can't handle it all." . . . He estimated that in 1956 "between 7 and 10 million Elvis Presley records will be sold—and look, we haven't even had him a year yet." . . . The fifth gold record's the most interesting: It was for "Love Me Tender," which was issued October 1 and for which Victor had more than 1 million orders on hand before the public ever heard it. Victor's income this year figures roughly at $60 million, of which 5 to 10 percent will be from Presley records. Elvis' director for *Love Me Tender* said, "We didn't know what to expect: he had a strike against him in a way. But he was very cooperative, very flexible, took directions like a trouper. . . . Once in awhile someone comes along—an Edison or a Bach who's been tapped on the shoulder, who's got a great gift. This boy's got it." . . . He was so polite, called everyone 'sir' or 'mam' . . . We loved him. . . . The studio is so high on Presley's film that although it was finished only a week ago, it is being processed in record

time for release for the Thanksgiving trade. Further, 20th Century is making more prints (575) than it ever has for any film in its history. . . . For Elvis has lifted Rock 'n' Roll right out of its nitch and slapped it into every home in the nation."

16 *The San Francisco News*, pp. 1, 8: WHAT MAKES ELVIS PRESLEY TICK — NO. 2 'CAN'T HE'P IT . . . AH JUST LOVE THAT BOY'. In part two of a three part series, the columnist commented on the performance in Dallas. Talking to a woman behind a cigar counter who said, "Ah can't he'p it. Ah just love that boy." Many of the fans "wore Rock 'n' Roll hats — colorful, quick-buck versions of the old pork pies — and lots of 'em wore pink shirts, heavy black shirts, or toreadore pants with the name 'Elvis Presley' stitched thereon." About 4,000 to 5,000 fans attended the performance in the Cotton Bowl. A pink and black stage was on the 50 yard line. A cadillac entered the stadium and a spotlight picked up Elvis sitting in the convertible. "The car circled the field and stopped in front of the stage. Elvis hopped out, took the microphone, and started to say something, but you could never figure out what he was fixing to say, because the girls in the stands kept hollerin'. . . . He was wearing a kelly green tweed coat, white three-quarter buckskin soles with red soles, navy blue pants, a black-and-gold cummerbund, a ruffled white shirt, and a navy blue string tie." He clowned around with the musical group and then began singing. "The shrieks would die down a little, and Elvis would swivle himself into a bump and a grind, bringing forth new shrieking ecstasies. He was real loose. He kidded with the Jordanaires who jointed him for a couple of numbers, but he was working hard, you could see." . . . After he had sang for a half hour, he began "Hound Dog," and bounced off the stage, carrying the mike with him. There, on the 50-yard line, he sank to his knees, rose, wove, bumped, ground, and sank again, time after time. The girls screamed themselves silly. One person remarked "It's unfortunate, but we've got to protect Elvis, otherwise they'd tear him apart."

17 *Variety*, pp. 1, 76: BAPTIST MINISTERS SERMON VS. ELVIS: HE'LL HIT THE SKIDS. A Baptist minister in his sermon on Sunday (October 14) predicted that Elvis would soon hit the skids. "The music and beat of Elvis Presley's singing seems to me a reflection of the turmoil and confusion that is present in the lives of young people today. . . . Presley is on top today but in 1 or 2 years he will be far less popular. . . . Elvis is now an expression of the subconscious nature of modern youth in a time of turmoil." The minister remarked that a larger than normal number of teenagers attended the morning service.

17 *The San Francisco News*, p. 1: WHAT MAKES ELVIS PRESLEY TICK — NO. 3. THE PELVIS EXPLAINS THAT 'VULGAR' STYLE. Following an interview with Elvis, a

columnist wrote "Today he's a polished showman, with a great sense of timing, lots of humor, and a seemingly easy manner. This easiness is deceptive. He told me: "I get a little nervous in a crowd. I always do, I always will. . . . I don't get, much relaxation . . . I wish I could relax. . . . I'd like to get me a home some time.' To his fans, especially, he's very kind, signing autographs, for instance, he'll say: 'Honey, what's your name? Where's your home?'—And the girls, and boys too, warm up to him fast. When asked about his philosophy on life and about his business, Elvis remarked, "I'm learning it and lots of people are helping me. I don't know how long this'll go on. I may be back driving a truck next year this time or I may be back herding sheep. But I know this. All good things come from God. You don't have to go to church to know right from wrong.' When asked about his sideburns, Elvis said 'I don't like 'm real well, but I've been a success with 'em so I guess I'll keep 'em.' He told a 13-year old: 'The fan clubs played a big part, honey, in my success . . . they do in anybody's. That's no joke.' Elvis was sensitive to a picture in *Life* magazine of a minister denouncing Elvis "That hurt me bitter, . . . God gave me my voice. I never danced vulgar in my life. I've just been jigglin'." Nick Adams, commenting on Elvis said, "He's the greatest guy I've ever met."

19   *The New York Times*, p. 53: PRESLEY INVOLVED IN MEMPHIS FIGHT. The article reviews what happened at the service station when Elvis and Ed Hopper and his assistant had a confrontation.

19   *San Francisco Chronicle*, pp. 1, 6: ARREST IN MEMPHIS ROW. ELVIS WINS IN BRAWL, WINS ON POINTS. Elvis Presley slugged it out with two service station attendants tonight. He was way ahead when the cops broke it up and charged all three with assault and battery. The Rock 'n' Roll teenage idol had a slight scratch on the side of his face.

19   *Tupelo Daily Journal*, p. 1: ELVIS SHOWS FISTIC PROWESS IN SLUG FEST. "Rock 'n' Roll singer Elvis Presley slugged it out with two filling station attendants tonight and proved he was as handy with his fists as with a song."

20   *The New York Times*, p. 16: PRESLEY ROLLS IN CLEAR. COURT ROCKS HIS OPPONENTS IN FIGHT WITH FINES. This article reviews Elvis' confrontation with the service station attendants in Memphis where Elvis was found not guilty, and the other two individuals were fined $25 and $15 each.

22   *San Francisco Chronicle*, p. 4: GIRLS SMEAR ELVIS' CADILLAC. While Elvis watched himself on a movie screen in Memphis, his fans scrolled love messages in lipstick over his white cadillac and ripped the upholstery as well.

24   *Variety*, p. 55: R 'n' R WORTH 5 GOLD DISCS, 450G IN 1 YEAR TO ELVIS, 'LOVE ME TENDER' CLINCHER. Elvis continues to break all sales records and will receive his fifth

gold disc in one year on the next "The Ed Sullivan Show" (October 28). "Love Me Tender" is the latest record to pass the one million sales mark. What was unique about "Love Me Tender" is that it received over one million orders from distributors even before it had been pressed. Other one million records for Elvis include: "Heartbreak Hotel," "Don't Be Cruel," "Hound Dog," and "I Want You, I Need You, I Love You." Elvis has sold 10 million records for RCA possibly earning him $450,000 in record royalties for the last 12 months.

24 *Variety*, pp. 1, 78: ELVIS A MILLIONAIRE IN 1 YEAR. Elvis Presley will earn $1 million in gross income this year. Despite critics who have repeatedly said he can't last, it is reasonable to project that his future income will be just as significant. Elvis had been a rising entertainer for several months prior to "The Milton Berle Show" this past summer; however, since the Berle show, his record sales and popularity have soared. It is felt that his $1 million in 1956 earnings is aided by the almost one million advanced record sales for "Love Me Tender" and the estimated 10 million record sales for 1956. In addition, there are advances for television guest performances and movie contracts. Merchandisers estimate a possible $40 million in retail for Elvis-related products in the next 15 months. There are 51 items with Elvis' name, 80 percent aimed at the female market and 20 percent at the male market. The estimated $40 million in retail sales is at the domestic level only. Elvis will probably earn $2.5 million for the years 1956 and 1957.

24 *Variety*, p. 78: GOD-LOVING JELLY-KNEED KID: PARKER ON PRESLEY. Colonel Tom Parker wants merchandising hustlers not publicity personnel now that Elvis has made the big time. A columnist from *The San Francisco News* in a series on Elvis writes of him as "'A God-loving, jelly-kneed kid' who's taken Rock 'n' Roll out of the category of "race" or Rhythm-and-Blues music and made it into pops." This has been Elvis' main influence, stated the writer, that Hollywood, reluctant to accept Elvis initially, has finally accepted him and invested money in him.

24 *Variety*, p. 78: DEUTSCHE PITCH FOR ELVIS. RCA in a promotion trailer stated, "He walks like Marilyn Monroe but at home he is a model son!"

24 *Tupelo Daily Journal*, p. 6: SULLIVAN HAS PRESLEY ON SHOW AGAIN SUNDAY. "It may be a good thing for Ed Sullivan that Elvis Presley is coming back next Sunday. After last Sunday's show and with the change in time, he'll need him."

24 *Tupelo Daily Journal*, p. 1: ELVIS SEES DRAFT CALL "GETTING PRETTY CLOSE." "Rock 'n' Roll idol Elvis Presley told United Press tonight he had received his draft questionnaire 3 weeks ago and that he figured army service

was getting pretty close. . . . When the times comes they can bring on the Khaki. . . . I got the papers while I was out in Hollywood shortly before I finished my picture, *Love Me Tender*. . . . The papers came just before I went on my Texas tour, that was about three weeks ago. . . . I honestly don't know what the questionnaire means. . . . I haven't heard anything since the questionnaire or about when to appear for a physical.' He said that he would be 'just as happy in the army as anyplace else.' I'm no different from anyone else. . . . When they want me, I'm ready. I'll have a ball until they call me and after they call me.'"

26   *Colliers*, Vol. 138, pp. 109–111: ROCK 'N' ROLL BATTLE. BOONE VS. PRESLEY. Currently, the top singer is Elvis Presley, who a year ago was almost unknown. Since the start of 1956, he has sold more than 7 million records, has become a major television attraction, has boosted the ratings of any show on which he appeared, bought 5 new Cadillacs and a Lincoln Continental, has been paid $100,000 to make a movie (*Love Me Tender*) for 20th Century Fox, "and has exerted such a sweeping influence on American teenagers that sociologists and psychologists have once again begun to debate the fate of our youth as fainting fits and Presley hairdo's sweep the nation. As "brief as Elvis' reign has been, a new young singer named Pat Boone has fast been gaining on him." "In the battle for first place in the affections of Rock 'n' Roll fans, it would be hard to find two more dissimilar rivals than Boone and Presley.

26   *Tupelo Daily Journal*, p. 1: FILLING STATION SLUGGER FIRED DESPITE ELVIS' PLEA. "Singer Elvis Presley tried in vain today to save the job for a 42-year-old filling station worker who got a black eye in a fisticuffs exchange with the Rock 'n' Roll teenage idol. 'I asked the owner not to fire the man,' the 21-year-old Presley said in an interview."

27   *The Billboard*, p. 1: ARMY TO GIVE ELVIS PRESLEY A G.I. HAIRCUT. When Elvis Presley reports as an Army inductee in early December, he will have his famous sideburns shaved. After a short basic training, he is scheduled to join Special Services on an entertainment tour. He will be allowed to continue his television and recording engagements. Elvis is to enter the Armed Forces "under as much secrecy as possible," the time of his arrival at Fort Dix known only to a handful of Army officers and his own business staff. It has been suggested that a last minute switch may take place, placing Elvis in another training camp, thus insuring a minimum of publicity and disturbance.

27/28   *Tupelo Daily Journal*, p. 1: ELVIS SAYS HE WANTS FARM FOR FATHER. "Rock 'n' Roll star Elvis Presley said today he was looking for a farm for his father because 'Daddy was raised in a cotton patch.'"

29	*Time*, p. 47: PEOPLE. In this section, there was a long paragraph dealing with Elvis' confrontation in the parking lot in Memphis.
29	*The New York Times*, p. 33: PRESLEY RECEIVES A CITY POLIO SHOT. Elvis received a Salk polio vaccine shot. He was personable, quick-witted, charming, and polite to reporters much to their surprise. "He is setting a fine example for the youth of the country," stated a doctor regarding Elvis getting the vaccine. Yesterday at noon in Times Square, in front of the Paramount Theater, a 40-foot "statue" of Elvis was unveiled over the theater marquee.
30	*The Philadelphia Inquirer*, p. 32: PRESLEY'S RATING TOPS THAT OF MARY MARTIN. "Elvis Presley and excerpts from 'The Most Happy Fellow' on "The Ed Sullivan Show" Sunday night trounced Mary Martin and "Born Yesterday" in the Trendex Ratings 39.1 to 18.4 for the hour they were competing.
30	*Tupelo Daily Journal*, p. 1: GRAHAM SEES PRESLEY AS 'GREAT EVANGELIST.' "Evangelist Billy Graham said today singer Elvis Presley would make a great evangelist."

November

	Motion Picture (November) Vol. 46, pp. 4, 5: UNDER HEDDA'S HAT. The columnist stated she was revolted by Elvis' gyrations on Milton Berle's show.
	The New Yorker, Vol. 32, pp. 196–197: THE CURRENT CINEMA. The columnist reviewed *Love Me Tender* and Elvis' performance. While the columnist was on the negative side for Elvis' performance, he did comment on the extremely positive response for Elvis' fans for Elvis' performance. "As soon as the fellow's name appeared on the screen, everybody around me started mewling. . . . I do know that on various occasions Mr. Presley got applause for such lines as 'You ain't got no right to do this,' and 'Yeah, what about it?'—and, indeed, once received an ovation for clearing his throat."
2	*The San Francisco News*, p. 5: A picture of Elvis with Natalie Wood after she flew to Memphis to visit Elvis. Friends said that wedding rumors are to be discounted. They're "just good friends."
5	*Newsweek*, p. 67: "GI JIVE." The article stated that Elvis is to be called to Fort Dix, NJ for duty in the army in December and will have his sideburns shaved. He is also to have extensive dental and periodontal work done. The draft board in Memphis, TN had 86 letters and phone calls from people who wanted to know when Elvis would be leaving.
7	*Variety*, p. 46: "AS TO THAT PRESLEY LONG-TERMER . . ." IT SEEMS THAT THE "$1,000-PER-WEEK

20-YEAR DEAL." that Elvis and RCA Victor arranged is actually a way to spread Elvis' $430,000 earnings in record royalties for his first year over a decade. By spreading the almost half-million earnings over a 10-year period, the earnings amortize over a long-term, thus, reducing his earnings for tax purposes. Elvis has earned in the first year from his 10-million record sales the entire sum that RCA Victor "guarantees" him for the next 10 years.

7   *Tupelo Daily Journal*, p. 11: FAVORABLE COMMENTS ON ELVIS IN NEW YORK TIMES. "Some of the most caustic comments about Elvis Presley have been found in the television columns of *The New York Times*. . . . Thus, it was with some surprise that we noticed some favorable comments on Elvis creeping into television columns of the *Times*." He was not without the humility and gentle humor of a small town boy." Remarking that Elvis had said, "I just wish that I had a chance to try to change the minds of these adults. If I thought that I was leading anyone astray, I'd quit this business and go back to driving a truck. I've searched my heart about this thing and don't think I am a detriment. You know, there's a verse in the Bible that says you will reap what you sow. I believe it, and I try to be careful about what I sow."

8   *Tupelo Daily Journal*, p. 12: $1,000 A WEEK FOR 20 YEARS FOR PRESLEY. "Victor tossed Elvis Presley's old contract into the wastebasket and typed him up a new one that calls for $1,000 a week 52 weeks a year for 20 years, and he will get the weekly check even if he is drafted into the army!"

13 *Look*, Vol. 20, pp. 99–107: THE GREAT ELVIS PRESLEY INDUSTRY. Colonel Tom Parker and Hank Saperstein with a minium investment and operating expenses expect to sell between 19 and 24 million dollars worth of merchandise to teenagers in the next 12 months. This does not include income from Elvis' recordings that should be around $900,000 this year or from personal appearances that bring in about $25,000 a week at times. Or from TV appearances or movie contracts ($750,000 for three pictures with 20th Century Fox).

14 *Variety*, p. 54: AROUND NASHVILLE IN THREE DAYS. It was rumored that Elvis was to make an appearance in the lobbies of the Heritage and Andrew Jackson hotels. Teenagers packed the lobbies waiting for autographs.

14 *Tupelo Daily Journal*, p. 20: ELVIS PONDERING MAJOR OFFER FROM ENGLAND. Elvis Presley is considering an offer to appear from 2 to 4 weeks at Empress Hall, London, at 4,000 pounds ($11,200).

16 *The New York Times*, p. 23: THE SCREEN: CULTURE TAKES A HOLIDAY. The critic critisized *Love Me Tender*, which opened at the Paramount Theatre yesterday, and Elvis. However, he did say of Elvis "he certainly goes at this job with

	a great deal more zeal and assurance than the rest of the actors show."
17	*Tupelo Daily Journal*, p. 18: ELVIS, JOURNAL ROVING REPORTER DRAW ATTENTION AS 700 GIRLS GATHER. When one of the young women from Future Homemakers of America was asked, "What would you like to have in your home that begins with an 'E'?," she yelled "Elvis!"
17/18	*Tupelo Daily Journal*, p. 1: JUDGE UPHOLDS SCHOOL'S RIGHT TO EXPEL BOY FOR WEARING ELVIS PRESLEY HAIRCUT; MOTHER MAY APPEAL. A judge "upheld the right of a school board to expel a teenage boy for wearing an Elvis Presley haircut." After hearing the judge's ruling, his mother hinted "she may take further legal action."
17/18	*Tupelo Daily Journal*, p. 7: ELVIS RECORDS SOOTH MENTAL PATIENTS. "Elvis Presley and his Rock 'n' Roll could go to work for science. So says a doctor at an Iowa Mental Health Institute. A doctor said, "Presley and his guitar have a soothing affect on mental patients."
19	*Ledger–Enquirer*, p. 16: "PELVIS" ROCKING MERCHANDISING WORLD. BOOM FORECAST IN ELVIS PRODUCTS. Elvis Presley is rocking the merchandising world with as much impact as he Rocks 'n' Rolls the bobby socks set. . . ." The Elvis Presley line of lipsticks are named after the titles of his songs . . . 'Hound Dog Orange', 'Heartbreak Pink', 'Lov Ya Fuchsia' and 'Cruel Red.' He also endorses cologne and "Presley Pressed Down—a pomade for kids with unruley hair."
19	*Ledger–Enquirer*, p. 16: MANAGER TALKING NEW MOVIE FOR ELVIS AFTER FANS RIOT AT NEW YORK OPENING. Following a riot at the Paramount Theater in New York after the opening of Elvis Presley's picture *Love Me Tender*, Colonel Parker flew to Hollywood to talk about Elvis making another movie. "I hear that Elvis' price has gone up, up, up."
19	*Tupelo Daily Journal*, p. 19: *LOVE ME TENDER* PREMIERE AT TUPELO ON WEDNESDAY. "Rumors have been circulated that Elvis will appear in Tupelo in person for the opening, but local theater officials emphasize that this was not correct." . . . One of the highlights of this production is a picnic scene in which young Presley entertains by playing his guitar and singing songs. His numbers in this and other scenes in the picture include the title song, "Love Me Tender," "Poor Boy," and "We're Gonna Move," and "Let Me."
20	*Tupelo Daily Journal*, p. 1: ELVIS FARM PURCHASE SAID JUST A RUMOR. Elvis is not buying a farm in Hickory Flat, MI for his father.
23	*San Francisco Chronicle*, p. 29: ELVIS TANGLES WITH A DEFIANT HUSBAND. A fight between Elvis Presley and a 19-year-old was broken up by police today in Toledo, OH. The

	youth was upset, claiming his wife carried a picture of Elvis in her wallet and didn't carry one of him. Elvis said he was not going to press charges.
23	*San Francisco Chronicle*, p. 21: LOVE ME TENDER AT THE FOX. FIRST PRESLEY A MODEST FILM. In a review of *Love Me Tender*, the reviewer felt that although the film was not tailored specifically for Elvis' talents, his presence in the movie was enough to "electrify" his followers. "His occasional smile is quick and touching." In the movie, he sang four songs: "Love Me Tender," "Poor Boy," "We Are Gonna Move," and "Let Me."
24	*The New York Times*, p. 16: PUNCH MISSES PRESLEY. The article reviews Elvis' confrontation with a 19-year-old who resented that his wife, from who he was separated, carried Elvis' picture instead of his. Elvis stated that he did not want to press charges.
25	*Ledger–Enquirer*, p. D-5: HOLLYWOOD IS TALKING ABOUT: PRESLEY RAGE SPREADING TO NEW LIPSTICK SHADES. The Elvis Presley rage is spreading even to beauty products with the market now offering lipsticks in the shades of "Hound Dog Orange," "Heartbreak Pink," and "Cruel Red." There is even a "Presley Press Down for Unruly Hair."
29	*Tupelo Daily Journal*, p. 1: PRESLEY RAGE. 'JUST ANOTHER PHASE.' BING CROSBY SAYS. "Bing Crosby . . . shrugged off the Elvis Presley rage among teenagers as 'Just another phase.' He described Presley's style as 'Jaz, only a little louder with more definition on the beat.'"
29	*Tupelo Daily Journal*, p. 19: ELVIS AID DENIES FIGHT WAS STUNT. "A member of Elvis Presley's staff said today the report that Presley's Toledo, OH slugging match with Louis Balint was a frame-up was "ridiculous."
30	*Ledger–Enquirer*, p. 6: ELVIS SEEN AS SYMBOL OF OUR TIMES. "Maybe this will become known as the Elvis Presley Century. . . . Maybe, like the groaning post-adolescent from Tennessee, the 20th Century is more a fad than a reality. Maybe we will get over it by the year 2,000, which is no encouragement to those of us who don't expect to be around that long. . . . History may say that this sideburned youth who wiggles hips while singing popular songs was a symbol of this time — that this century does a lot of wiggling and squirming without even getting anywhere. . . . But let's not be too hard on Mr. Presley. Doubtless he does the best he can, and nobody should interfere with his right to do it."

December

TV Radio Mirror, (December), pp. 28, 84–85: THE GIRL WHO GOT TO PRESLEY. Recounting the story of an 18-year-old girl who met and befriended Elvis and was invited on a southern tour of 6 cities in August, 1956. The article recounted how she got to meet Elvis after he appeared at a local theatre in Biloxi in 1955. She snuck through the door backstage and found a crowd milling around. Instead of joining the crowd and taking her chances, she entered the Ladies room and waited until there was no more noise in the corridor. "And when I went out, . . . there he was . . . Five minutes later . . . he asked me to show him the town, and, of course, I accepted." Of Elvis she said, "He's a wonderful guy when you get to know him. I mean if you really know him. He's a warm individual and treats everyone so nice."

Cosmopolitan (December) Vol. 141, pp. 54–62: WHAT IS AN ELVIS PRESLEY? In this article, the columnist reviews Elvis' success, his 13-year-old daughter's discovery and admiration of Elvis, and his own concerns. He commented on an article to a columnist in which a girl stated that "Elvis' freedom and lack of inhibitions meant a lot to her—simply because she herself was neither free nor uninhibited." He then commented, "But that still doesn't take the curse off his bumps and grinds. These gyrations have to concern parents . . . I don't think for a minute that my 13-year-old . . . is going to become a delinquent because she's batty over Elvis. But I think if she were older, and not as strictly supervised as she is now . . . I might be a trifle worried."

Photo Play (December) Vol. 50, pp. 40–41: Multiple cut out pin-up pictures of Elvis.

Motion Picture (December) Vol. 46: pp. 40–43, 60–61: ELVIS PRESLEY. THE BIG NOISE FROM TUPELO. The article comments on Elvis' presence at the 20th Century Studio lot preparing for the filming of *Love Me Tender*. "Even before Elvis arrived on the lot, the phones began ringing like crazy. And letters by the thousands arrived daily. Stage-door-Jennies lined the entrance all day long. They stopped studio personnel and asked if they worked on Elvis' set. If the answer is yes, one will yell to another, "Touch him! Maybe he touched Elvis." Elvis carries a comb in his pocket and "is forever taking one or more swipe through his dark shock of heavily brilliantined hair. His hair is his trademark—a heavy mop over the forehead, duck tail in the back and long sideburns. But it is his deep-set, heavily-lidded boudoir eyes that hold one's interest . . . Talk with Elvis and you can't help being drawn to him. He never uses first names with older, coworkers, addresses men as 'Sir' and women as 'Ma'am' . . . He warmly presses one's hands in both of his when saying goodbye." A friend commenting about Elvis said, "On stage, Elvis is an explosion; back at the hotel, he's a shy, uncertain country boy." "Elvis gets so intense about his five or six shows a day that he completely ignores food. Then, after not eating all day, he'll have six cheeseburgers and three malteds." Elvis had remarked,

"You've got to be different, . . . if you want to stand out from the crowd. Take mah sideburns, . . . When Ah was at Humes High, the boys all wore GI haircuts. But Ah wanted to look grown up and different."

Photo Play (December) Vol. 50: pp. 42–43, 93–94: PRESLEY TAKES HOLLYWOOD. "They're calling him the greatest threat to established stars since Tyrone Power. They were all set to hate him, but they loved him." "It was a first day of work on *Love Me Tender*. Elvis remarked that "I don't know much about this business, so I learned the whole script—everybody's parts." He smiled, and his smile, too, was shy, almost ashamed. Elvis was well dressed; when interviewed, "he was wearing black and white shoes, brown slacks, and a pink satin shirt, cut like a doctor's or barber's jacket. A fan, he confessed, had made it for him." Elvis remarked, "I was plenty scared that first day," for he had not acted previously. There was debate as to whether Elvis should be coached in acting. The director and producer had considered this but felt that Elvis would display enough "natural acting ability" on his own. So the decision was reached after reviewing Elvis' first scene that he would not be coached as long as he continued to handle things well. Richard Egan, the lead in the movie remarked, "he's a real nice fella," and Debra Paget, the lead actress stated, "The best way to describe his work, I think, is to say it's inspired." Elvis confided to the columnist that his latest ambition was to portray James Dean in a movie. When it was known that Elvis was staying at the Hotel Knickerbocker in Hollywood, he received 237 phone calls on the first day.

1 *Melody Maker*, p. 8: LET'S BE FAIR TO MR. PRESLEY. "I am grateful to the producers of *Love Me Tender* for giving me a chance to observe the Presley that exists behind the rather vulgar, gimmick-ornamented facade that has become his recorded substance. . . . "His performance in *Love Me Tender* gives the first indication . . . that Presley has secretly been nourishing the seeds of artistry . . . Presley, in fact, emerges from his first film with credit. He has demonstrated much more talent than most of his detractors were prepared to concede to him. And, as I have been one of them, I must be among the first to raise a cheer. Let us, I say, be fair to Presley."

3 *Tupelo Daily Journal*, p. 9: PRESLEY ASKS $250,000 FOR 3 SULLIVAN SHOWS. "Elvis Presley got $50,000 for three appearances on . . . "The Ed Sullivan Show" . . . Now Sullivan has phoned to discuss another series of guest shows for Elvis and the conversation went something like this: Sullivan, "How much do you want?" Parker, "Are you sitting down, Ed?" Sullivan, "Yes." Parker, "$250,000."

8 *Saturday Review*, p. 30: SR GOES TO THE MOVIES. A columnist reviews *Love Me Tender* and states that Elvis is a "triple threat man in this one: he sings, he wiggles, and he

	acts." He then goes on to review the plot of the movie.
8	*The Billboard*, p. 24: PRESLEY DISKS SET CANADA SALES MARKS. Elvis Presley records are setting sales marks in Canada. Two of Elvis' records, "Hound Dog," and "Don't Be Cruel," have sold over a 100,000 records and "Love Me Tender" has sold 135,000 in 6 weeks. Unusually, top records in Canada may hit 100,000 sold. RCA stated that "Don't Be Cruel" is probably the biggest single record sold in the history of the company in Canada. Dealers have stated that the interest in Elvis records has accounted for the boom in the entire record industry. Sales of guitars in some cities have also boomed and dealers are sometimes 6 weeks behind in orders. Elvis appeals to both the English and French populations.
11	*Look*, Vol. 20, p. 130: The magazine showed a profile of Elvis and a comparable view of the statue of *Discobolus* (the discus thrower) and compared the features of Elvis with the statues of *Discobolus* and Michelangelo's *David*.
16	*The Shreveport Times*, p. 10A: EVERYBODY AND HIS DOG TURNS OUT FOR ELVIS. Everyone was out to see Elvis perform on "Louisiana Hayride" last night at the Louisiana State fairgrounds. It is the only structure large enough to hold Elvis' screaming following. Elvis sang "Love Me Tender," "Don't Be Cruel," and "Heartbreak Hotel" among other songs and was accompanied by The Jordanaires.
16	*The Shreveport Times*, p. 1A: MASS HYSTERIA. FRENZIED ELVIS FANS ROCK YOUTH CENTER. "Elvis (the Pelvis) Presley came to town yesterday, and last night 9,000 Rock 'n' Rollers "flipped" as he performed at the "Louisiana Hayride." It was one of the greatest displays of mass hysteria in the history of Shreveport. He was barely audible over the screams of the frenzied 9,000 fans. A press conference resembled a mob scene. Elvis wore a green coat, blue pants, a white shirt, tie, and silk scarf and white shoes with blue shoes during his appearance on the "Louisiana Hayride." During an interview, Elvis was friendly and demonstrated a good sense of humor. An interview with the president of the Shreveport-Bossier Presley Fan Club stated that Elvis is "the most fascinating human I've ever known . . . Elvis is a living denial of the notion teenagers should be seen and not heard."
16	*The Shreveport Times*, p. 12A: TO AID YMCA. Elvis Presley who has supposedly earned a million dollars in the last couple of years has performed for free. Both Elvis and the members of KWKH Hayride contributed the receipts to Shreveport's YMCA. Elvis performed for 35 minutes in what was described as an "unforgettable" performance.
17	*The New York Times*, p. 28: PRESLEY TERMED A PASSING FANCY. A minister in Greenwich Village stated that the Elvis Presley craze will pass. "Using innuendo and suggestion, by curl of lip and shake of hip, represents the revolt from the

tried and true." He stated that Elvis' appeal gave many images to the viewer: someone who earns more than the President of the United States and the entire cabinet; someone who is reminiscent of the late James Dean; "a whirling dervish of sex"; someone who represents the 'Pied Piper.'

24 *The New Republic*, p. 22: A STAR IS BORN. The columnist reviews *Love Me Tender* and likes it very much. "I went to see *Love Me Tender* last night, and I liked it enormous." He noted that Elvis was not obscene or lewd and that he stood out from everybody in the picture. "Elvis didn't just *memorize* his lines. He seemed to sense, deep down inside somewhere, what almost every word meant. That's while his portrayal of Clint, . . . was so moving."

30 *Tupelo Daily Journal*, p. 5: GI's IN ALASKA ASK BOB HOPE: WHEN IS PRESLEY GOING TO BE DRAFTED INTO ARMY? Bob Hope conducted a question and answer seminar on Hollywood for the GI's. One of the things they wanted to know was when Elvis was going to be drafted.

31 *The Wall Street Journal*, pp. 1, 8: HEARTBREAK, HOUND DOGS PUT SALES ZIP INTO PRESLEY PRODUCTS. Today, Elvis Presley, is a business. It is felt that the Presley craze will remain at a high level for about 2 years if first class merchandising programs continue, and then it will taper down. Many merchandisers are worried about being burned similar to the Davy Crockett phase where his popularity suddenly diminished. Mr. Saprestin recalled that on one occasion they noted teenagers writing "'We love Elvis' with lipstick on the side of a building." That gave them the idea to start the lipstick business. "Lipsticks, in the shades of Hound Dog Orange, Heartbreak Hotel Pink, and Tutti Frutti Red (titles of Elvis' records) and with the Presley signature on the case, started rolling out . . ." A manufacturer from New York has sold about 12,000 pairs of black twill jeans with emerald green stitching that retail for $2.00 a pair. Elvis' signature is stamped on a leather pocket patch, and a four-color photo of Elvis is on a tag. About 350,000 Elvis charm bracelets have been turned out over the last 3 months. However, some requests for licenses have been turned down. Two men wanted a license for a life size "mechanical Elvis' which would wiggle its hips while a Presley recording" played. They wanted the machine to play before an audience and guaranteed 250 days of use. A brewery wanted to make a "Presley's Rock 'n' Roll malt," which was a non-alcoholic beer.

Bibliography

Newspapers – 1956

Atlanta Journal
The Charlotte News
The Dallas Morning News
The Dallas Times Herald
The Florida Times-Union
The Houston Press
Jacksonville Journal
Ledger – Enquirer
The New York Times
Oakland Tribune
The Philadelphia Inquirer
San Francisco Chronicle
The San Francisco News
The Shreveport Times
Tupelo Daily Journal
Wall Street Journal

Periodicals – 1956

America
The Billboard
Collier's
Coronet
Cosmopolitan
Down Beat
House and Garden
Life
Look
Melody Maker
Motion Picture
The New Republic
Newsweek
The New Yorker
Photoplay
Saturday Review
Screenland – TV Land
TV Guide
TV Radio Mirror
Time
Variety

Books

Cotten L. *All Shook Up. Elvis. Day-By-Day, 1954–1977.* 1985, Pierian Press, Ann Arbor, MI.

Escott C, Hawkins M. *Sun Records. The Discography.* 1987, Bear Family Records. Bollersode, West Germany.

Jorgensen E, Rasmussen E, Mikkelsen J. *Reconsider Baby. The Definitive Elvis. Sessionography. 1954–1977.* 1986, Pierian Press, Ann Arbor, MI.

Sauers W. *Elvis Presley. A Complete Reference. Biography, Chronology, Concert List, Filmography, Discography, Vital Documents, Bibliography, Index.* 1984, McFarland and Company, Inc., Jefferson, NC.

Whisler JA. *Elvis Presley. Reference Guide and Discography.* 1981, The Scarecrow Press Inc., Metuchen, NJ.

Worth FL, Tamerius SD. *Elvis. His Life from A to Z.* 1990, Contemporary Books Inc., Chicago, IL.